"When Jesus saw people's physical and spiritual needs, the Holy Spirit burned within Him." He had a desire for others to know the source of their strength. Nancy's devotions are one of a kind, a journey to the very heart of God. They are tender, practical, creative and spiritually profound in their insight to God's heart, filled with mercy. You will be transformed by reading Never the Same Again by Mrs. Rowland.

—Norene Humphries,
Career Missionary to East Asia, Hong Kong, Taiwan, Korea, Japan and China, International Mission Board, SBC, Richmond, Virginia

In this book, the author Nancy Rowland follows again a pattern different from many devotional books. Where most begin with a Scripture text, and then expound on or apply it, she begins with a narration, usually of a personal experience, and then applies a text to it. The result is to make Scripture pertinent and alive. Hand a copy to a troubled friend, and expect to see a transformation begin.

—Carl F. Rupprecht,
Retired Writer/Editor

Nancy's observations of life and faith remind me of Brother Lawrence, who knew the power of practicing the presence of God. She truly is a woman who walks closely with the Lord and is able to communicate the joy of the Lord through her devotions.

—Kelly King,
Women's Missions and Ministries Specialist for the Baptist General Convention of Oklahoma

Never the Same Again offers a unique look into Nancy Rowland who loves Truth and lives what she writes. Her words intertwined with God's Word touch on the everyday and the eternal. How?
—Death and Life
—Bad Things and Blessings
—Aloneness and Relationships

—Carolyn Teague,
Founder and Director, INNERchange, Inc., Fort Worth, Texas

As Nancy's pastor, it is a joy to recommend *Never the Same Again.* It is a powerful, practical, and penetrating anthology of daily life as seen through the Word of God. Read it and be blessed.

—Doug Miller,
Pastor, First Baptist Church, Wilburton, Oklahoma

I first met Nancy Rowland on a trip to Malawi, Africa. I had the opportunity to see Nancy in every type of situation. We traveled together, ministered together, prayed together and shared life experiences together. Nancy is a loving and caring person. What you read in the pages of this book is from the heart of a woman who has a genuine passion for God and others.

—Rob Miller,
Print Communications Specialist,
Baptist General Convention of Oklahoma

never
the same
again

Michelle,
It has been great getting to know
you and Steve. I pray God will
bless your marriage. I pray God will
speak to your heart as you read
what He gave to me. It has been
an incredible journey with the
Lord in His Word. We serve an
amazing God.
Jeremiah 15:16
Nancy Rowland

NANCY ROWLAND

never the same again

TATE PUBLISHING & *Enterprises*

Published by Tate Publishing & Enterprises, LLC
127 E. Trade Center Terrace | Mustang, Oklahoma 73064 USA
1.888.361.9473 | www.tatepublishing.com

Tate Publishing is committed to excellence in the publishing industry. The company reflects the philosophy established by the founders, based on Psalm 68:11,
"The Lord gave the word and great was the company of those who published it."

Published in the United States of America

ISBN: 978-1-60696-674-7
Religion / Biblical Studies / General
09.03.31

Dedication

I dedicate this book to my husband, Doyal, who loves me and supports me in all I do. I thank him for his prayers, his listening ear, his encouragement, and his continual financial support of my journey in writing. The opportunity God opened for me to write seemed impossible, but with God in control, Doyal and I walked this journey together. God has been faithful to us every step of the way. I thank God for a husband who loves the Lord and believes "all things are possible with God" (Mark 10:27b, NASB).

I dedicate this book to God my Father, because without his inspiration and guidance, it would not have been written.

Acknowledgements

To my dear friend, Cecilia Morris, who has spent many hours editing my manuscript. She has prayed for me and encouraged me to continue this endeavor. To my special friend, Becky Minton, who has been one of my greatest encouragers. She has diligently read every devotional I have written, giving feedback concerning the application of illustrations and scriptures. To all my friends and family who have encouraged me to continue writing as God leads me.

Contents

Foreword

There is nothing more vital to a Christian's relationship with the Lord than time spent consistently with him in prayer and in his word. The daily demands and stresses of life seem to eat away at this precious time, leaving us all the more weary. In *Never the Same Again,* Nancy has penned devotionals that not only help you to unwind, but guides you directly to the Lord and true refreshment through continuous use of Scripture. Her use of personal reflections on experiences and people in her life are warm and engaging and will at times give you a good laugh or cry. The Scripture and message woven in each devotional causes you to reflect on the Lord and your relationship with him.

I first met Nancy through my work in the women's office at the Baptist General Convention of Oklahoma. Nancy is a tremendous servant-leader in our state. It's only natural that she was asked to serve on the state women's leadership team. Through these meetings and retreats, I got to know Nancy better. We soon became close friends and prayer partners. My relationship with Nancy has been both an answer to prayer and a great thrill for me. The simple, yet powerful ways she has taught and encouraged me has renewed my passion to see all women partaking in the fullness of life in Christ.

Every aspect of Nancy's life is one of ministry, unabashedly proclaiming Jesus is Lord, and oh, he is good. Through reading her testimony in the title devotional of this book, *Never the Same Again,* and the others that follow, you will see how Nancy has allowed every experience in her life, both good and bad, to make her the woman of God she is today. Take note of how every resource she has used is for the building up of others. I pray we will be encouraged that, with the Lord's guidance, we too can take all our experiences and become a person after God's own heart.

Nancy, my friend, I love you dearly and am so deeply humbled to be writing the foreword for your first published book. I am so thankful that the Lord brought you into my life. May each one of us who reads these pages find rest and refreshment in the Lord. Through our encounter with him, may we never be the same again!

Stephanie Pruitt
Former Women's Missions & Ministries Assistant
Baptist General Convention of Oklahoma

Never the Same Again

The other morning, while driving my husband to church for a men's breakfast, I was listening to a Christian radio station. They were broadcasting a 1979 Billy Graham crusade. Evie Karlsson and her husband were singing the song "Never the Same Again." The Spirit of the Lord gripped my heart and tears began to flow down my cheeks as God clearly showed me this was to be the title of my next devotional book. Thinking back as to why I would never be the same again, I knew God had led me step by step through life, preparing me for where I am today. I asked the Lord for the assurance that this was truly what he was saying to me. A peace came over me as I realized it was definitely the Lord stirring this thought within me. "And all of us have had that veil removed so that we can be mirrors that brightly reflect the glory of the Lord. And as the Spirit of the Lord works within us, we become more and more like him and reflect his glory even more" (2 Corinthians 3:18, NLT).

As a young child, my parents taught me the Bible and to pray. When I was eight years old, I came to know Jesus as Savior, and because of my decision, I will never be the same again. The Holy Spirit convicted my heart of the sin in my life, "for all have sinned and fall short of the glory of God" (Romans 3:23, NASB). For one who knows little about the Bible, it is more understandable in "everyone has sinned, everyone falls short of the beauty of God's plan." (J. B. Phillips, *The New Testament In Modern English*).

My father, who was a preacher, explained the Scriptures to me, making sure I understood what it meant to become a Christian. He then helped me to pray and ask Jesus to be my Savior and Lord. Being only eight years old, I did not understand all it meant. God gave me a much clearer understanding as I walked with him step by step. My whole life has been a learning experience. I cannot say I have not made mistakes along the way because I certainly have. I am thankful, though, that our God is patient and understanding and loves us with an unconditional love.

My mom and dad taught me well as I was growing up. I praise God I never had any regrets about being a preacher's kid. Many preachers' children rebel because they are always on display and people feel they should be perfect. I felt so blessed by the opportunities I was given as a preacher's kid. I traveled a lot with my dad to different meetings, but I also spent time with him fishing and working in the yard. Of course, my mom was always teaching me the things a girl should know. "Train up a child in the way he should go, even when he is old he will not depart from it" (Proverbs 22:6, NASB).

Parents are to teach their children as they grow. They are to dedicate them to the Lord and teach them the Word of God. In time, they will make their own decisions. We pray what they have learned from the Bible will bring conviction in their hearts about how they are to live. Every Christian parent who has taught their children the Word of God desires for them to live according to the instruction of the Lord.

When I had one remaining semester of college, I married a man I went to college with. I graduated from college in 1967 and began teaching school. Six years later, I gave birth to our first son, and our second son was born three years later. When the first son was five years old and the second was two years old, their father died from a massive blood clot in the lungs after back surgery. My whole life took a sudden change. I believe God used this time to really get my attention. I prayed daily that God would be my constant companion and fill the emptiness left in my life by the death of my husband. The following verse expresses what we must do if we desire God's constant companionship and friendship: "And [so] the

Scripture was fulfilled that says, Abraham believed in (adhered to, trusted in, and relied on) God, and this was accounted to him as righteousness (as conformity to God's will in thought and deed), and he was called God's friend" (James 2:23, AMP).

For too long I had been trying to do things in my own strength and not depending on the Lord for his direction and guidance. I was not spending the time in the Word of God I needed to spend. My prayer life was rather dull and not nearly as consistent as it needed to be. God definitely got my attention. "You are my friends if you keep on doing the things which I command you to do" (John 15:14, AMP).

I so desired the friendship of the Lord, for I had lost my closest companion and friend. "For the eyes of the Lord range throughout the earth to strengthen those whose hearts are fully committed to him" (2 Chronicles 16:9a, NIV). I truly began a journey of walking more closely to the Lord than I ever had in my life.

The boys and I moved to Oklahoma where I met my present husband, Doyal. God blessed me with a great companion, a good Christian man, and a loving husband. Doyal's wife had died some months earlier, and after our marriage, we began blending our families, which was not an easy task. The Lord really drove me to my knees during that time. I learned what it was to pray continually and the power of prayer. "Be earnest and unwearied and steadfast in your prayer [life], being [both] alert and intent in [your praying] with thanksgiving" (Colossians 4:2, AMP).

I am so thankful God is patient and does not give up on us. Step by step he was preparing me for things ahead. I also came to realize that my life must be built on the foundation of the Word of God. In order for this to happen, I needed to immerse myself in the Bible. It did not happen immediately. It was a gradual, learning experience for me.

The grass withers, the flower fades, but the word of our God will stand forever.

Isaiah 40:8 (AMP)

For all flesh (mankind) is like grass, and all its glory (honor) like [the] flower of grass. The grass withers and flower drops off. But the Word of the LORD (divine instruction, the Gospel) endures forever. And this Word is the good news which was preached to you.

1 Peter 1:24–25 (AMP)

I had a long way to go to arrive where God wanted me to be, but I began my journey with faith that the Holy Spirit would guide me all the way. "Whether you turn to the right or to the left, your ears will hear a voice behind you, saying, "This is the way; walk in it" (Isaiah 30:21, NIV).

After our children left home, God did an amazing thing in Doyal's and my life. God singled us out and said, "Therefore, go and make disciples of all the nations, baptizing them in the name of the Father and the Son and the Holy Spirit. Teach these new disciples to obey all the commands I have given you. And be sure of this: I am with you always, even to the end of the age" (Matthew 28:19–20, NLT).

We began going on mission trips, building chapels in different countries, doing evangelism, digging wells, and teaching people to be obedient and serve the Lord. God has grown us in so many ways through these experiences.

The journey God has led me on has not been easy. God has revealed things in my life that I needed to let go. Having grown up in a very traditional Baptist preacher's home, I had a narrow view of life and was bound by traditional beliefs. As God began to speak to my heart, he revealed those things he wanted to remove from my life. I learned to step out of the box I had lived in for so long and allowed myself the joy of accepting others of different faiths as God's children also. Really, I released God from the box I had placed him in, realizing he was the God of all people, not just Baptist. God took me out of my comfort zone and led me to step out on faith to accomplish what he had in mind for me. I have never been a transparent person, but the writing of these devotional books has changed that. This has given me opportunities to minister to others, because they see that I have experienced many of the same problems as they have. I have come to accept others with different backgrounds just as they are. Many of them have encountered situations in life I have never been exposed to. I love helping them see who they are in Christ Jesus and what he desires to do in their life. God has given me freedom to be myself, but doing so according to his leading. Let me assure you, I am still not totally where God wants me to be. I have a long way to go, but God is so faithful and very patient with me. As a result of my many experiences, God has led me to write devotional books; rather, God and I have written together. What an awesome experience it has been! "But this thing I did command them: Listen to and obey my voice, and I will be your God and you will be my people; and walk in the whole way that I command you, that it may be well with you" (Jeremiah 7:23, AMP). Jeremiah delivered the Word of the Lord to Judah, but it speaks to our hearts today. We must listen and be obedient to the Lord in all things.

Why will I never be the same again? The Lord has become my very top priority in life. He alone is my reason for living. I know when I serve him with all my heart, soul, and strength that all other things in life will fall in place. I will be the wife, mother, friend, and servant I need to be. I had to first learn to listen to the Lord and hear him speak to me. "And the Lord came and stood and called as at other times, Samuel! Samuel! Then Samuel answered, Speak, Lord, for your servant is listening" (1 Samuel 3:10, AMP).

How has God changed your life?

Are there areas of your life you need to allow God to control so you will never be the same again?

What is your first priority in life?

Happenings in Life that Call for Change

Different things that happen in life make a great impression on how we think and what we do. As a teenager, I remember reading the book *Through Gates of Splendor* by Elisabeth Elliot. Five men and their wives had gone to Ecuador as missionaries to the Auca Indians. They worked hard developing a strategy to reach these primitive, savage people for the Lord. Each step they took was well thought out and of great importance in building a relationship with Auca Indians who were killing off their own people. They knew if they did not reach them with the Gospel of Jesus Christ very soon, the tribe would be extinct. The moment they thought they had made great accomplishments toward this relationship; all five missionary men were savagely killed by the Auca Indians. Three years later, Elisabeth Elliot and Marj Saint, two of the wives, were invited to come live among the Auca Indians. They took their children and went to join them, along with Rachel Saint, a single missionary living there. God did amazing things in the lives of the people. Those who had actually killed the missionaries came to know Jesus. What happened in Ecuador with the death of the missionaries was not by accident. This story has affected so many different people. Not only have many come to know Jesus because of what happened, but many have come to serve the Lord in missions. The lives of the wives of these five missionaries would never be the same again, but God proved his faithfulness to each of them. They were able to see the fruit of their husband's efforts.

One of the most radical changes to take place in a person's life is found in the Bible. Saul persecuted those who believed in the Lord. Believers scattered in many directions when the persecution began.

Saul would drag both men and women believers off to prison. He went directly to the high priest to ask for letters addressed to the synagogues in Damascus in order that they would cooperate with him in the arrest of any people of the Way (believers in the Lord). Saul had a most unusual experience on the way to Damascus. God had a special plan for Saul's life and an event took place that would change him forever.

> As he was nearing Damascus on this mission, a brilliant light from heaven suddenly beamed down upon him! He fell to the ground and heard a voice saying to him, "Saul! Saul! Why are you persecuting me?" "Who are you, sir?" Saul asked. And the voice replied, "I am Jesus, the one you are persecuting! Now get up and go into the city, and you will be told what you are to do." The men with Saul stood speechless with surprise, for they heard the sound of someone's voice, but they saw no one! As Saul picked himself up off the ground, he found that he was blind. So his companions led him by the hand to Damascus. He remained there blind for three days. And all that time he went without food and water.
>
> Acts 9:3–9 (NLT)

God sent Ananias to lay hands on him so he would be able to see again: "But the Lord said, 'Go and do what I say. For Saul is my chosen instrument to take my message to the Gentiles and to kings, as well as to the people of Israel. And I will show him how much he must suffer for me'" (Acts 9:15–16, NLT).

Saul would later become known as Paul and would suffer much for the Lord. The man who had persecuted and murdered Christians was now sharing Jesus with them. Saul was never the same again.

Another instance of radical change was seen in the life of Horatio Spafford, even as he and his wife were grieving over the

NEVER THE SAME AGAIN

death of their son. Spafford was a very successful lawyer in Chicago and had invested heavily in real estate. On October 8, 1871, the Great Chicago Fire swept through the city, and destroyed almost everything he owned. It appeared that his life was being destroyed, but he was a man of great faith.

> Fix your thoughts on what is true and honorable and right. Think about things that are pure and lovely and admirable. Think about things that are excellent and worthy of praise. Keep putting into practice all you learned from me and heard from me and saw me doing, and the God of peace will be with you.
>
> Philippians 4:8b–9 (NLT)

Horatio Spafford began to pick up the pieces of his life, caring for his wife and four daughters. Two years later, he decided to take a holiday in Europe. He selected England because he knew Dwight L. Moody would be preaching there. He was delayed because of business, so he sent his wife and four daughters ahead on board the ship *S. S. Ville Du Havre*. As they crossed the Atlantic, the ship was struck by an iron sailing vessel and two hundred twenty-six people lost their lives, including his four daughters. His wife survived and sent a telegram to Spafford saying, "Saved Alone." Once again, disaster had come into his life. He took another ship to England and as they crossed the place where the ships had collided, the captain called it to his attention. Spafford returned to his cabin and composed the song "It Is Well With My Soul."

"It Is Well With My Soul"
When peace, like a river, attendeth my way,
When sorrows like sea billows roll;
Whatever my lot, Thou hast taught me to say,
It is well, it is well with my soul.

Many people would have blamed God after such tragedy, yet Spafford could still say all was well with his soul because of his faith in the Lord. "Beloved, I pray that you may prosper in every way and [that your body] may keep well, even as [I know] your soul keeps well and prospers" (3 John 2, AMP).

Because of all that had happened, he would never be the same again, but because of his relationship with the Lord and his dependence on him, his faith was strengthened.

What happens in your life when bad things happen? Do you look for someone to blame? Do you ever blame God?

What verse do you claim when bad things happen in your life?

Snagged by the Luscious Delicacy Dangling Before Them

One of my greatest joys in the past was to spend time fishing the old fashioned way with a cane pole. In later years, I fished with a rod and reel. I enjoyed fishing with live bait on my hook and a bobber a few feet above it. I would throw it out in the pond, relax, and wait for a fish to snag my bait and pull the bobber under. The fish were tempted by the delicious-looking worm or minnow on my hook. There were times they would play with it, nibbling at the bait and causing the bobber to move around. Other times they would grab the bait, unsuspecting of a hook underneath that would get caught in their mouth or throat. They were so attracted to the luscious delicacy dangling in front of them; they grabbed it with great enthusiasm. It brought me great joy to reel them in and rejoice in the catch of the day, particularly when the fish was big enough to eat.

When we partake of the luscious delicacy provided for us in the Word of God, our life will be changed. One of the first verses we learn as children contains the greatest story ever told: "For God so greatly loved and dearly prized the world that he [even] gave up his only begotten (unique) Son, so that whoever believes in (trusts in, clings to, relies on) him shall not perish (come to destruction, be lost) but have eternal (everlasting) life" (John 3:16, AMP).

As a child, it amazed me how God gave the only Son he had to die on the cross for me. It was good to know that if I would simply place my faith and trust in him I could have everlasting life.

We went to Brazil in 1995 to share with people gathered in homes the message of this simple verse. God, who created all things, loved us so much he was willing to send his only Son to die upon the cross to pay the price for our sin so we might have everlasting life: "For God so loved the world that he gave his only Son, so that everyone who believes in him will not perish but have eternal life" (John 3:16, NLT).

Many people accepted Jesus as Savior when this message was presented to them. They chose to partake of the luscious delicacy from the Word of God. Their lives would never be the same again.

Thinking about the delicacies found in the Word of God reminds me of: "The grass withers, the flower fades, when the breath of the Lord blows upon it; surely the people are grass. The grass withers, the flower fades, but the word of our God stands forever" (Isaiah 40:7–8, NASB).

People's lives change, and one day they will die. In the spring and summer, grass grows at a rapid speed, but as the fall of the year comes, it begins to lose its rich green color, and by winter most of it withers and dies. Isaiah assures us that even though the grass withers and the flower fades, the word of our God will stand forever, it will not die.

The Word of God starts at the very beginning of life. It talks about God creating all things: "In the beginning God created the heavens and the earth" (Genesis 1:1, NASB).

God not only created all the heavens and the earth, but he also created every living thing that walked upon the earth and swam in the streams, lakes, rivers, and oceans. Lastly, he created man: "And God created man in his own image, in the image of God he created him; male and female he created them" (Genesis 1:27, NASB).

God created man and desired that man would obey his commands, but many times man failed. Temptation came and man allowed himself to be snared by sin, just as the fish mentioned above was tempted and caught by the luscious delicacy dangling in front of him. "But each one is tempted when he is carried away and enticed by his own lust. Then when lust is conceived, it gives birth to sin; and when sin is accomplished, it brings forth death" (James 1:14–15, NASB).

All flesh is confronted with temptation. God provides encouragement from his Word when we are tempted and inclined to give over to Satan's desire for our life. "So humble yourselves before God. Resist the devil, and he will flee from you. Draw close to God, and God will draw close to you" (James 4:7–8a, NLT).

We come humbly before the Lord, realizing we cannot do it on our own, and ask him to help us resist the temptation Satan is putting before us. When we stand on the Word of God, Satan will flee from us. God promises that if we will walk closely with him, he will stay close to us.

Every provision a Christian needs to stand strong in this world is found in the Word of God. "For, 'All flesh is like grass, and all its glory like the flower of grass. The grass withers, and the flower falls off, but the word of the Lord abides forever'" (1 Peter 1:24–25a, NASB).

Believers can depend on the Word of God because it will stand forever. God's Word will do exactly what he sends it out to do.

As the rain and the snow come down from heaven, and do not return to it without watering the earth and making it bud and flourish, so that it yields seed for the sower and bread for the eater, so is my word that goes out from my mouth: It will not return to me empty, but will accomplish what I desire and achieve the purpose for which I sent it.

Isaiah 55:10–11 (NIV)

There is convicting power in the Word of God. When a person reads the Scriptures, the Holy Spirit will use the Word to convict his or her heart.

The heart cry of the Lord is that all people will know him for he is the only way, the only truth, and the only life. Our conversion experience is not the end. God expects us to meditate upon his Word because as a believer we should have a hunger and a thirst for him.

> O God, you are my God; I earnestly search for you. My soul thirsts for you; my whole body longs for you in this parched and weary land where there is no water. Your unfailing love is better to me than life itself; how I praise you! I will honor you as long as I live, lifting up my hands to you in prayer. You satisfy me more than the richest of foods. I will praise you with songs of joy.
>
> Psalm 63:1, 3–5 (NLT)

Do you really have an insatiable desire to know God? Do you search the Scriptures seeking to know the Lord better? The more time we spend with him in his Word, delving deeply into the sweet, tasty morsels provided to satisfy our hunger, the better we will get to know our Father. The better we know him, the more we will love him and desire to serve him.

When a fish is tempted by the luscious delicacy dangling in front of him, he grabs hold with great gusto, even though it may mean death. When we sink our teeth into the scrumptious, delicious meal God has set before us in his Word, we will die to self and have an insatiable desire to walk with the Lord. I invite you to come and dine with me at the table God has prepared for us. Don't worry about your appearance or how dirty you are; just come as you are, because God will clean you from inside out as you feast upon his Word. As God speaks to you through the Scriptures and the Holy Spirit convicts your heart, you will never be the same again.

Think about the scriptures presented. What is God saying to you? Which scripture truly spoke to your heart concerning some change you need to make in your life?

What does the Bible mean to you? Why is it important to you? Maybe it is not important to you, why is that so?

One in Spirit,
One in the Bond of Love

From time to time, people come into our life that we are automatically drawn to. We develop a sweet relationship with them. We could compare it to a honeybee drawn to a flower from which it will extract nectar. This nectar is used by the bee to manufacture honey. It makes me think of the special relationship I have had with two sweet friends the past few years. They have been two of my greatest encouragers and cheerleaders in the writing of my devotional books. God did a special work in drawing us to one another, for it has been a very sweet friendship. I have been able to go by almost daily to visit with them, sharing with them things in my life and having a time of prayer together. Especially through these times of prayer, our relationship has become very strong. Recently, the Lord called Ray home to heaven to be with him. After sixty-three years of marriage, Juanita has emptiness in her life right now. She is a strong believer and is depending on the Lord to carry her through the valley to the mountaintop once again. Our relationship with one another has grown sweeter each time we have prayed together. The power of prayer has a way of creating oneness in the Lord between people and at the same time building a strong relationship. It seems each of us has drawn "sweet nectar" from one another that produced a beautiful bond of friendship. "The heartfelt counsel of a friend is as sweet as perfume and incense" (Proverbs 27:9, NLT).

I think of the relationship between Boaz and Ruth. Ruth was a Moabite and the daughter-in-law of Naomi. Naomi's husband died and about ten years later, the two sons who were married to Ruth and Orpah also died. Naomi decided to return to the land of Judah. She told the two daughters-in-law to return to their families.

Orpah did as Naomi said, but Ruth refused to leave her mother-in-law: "But Ruth replied, 'Don't ask me to leave you and turn back. I will go wherever you go and live wherever you live. Your people will be my people, and your God will be my God'" (Ruth 1:16, NLT).

Ruth and Naomi arrived in Bethlehem at the time of the barley harvest. Ruth took the initiative to go to the fields to pick up grain so she and Naomi would have food. The harvesters were instructed to leave the corners of the fields for the poor to harvest and also leave any grain that was dropped for them to pick up. Ruth, being a widow, had the right to go to the fields and pick up this grain. Ruth worked very hard, and when Boaz returned to his field, he asked the man in charge who she was. The foreman for Boaz told him she was the woman from Moab who had returned to Bethlehem with Naomi. He told Boaz she had been working very hard since early morning.

> Boaz went over and said to Ruth, "Listen, my daughter. Stay right here with us when you gather grain; don't go to any other fields. Stay right behind the women working in my field. See which part of the field they are harvesting, and then follow them. I have warned the young men not to bother you. And when you are thirsty, help yourself to the water they have drawn from the well."
>
> Ruth 2:8–9 (NLT)

Ruth found favor in the heart of Boaz. He showed kindness toward her and took a special interest in her. This did not happen by accident, but it was part of God's plan. When Naomi heard what Boaz had said to Ruth, she was encouraged because his words revealed his love for Ruth and his desire to make her happy. Boaz was well-to-do and a near relative of Naomi's deceased husband. Boaz made provision in the instruction he gave to his workers for Ruth to work only in his fields. Naomi could see he was making plans for her and Ruth. Ruth may not have recognized God's leading in all the events in her life. It was not by accident she went to Boaz's field to glean the grain, nor was it an accident that Boaz was a close relative of Elimelech. God's plan was being put into action; a bond of love formed between Boaz and Ruth. Boaz was considered to be the kinsman redeemer and could redeem the property Elimelech had mortgaged when he took his family to Moab. Naomi did not have the money to do this. If Boaz bought the property back, it would remain in the family. He would also be responsible for taking the wife of the deceased. The Scripture does not explain how Mahlon, Ruth's husband, was connected to his father's property. After all the different aspects of this plan were completed, Boaz took Ruth to be his wife.

> So Boaz took Ruth and she became his wife. Then he went to her, and the LORD enabled her to conceive, and she gave birth to a son. The women said to Naomi: "Praise be to the LORD, who this day has not left you without a kinsman-redeemer. May he become famous throughout Israel!"
>
> Ruth 4:13–14 (NIV)

Not only was there a special bond of love between Boaz and Ruth, but there was a very special love between Ruth and Naomi.

Through all that happened God was making provision for the birth of King David and Jesus Christ: "The women living there said, 'Naomi has a son.' And they named him Obed. He was the father of Jesse, the father of David" (Ruth 4:17, NIV).

David was an ancestor to the Messiah. Jesus was to come from the tribe of Judah and David's family was chosen and our Redeemer, Jesus Christ, would be known as the son of David: "The book of the genealogy of Jesus Christ, the son of David, the son of Abraham" (Matthew 1:1, NASB).

Because of what happened in the Book of Ruth, Jesus was born in Bethlehem. He was sent by God the Father to be the Savior of the world and we are able to have an intimate love relationship with him.

I thank God for the bond of love and the oneness in spirit he brought between me, Ray, and Juanita. This came about because of our oneness in Jesus Christ. Even though Ray is gone, the strong bond of love continues between Juanita and me. God has a plan in all that happens in our lives. May we be patient and wait upon him to bring to fruition his entire plan.

Do you have special people in your life you can say you are one in spirit with and one in the bond of love? Who are they and why are they so special to you?

Do you have an intimate love relationship with Jesus Christ? If not, what needs to happen in your life to bring about this special relationship with Jesus?

Excruciating, Agonizing Pain

Stevie, our youngest son, called to tell us they had Tanner, his son, in the emergency room. Tanner was swinging and intended to jump forward out of the swing, but instead, he flipped backwards and landed on both his hands and feet. He landed with such great force that he broke both bones in his right arm about an inch above the wrist. He was in excruciating pain. Of course, there was a time of waiting at the emergency room. I visited with Stevie the next day and he said he never realized how much it hurt to see your child in so much pain and not be able to do anything to help him. His desire was to relieve Tanner of the pain he was suffering. Just talking about what Tanner had gone through the night before caused greater emotion to well up in Stevie. He loved his son so much he could not stand to see him hurt.

Abram and Sarai had no children. One day the Lord came to Abram with a special message: "And Abram said, 'Since thou hast given no offspring to me, one born in my house is my heir.' Then behold, the word of the Lord came to him, saying, 'This man will not be your heir; but one who shall come forth from your own body, he shall be your heir'" (Genesis 15:3–4, NASB).

Abram was a righteous man and believed what God said. As time passed by, they still did not have children and Sarai took it upon herself to remedy the problem. She sent her Egyptian maid, Hagar, to Abram and he lay with her. Hagar conceived and bore a son. Abram's name was changed to Abraham and Sarai became known as Sarah. Once again, God came to Abraham with a special message:

"And I will bless her, and indeed I will give you a son by her.

Then I will bless her, and she shall be a mother of nations; kings of peoples shall come from her." Then Abraham fell on his face and laughed, and said in his heart, "Will a child be born to a man one hundred years old? And will Sarah who is ninety years old, bear a child?"

Genesis 17:16–17 (NASB)

We know from the Scripture that Abraham and Sarah did have a child and they named him Isaac. We do not know how old Isaac was when God really put Abraham's faith to the test.

Now it came about after these things, that God tested Abraham, and said to him, "Abraham!" And he said, "Here I am." And he said, "Take now your son, your only son, whom you love, Isaac, and go to the land of Moriah; and offer him there as a burnt offering on one of the mountains of which I will tell you." So Abraham rose early in the morning and saddled his donkey, and took two of his young men with him and Isaac his son; and he split wood for the burnt offering, and arose and went to the place which God had told him.

Genesis 22:1–3 (NASB)

Abraham must have experienced great agony when God told him to sacrifice the son he and Sarah had waited so long to have. The pain would have been much greater than what Stevie experienced seeing Tanner suffer. This was a child they had wanted for so long and now God was asking them to relinquish this child to him. Abraham obediently did what God told him to do. When they came to the place where he was to build an altar and sacrifice Isaac, Abraham said some very important words to his servants: "And Abraham said to his servants, settle down and stay here with the donkey, and I and the young man will go yonder and worship and come again to you" (Genesis 22:5, AMP).

Did you notice what Abraham said? He said he and Isaac would go and worship and come back to them. Abraham believed the promise God had made to him in Genesis 12. God said he would be the father of many nations and there would be many descendants come from him. This promise definitely depended on Isaac having many children and there being many descendants through the years. Abraham was obedient to the Lord, so God spared Isaac's life. God wanted to see in Abraham the willingness to give up the son he had longed for. He wanted Abraham to sacrifice Isaac in his heart to him, thereby showing he loved God even more than his son.

Isaiah, a prophet, prophesied in the Book of Isaiah about a very important event that was going to take place: "Therefore the Lord himself will give you a sign: Behold, a virgin will be with child and bear a son, and she will call his name Immanuel" (Isaiah 7:14, NASB).

We know that the name Immanuel means "God with us." In the New Testament, Mary was betrothed to Joseph, but before they came together she was found to be pregnant by the Holy Spirit. Joseph did not understand this and was going to quietly divorce her in order not to bring embarrassment to her. One night an angel of the Lord appeared to Joseph in a dream:

> But when he had considered this, behold, an angel of the LORD appeared to him in a dream, saying, "Joseph, son of David, do not be afraid to take Mary as your wife; for that which has been conceived in her is of the Holy Spirit. And she will bear a Son; and you shall call his name Jesus, for it is he who will save his people from their sins."
>
> Matthew 1:20–21 (NASB)

Joseph was obedient and took Mary to be his wife and Jesus was born to them. The last phrase of verse 21 contains a very important message. How was Jesus going to save people from their sins? God had a definite plan in sending his one and only Son, in human form, to earth: "For even I, the Son of Man, came here not to be served but to serve others, and to give my life as a ransom for many" (Matthew 20:28, NLT).

Jesus explained to his disciples what must happen in his life. He told them he must die to redeem all people from the bondage of sin and death. It was only through the death of Jesus that others could be saved: "I have come to bring fire to the earth, and I wish that my task were already completed! There is a terrible baptism ahead of me, and I am under a heavy burden until it is accomplished" (Luke 12:49–50, NLT).

The baptism Jesus is referring to is his suffering and death. Jesus would be crucified, which was an excruciating death. The agony Jesus suffered on the cross is so apparent in the Scripture: "Then, at that time Jesus called out with a loud voice, '*Eloi, Eloi, lema sabachthani?*' which means, 'My God, my God, why have you forsaken me?'" (Mark 15:34, NLT).

He was quoting from Psalm 22. We are told that the whole twenty-second Psalm is the prophecy of the deep agony the Messiah would endure dying for the sins of the whole world. As Jesus took upon himself our sin, the separation from the Father brought deep agony for him. He not only suffered because of the separation from his Father, but the crucifixion itself brought terrible physical pain. It was a very important step in the process of his dying for the sins of all people. This was pictured by his baptism, the portrayal of the death, burial, and resurrection of Jesus in the Jordan River. "And I, the Son of Man, have come to seek and save those like him who are lost" (Luke 19:10, NLT).

It matters not what we have done in the past, Jesus meets us right where we are, and offers to us the gift of salvation. God the Father did not desire his Son to die on the cross, but he knew it had to be done. Jesus did not desire to go through this pain for us, but he was obedient to his Father and did exactly what God the Father told him to do. "But God demonstrates his own love toward us, in that while we were yet sinners, Christ died for us" (Romans 5:8, NASB).

We should be forever grateful for the great love shown towards us by Jesus's death on the cross. Jesus' resurrection from the grave brought us the hope of spending eternity with God in heaven: "As a result, I can really know Christ and experience the mighty power that raised him from the dead. I can learn what it means to suffer with him, sharing in his death, so that, somehow, I can experience the resurrection from the dead" (Philippians 3:10–11, NLT).

Write down a time in your life when you suffered or had to endure hardships, but through that experience you have come to know the Lord in a more intimate way.

Describe the relationship with the Lord you now have after what you have experienced. Can you say that Jesus is truly your master, your friend, or your companion?

The Testing of Your Faith

Doyal and I became acquainted with a special missionary couple, Joye and Herman Russell, at the Missionary Learning Center in Richmond, Virginia, when we were preparing to go as International Service Corp missionaries. They came to show slides of Malawi to those of us going to Africa. They loved their work in Malawi, but Herman, while out in one of the villages, had a stroke, causing him to lose his sight in the left eye. They served for another year before coming to the States on furlough. The stroke also affected his kidneys, leading to a kidney transplant some months later, preventing their return to Malawi. Joye has been going through treatments for ovarian cancer. Even in the midst of these trials, they continue to praise the Lord and serve him through the International Mission Board in the Office of Mission Personnel. They are an encouragement to candidates preparing to go and serve in missions. Romans 8:28 and Philippians 4:13 are two verses that have come to mean much to them during this time. The song that has meant so much to Joye is "Bring the Rain" by Mercy Me. It talks about people asking how they can make it through tough situations and how things that happen will forever affect who they are in Christ Jesus. It speaks of God's faithfulness in situations such as these.

> In this you greatly rejoice, though now for a little while you may have had to suffer grief in all kinds of trials. These have come so that your faith—of greater worth than gold, which perishes even though refined by fire—may be proved genuine and may result in praise, glory and honor when Jesus Christ is revealed.
>
> 1 Peter 1:6–7 (NIV)

I firmly believe their faith will be found strong and pure, and they will receive praise, glory and honor when Jesus Christ comes again.

Fanny Crosby was a living example of how God uses those who commit their lives to him even in the midst of a hardship.

Frances Jane "Fanny" Crosby (1820–1915) was an American hymn writer and poetess who wrote over 9,000 hymns during her life. One time a preacher sympathetically remarked, "I think it is a great pity that the Master did not give you sight when he showered so many other gifts upon you."
She replied quickly, "Do you know that if at birth I had been able to make one petition, it would have been that I should be born blind?"
"Why?" asked the surprised clergyman.
"Because when I get to heaven, the first face that shall ever gladden my sight will be that of my Savior!"[1]

Fanny Crosby wrote such hymns as "To God Be the Glory," "Jesus, Keep Me Near the Cross," "Praise Him! Praise Him!" "Redeemed, How I Love To Proclaim It," "Rescue the Perishing," "Jesus Is Tenderly Calling," and the list could go on and on. Fanny Crosby counted her disability to truly be a blessing, because Jesus' face will be the first face she will actually see. "Blessed is a man who perseveres under trial; for once he has been approved, he will receive the crown of life, which the Lord has promised to those who love him" (James 1:12, NASB).

It seems those who have allowed God to walk with them through life's trials have a much deeper knowledge and understanding of who God is and what he desires to do for them. Fanny Crosby exhibited great faith in the Lord.

Jesus knew what his future held, and many times he discussed this with his disciples. They did not really understand what Jesus was telling them. Jesus told them if they found the world hated them, they were to remember the world hated him first. If the disciples went along with the ways of the world, the people in the world would love them. Jesus had chosen them, set them apart from the world, so the people of the world hated them: "The people of the world will hate you because you belong to me, for they don't know God who sent me" (John 15:21, NLT).

Jesus tried to prepare the disciples for what they would face in the future. He wanted them to know when he went away he would send one to help them. "But I will send you the Counselor—the Spirit of truth. He will come to you from the Father and will tell you all about me" (John 15:26, NLT).

The disciples questioned Jesus as to what he meant. It was hard for them to understand because he spoke in parables. Finally, Jesus spoke in common terms, and they began to understand more.

> Jesus asked, "Do you finally believe? But the time is coming—in fact, it is already here—when you will be scattered, each one going his own way, leaving me alone. Yet I am not alone because the Father is with me. I have told you all this so that you may have peace in me. Here on earth you will have many trials and sorrows. But take heart, because I have overcome the world."
>
> John 16:31–33 (NLT)

We should not be surprised at life's difficulties we encounter because Jesus said we would encounter trials in life.

"I have fought a good fight, I have finished the race, and I have remained faithful" (2 Timothy 4:7, NLT). Most of us have not endured suffering to the extent Paul did. God gave him the strength to endure every trial. He was faithful to the Lord until he died, standing firm in his faith. May we do the same and continually praise the Lord for who he is. "I love thee, O Lord, my strength. The Lord is my rock and my fortress and my deliverer, my God, my rock, in whom I take refuge; my shield and the horn of my salvation, my stronghold" (Psalm 18:1–2, NASB).

Think of times in your life when you have suffered from health issues, a loss of a loved one, financial difficulties, the loss of your home and all your belongings by some natural disaster. How would your faith be described by those who know you?

Write a Bible verse you claimed to encourage you during that time. If you did not have a verse to claim at that time, search the Scripture so you will have a verse in time of need.

Called By God, Willing to Follow

The other day I was working with Daisy, our new blue heeler puppy. I put her on a leash and was trying to train her to follow me. Sometimes she would cooperate, and other times she would plant her body firmly on the ground. As I pulled her, she would pull in the other direction and become obstinate and disobedient to my commands. Of course, determined to make her follow me, I would yank on the leash and literally drag her. If she would follow when I called her, I would give her a little treat to reward her obedience. I will need to work at training her to immediately obey my commands. She needs to learn to follow where I lead.

Samuel became very upset with the children of Israel when they asked for a king to reign over them after Nahash, the king of the Ammonites, came against them. They decided they wanted an earthly king rather than having the Lord their God as their king. Samuel told them what they must do if they wanted to succeed: "Now if you will fear and worship the Lord and listen to his voice, and if you do not rebel against the Lord's commands, and if you and your king follow the Lord your God, then all will be well" (1 Samuel 12:14, NLT).

The Israelites had to stand in awe and reverence before the Lord and worship him. They and their king must listen to his voice and follow the Lord their God.

I truly believe God requires the same of us today. God calls plain, ordinary people to do his work. We must respect and worship the Lord with our whole heart. We must listen for his voice as he speaks to us and obey all he commands us to do. "But Amos replied, 'I'm not one of your professional prophets. I certainly never trained to be one. I'm just a shepherd, and I take care of fig trees. But the

Lord called me away from my flock and told me, 'Go and prophesy to my people in Israel'" (Amos 7:14–15, NLT).

Amos was a shepherd who cared for a flock of sheep and also took care of sycamore fig trees. He did not receive any special preparation for this job. He had not been raised by his parents to be a prophet, but God called and he followed in obedience. God will equip us for the task he calls us to perform.

> Strengthen (complete, perfect) and make you what you ought to be and equip you with everything good that you may carry out his will; [while he himself] works in you and accomplishes that which is pleasing in his sight, through Jesus Christ (the Messiah); to whom be the glory forever and ever (to the ages of the ages). Amen (so be it).
>
> Hebrew 13:21 (AMP)

In Hebrews 11, Barak is listed in the roll of the people of great faith. Ehud, a judge over Israel, had died and the Israelites did evil in the sight of the Lord. The Lord gave them over to King Jabin of Hazor, a Canaanite king. The leader of his army was Sisera and he oppressed the Israelites for twenty years. Deborah, a prophetess, sent for Barak.

> Now she sent and summoned Barak, the son of Abinoam from Kedesh-naphtali, and said to him, "Behold, the LORD, the God of Israel, has commanded, 'Go and march to Mount Tabor, and take with you ten thousand men from the sons of Naphtali and from the sons of Zebulun. And I will draw out to you Sisera, the commander of Jabin's army, with his chariots and his many troops to the river Kishon; and I will give him into your hand.'" Then Barak said to her, "If you will go with me, then I will go; but if you will not go with me, I will not go."
>
> Judges 4:6–8 (NASB)

Immediately, we think Barak is a coward and afraid to go by himself, but the Scripture does not say that. Deborah was a judge, and to our knowledge Barak was not, so this is why he received his orders from her. Barak was from Naphtali, one of the tribes sending men to the battlefield. Barak hesitated when he was told what God wanted him to do, but so did others such as Moses and Gideon. Wiersbe says in his commentary, "God's commandments are God's enablements." God will enable us to do what he commands us to do. Barak was not questioning God nor was he refusing to go. He believed God would deliver Sisera into his hands. It was simply that he was asking Deborah, the prophetess, to go with him. Possibly, he thought he might need to hear a word from the Lord while in battle. Deborah did not hesitate in going and Wiersbe says it is a good sign that his request was not out of the will of God. Deborah did tell him he would receive no honor for the victory, but it would go to a woman.

> When Israel chose new gods, war erupted at the city gates. Yet not a shield or spear could be seen among forty thousand warriors in Israel!
>
> Judges 5:8 (NLT)

> There were no blacksmiths in the land of Israel in those days. The Philistines wouldn't allow them for fear they would make swords and spears for the Hebrews.
>
> 1 Samuel 13:19 (NLT)

Because of this, there were very few weapons available for battle. There was no established army, simply volunteers. We know what Deborah and Barak did was an act of obedience and faith in our God. God had promised them victory in battle and they followed his leading and stood strong on his promise.

God's call on the life of Billy Sunday, the great evangelist, and his commitment to the Lord is a good modern day example. Billy Sunday was born on November 19, 1862, and his father died of pneumonia in an army camp on December 22 of the same year. Consequently, he never knew his father and his mother. He and his brother were sent to an orphanage as young children. He began his baseball career in 1883 with the Chicago White Stockings. He was led to the Lord by Sarah "Ma" Clarke at the Pacific Garden Mission in Chicago in 1886. In 1888, He was traded to the Pittsburgh Pirates and also married Helen Thompson, who they referred to as "Ma Sunday." In 1891, he set the record of ninety stolen bases in 116 games. He received offers of more money from the Philadelphia Phillies and from Cincinnati to play ball for them. He passed up both offers and went to work as secretary of the religious department for the YMCA for $83 a month. In 1894, the Pittsburgh Pirates offered Sunday $2,000 a month to play for them, but he accepted the job as an advance man for evangelist J. Wilbur Chapman for $40 a week. Billy Sunday held his first revival in 1897 in Garner, Iowa, and one hundred people accepted Jesus during the week. He was ordained as a minister in 1903 by a Presbyterian church. During his ministry, thousands of people came to know Jesus as Savior. During the famous ten-week evangelistic campaign in New York, 98,000 people came forward to accept Christ. Once God called him as his servant, no amount of money could steer him away from serving the Lord. Money was not important, but his commitment to the Lord was. He was called by God to follow him and be his spokesman and he was obedient. Think about the number of people who would not know Jesus if Billy Sunday had not accepted the Lord's call to preach and been faithful to follow him.[2]

How then shall they call upon him in whom they have not believed? And how shall they believe in him whom they have not heard? And how shall they hear without a preacher? And how shall they preach unless they are sent?

Just as it is written, "How beautiful are the feet of those who bring glad tidings of good things!"

Romans 10:14–15 (NASB)

Has God called you to serve him in some way? Have you been obedient to the Lord? Are you listening for God's voice? "Then the Lord came and stood and called as at other times, 'Samuel! Samuel!' and Samuel said, 'Speak, for thy servant is listening'" (1 Samuel 3:10, NASB).

Think about how you have responded to God's call.

The Measure of Greatness

The dictionary says to be great is to be beyond the average, markedly superior in character, quality, or skill. How do we measure greatness today? The other day I was visiting with our youngest son, and he told me he was putting a window in the door of his office at church. My first thought was that he might ruin the door. He proceeded to tell me how he was going to put tape on the door in the place where the window was to go and cut around it. I mentioned to him that he must have paid attention as a child to the way his dad did things. He replied, "Oh, Mom, I would not be the man I am today if it were not for Dad." In his eyes, his dad is a great man. He not only taught him different skills, but he set the example for him spiritually. Jesus gave the disciples an example of how they were to treat others: " …so he got up from the meal, took off his outer clothing, and wrapped a towel around his waist. After that, he poured water into a basin and began to wash his disciples' feet, drying them with the towel that was wrapped around him" (John 13:4–5, NIV).

Jesus knew the disciples would understand more clearly if he demonstrated how they were to serve others with a loving, compassionate heart. When he was finished, he said, "Now that I, your Lord and teacher, have washed your feet, you also should wash one another's feet" (John 13:14, NIV).

Stevie learned by watching his dad and by the example he set for him. The disciples learned from the example set by Jesus. As they traveled with him, they listened to his teaching and watched the way he did things.

My parents were the greatest example I had growing up. They taught me about life and how to love others in spite of things in their lives that make them appear unlovable. They demonstrated to me how one could have a forgiving spirit. Their lives were an example of great joy in the Lord because of the relationship they had with him. They showed gentleness, meekness, humbleness, and a desire to bring peace to all around them. "But the fruit of the Spirit is love, joy, peace, patience, kindness, goodness, faithfulness, gentleness, self-control; against such things there is no law. If we live by the Spirit, let us also walk by the Spirit" (Galatians 5:22–23, 25, NASB). They exemplified the greatness of the Lord in their lives.

When I think of greatness in ordinary people that God has used, I think of Corrie ten Boom. She and her family risked their lives to help the Jews escape from the Nazis during World War II. What was the reward for what they did? They were put in a concentration camp and treated badly. Through all that happened, Corrie stood strong and exemplified Christ-likeness in the most terrifying of circumstances. Corrie said, "Every experience God gives us, every person he puts in our lives, is the perfect preparation for the future only he can see." She was a great witness for the Lord, even in the midst of suffering in the concentration camp. One day, Corrie and two other prisoners who were ill were taken outside the prison walls to see a doctor. While waiting to see the doctor, Corrie asked to use the lavatory. The nurse who took her to the bathroom asked very discreetly if there was any way she could help her. Corrie replied, "Yes. Oh, yes! A Bible! Could you get me a Bible? And a needle and thread! And a toothbrush! And soap!" Corrie saw the doctor, and as she was leaving the nurse rose quickly, swishing by her, placing something wrapped in paper in Corrie's hand. Corrie felt it in her pocket and thought she felt the outline of a book and wondered if it could be a Bible. Upon returning to prison, she opened the paper, and to her and her cellmates' delight there was soap, a package of safety pins, not a whole Bible, but the four Gospels in four little books. She was elated and shared the soap and safety pins with her cellmates. She offered to share the Gospels, but they were afraid to be caught with them. Two nights later, Corrie ten Boom was put in solitary confinement. She was very sick and continued to run a fever. Gradually as her health returned, she could see well enough to read the Gospels she had been given. She could see the whole drama of salvation unfold within the words of the Gospels. She pondered how all of this could even be a part of Jesus's plan to show how in the midst of defeat, the Lord was victorious over death. What was it God was trying to show her?

> "For I know the plans I have for you," declares the LORD, "plans to prosper you and not to harm you, plans to give you hope and a future. Then you will call upon me and come and pray to me, and I will listen to you. You will seek me and find me when you seek me with all your heart."
>
> Jeremiah 29:11–13 (NIV)

In the writings about Corrie, it tells us she found solace there in solitary confinement in the words of the Gospels. She realized Jesus faced things similar and even worse than what she was facing. When she was released from the concentration camp, she spent her time telling people about Jesus and sharing with them what the Lord had done for her while she was in prison. She was a living example of Christ-likeness.

The Bible tells us Solomon was a great king and became greater than any of the kings who ruled in Jerusalem. Whatever he wanted, he took. He accumulated homes, vineyards, gardens, and orchards, and he planted all kinds of fruit-bearing trees. He had flocks and herds of different kinds of animals. He sought happiness in the things men enjoy. He was not afraid of work and worked very hard to get what he wanted. One day, he sat down and evaluated all he had obtained: "But as I looked at everything I had worked so hard to accomplish, it was all so meaningless. It was like chasing the wind. There was nothing really worthwhile anywhere" (Ecclesiastes 2:11, NLT).

He decided that whether one was wise or a fool, each one would die, so everything was meaningless. He came to the conclusion that even when we enjoy the pleasure of food and drink, it is from the hand of God: "God gives wisdom, knowledge, and joy to those who please him" (Ecclesiastes 2:26a, NLT).

Solomon concluded there was a right time for everything in life. In the third chapter of Ecclesiastes he listed many of those things. He was really evaluating all he had done and he came to this conclusion:

> I have seen the burden God has laid on men. He has made everything beautiful in its time. He has also set eternity in the hearts of men; yet they cannot fathom what God has done from beginning to end. I know that there is nothing better for men than to be happy and do good while they live. That everyone may eat and drink, and find satisfaction in all his toil—this is the gift of God. I know that everything God does will endure forever; nothing can be added to it and nothing taken from it. God does it so that men will revere him.
>
> Ecclesiastes 3:10–14 (NIV)

To me, one of the wisest things Solomon said in Ecclesiastes is that when we come before God, we are to come in reverence, prepared to listen to what he has to say to us: "As you enter the house of God keep your ears open and your mouth shut! Don't be a fool who doesn't realize that mindless offerings to God are evil. And don't make rash promises to God, for he is in heaven, and you are only here on earth. So let your words be few" (Ecclesiastes 5:1–2, NLT).

Many come to church and go through the motions of worshipping by praising God, praying to him, and making promises to him, but they are not sincere. They leave the place of worship actually in worse condition because they did not give God the reverence and honor he deserves. Warren Wiersbe wrote, "The worship of God is the highest ministry of the church and must come from devoted hearts and yielded wills." Many times we come to church with no thought of what God desires to do in our lives while we are there. We do not plan to devote our hearts to the Lord or allow him to bring about what he desires for our life. We are simply there. To end his writing, Solomon said,

> Here is my final conclusion: Fear God and obey his commands, for this is the duty of every person. God will judge us for everything we do, including every secret thing, whether good or bad.
>
> (Ecclesiastes 12:13–14, NLT)

Solomon was a great king and wrote with great wisdom.

What standards do you use to measure greatness?

Who is the greatest person you have known, and what made that person great in your eyes?

Superabundant Source of Strength and Nourishment

Autumn is here and the leaves are beginning to change. We have all types of small, leafy limbs lying in our yard, and the leaves on these small limbs have already turned brown. My husband said the cutworms were cutting off the small limbs. A cutworm is a dull-colored caterpillar with smooth skin. Sometimes they are gray and sometimes black. Some of them have spots and some have stripes. The cutworm can be very destructive, and if you were to look at our front yard under our hickory trees, you would see how destructive they are. They can destroy entire fields of corn, wheat, or vegetables overnight. They can also cause great damage to tobacco, cotton, and many varieties of fruit trees. The cutworm chooses the tender, small limbs to chew on. When it chews a branch off the tree, the leaves turn brown quickly because the severed branch has no source of nourishment. When I mowed the yard, I picked up many small branches from the ground and threw them over the fence. It was amazing at the perfect cut on the branch, except for a few jagged pieces in the middle, where it broke when it got too heavy to bear its weight. The cutworms are a masterful demolition crew. The same process can take place in the life of a believer. "I am the vine; you are the branches. Whoever lives in me and I in him bears much (abundant) fruit. However, apart from me [cut off from vital union with me] you can do nothing" (John 15:5, AMP).

Our lifeline as a believer is the Lord Jesus Christ. He is the vine to which we, the branch, are connected. He is our source of strength and nourishment. If we do not nourish our intimate, love relationship with the Lord, we become as deadwood. Satan relishes this in the life of a believer. I am sure each of us has known people who claim to know Jesus, but yet, they appear dead, disconnected from the Lord. Possibly, we have gone through such times ourselves. How do we keep the reservoir of strength and nourishment full from the Lord? Ezekiel was commissioned by God to deliver God's message to the children of Israel.

> The voice said to me, "Son of man, eat what I am giving you—eat this scroll! Then go and give its message to the people of Israel." So I opened my mouth, and he fed me the scroll. "Eat it all," he said. And when I ate it, it tasted as sweet as honey. Then he said, "Son of man, go to the people of Israel with my messages."
>
> Ezekiel 3:1–4 (NLT)

Ezekiel first had to let God's message sink deep into his heart before he was able to go and deliver God's message to others. He had to meditate on what God was saying. Not only did he receive the message God wanted him to deliver, but he also received strength from the Lord for the task he had to perform.

We must spend time with the Lord in his Word in order to hear God speak and give us direction in life. He will equip and strengthen us for any task he calls us to do. If we do not spend time with the Lord in his Word and in prayer, we become weak and begin to fall away from him. The intimate fellowship we once had becomes more distant and disconnected. Soon we are as a branch severed from the vine and we begin to dry up, producing less and less fruit for the Lord.

> And we pray this in order that you may live a life worthy of the LORD and may please him in every way: bearing fruit in every good work, growing in the knowledge of God, being strengthened with all power according to his glorious might so that you may have great endurance and patience.
>
> Colossians 1:10–11a (NIV)

God the Father wants us to live a life worthy of him and bear fruit for him. He desires to be glorified by what we do as his children. The only way we can do this is to stay connected to our source of strength, the Lord Jesus Christ, our vine.

We must continually voice our praise and our concerns in life to the Lord. "The Lord hates the sacrifice of the wicked, but he delights in the prayers of the upright. The Lord despises the way of the wicked, but he loves those who pursue godliness" (Proverbs 15:8–9, NLT).

God, our Father, enjoys hearing from his children and has great love for all who desire and strive to live godly lives. He promises he will be there to give us the strength we need for life. "Yet those who wait for the Lord will gain new strength; they will mount up with wings like eagles, they will run and not get tired, they will walk and not become weary" (Isaiah 40:31, NASB).

When Jesus had finished feeding the 5,000 men, plus women and children, he went to the mountain by himself to pray: "And after he had sent the multitudes away, he went up to the mountain by himself to pray; and when it was evening, he was there alone" (Matthew 14:23, NASB).

Jesus felt the necessity to spend time alone with his Father. Prayer was a very important part of Jesus's ministry. When he was preparing to choose the twelve apostles, he prayed: "One day soon afterward Jesus went to a mountain to pray, and he prayed to God all night. At daybreak he called together all of his disciples and chose twelve of them to be apostles ... " (Luke 6:12–13a, NLT).

Jesus felt such a need for God's direction that he prayed all night. Sometimes, it is hard for us to pray for five minutes. As children of God, we must find time daily, by ourselves, and spend time with the Lord in prayer. We express our concerns to the Lord, but we must also listen to what the Lord has to say to us. Prayer is not just us talking to the Lord, but it also includes us listening to him.

Our continual strengthening and nourishing from the Lord

comes through the avenues of meditating on the Word of God and praying from the depths of our heart to him. The only way we can receive this nourishment is by abiding in him: "If you abide in me, and my words abide in you, ask whatever you wish, and it shall be done for you" (John 15:7, NASB).

How much time do you spend daily abiding with the Lord? The only way God's Word can abide or live in us is for us to spend time saturating our minds and hearts with his Word. Then we can ask whatever we desire and it will be done for us through the avenue of prayer. Will you make a covenant with the Lord to spend more time with him daily? If you feel the need for more of this sweet time with the Lord, write it on a card, sign and date it. Put it in your Bible to remind you of your agreement with the Lord. Be diligent about praying and meditating on the Word of God.

"Now to him who is able to do immeasurably more than all we ask or imagine, according to his power that is at work within us" (Ephesians 3:20, NIV). What does this verse mean to you in regards to the source of our strength and nourishment?

Fear of the Unknown

We bought our new blue heeler puppy when she was six weeks old. She is now four months old and we are trying to train her to eat from our dog feeder. There are times we need to be gone and it is hard to ask people to feed the dog. The past two days we have been coaxing her to eat from the feeder with different things. We propped the flap back so she can see the food. If we coax her to it with food in our hand, she will eat from our hand inside the feeder. She appears to be very hungry, but I guess she is not hungry enough. It is difficult not to give her other things because we know she is hungry. But, the only way to train her is to have her get so hungry that she will lose her fear of the feeder and eat the food. I was able to get her to eat a few bites of turkey off the top of the food in the feeder. Why? Because she was so hungry and it was sweet to the taste. For a moment, her fear left her.

We all remember the story of Joseph and his jealous brothers. His father, Jacob, showed much love for him and gave him a coat of many colors. Also, Joseph had brought back bad reports to their father about them. Joseph had a dream that his brothers would bow down to him and this made them angrier. Joseph had another dream and his mother, father, and brothers would all bow down to him. They thought their father showed favoritism toward Joseph and determined in their hearts to do bad toward him. One day Jacob sent Joseph to check on his brothers: "So it came about, when Joseph reached his brothers, that they stripped Joseph of his tunic, the varicolored tunic that was on him; and they took him and threw him into the pit. Now the pit was empty, without any water in it" (Genesis 37:23–24, NASB).

Some Midianite traders came along and the brothers took

Joseph out of the pit and sold him to the Ishmaelites for twenty shekels of silver. Joseph was only seventeen years when he was sold into slavery in Egypt to Potiphar, pharaoh's officer. Thirteen years later, after several difficult situations were resolved, he was promoted to governor of Egypt. There was a famine in the land and Jacob sent his sons to Egypt to buy grain because they had no food.

> Now Joseph was the ruler over the land; he was the one who sold to all the people of the land. And Joseph's brothers came and bowed down to him with their faces to the ground. When Joseph saw his brothers he recognized them, but he disguised himself to them and spoke to them harshly. And he said to them, "Where have you come from?" And they said, "From the land of Canaan, to buy food." But Joseph had recognized his brothers, although they did not recognize him.
>
> Genesis 42:6–8 (NASB)

In the Bible, it tells us Joseph remembered the dreams he had in the past. He accused them of being spies. Can't you imagine the fear that came over them when he made this accusation? They had no idea about what would happen to them because they were out of their own personal surroundings. They feared the unknown. Many things transpired before they ever realized it was Joseph talking. The time finally came when Joseph could stand it no longer and he made himself known to his brothers. He wept so loudly that all of the people in the household heard him.

> Then Joseph said to his brothers, "I am Joseph! Is my father still alive?" But his brothers could not answer him, for they were dismayed at his presence. Then Joseph said to his brothers, "Please come closer to me." And they came closer. And he said, "I am your brother Joseph, whom you sold into Egypt. And now do not be grieved or angry with

yourselves, because you sold me here; for God sent me before you to preserve life."

Genesis 45:3–5 (NASB)

I can just imagine how they must have feared for their lives because of what they had done. What they had intended for evil was a part of God's plan to preserve the nation of Israel.

I remember the time seven members of our church went to Brazil on a mission trip. We were going to Aracaju to do evangelism. When we got off the plane, we went through customs and walked down a very narrow pathway amidst a throng of onlookers. There must have been someone important coming off the plane because there were hundreds of people there. It seemed when we walked down the pathway we were knocking elbows with the people because they were so close. All seven of us really had a fear of the unknown. They appeared to have a look of anger on their faces, as if they felt like we did not belong there. We were not accustomed to traveling in foreign countries. We had to fly into Brazil alone because of a canceled flight in Tulsa that separated us from the group we were to travel with. Every time we arrived in an airport, we had to make changes because our flight had left or been canceled. In times such as these, it is good to recall verses that assure us of God's presence with us: "Do not fear, for I am with you; do not anxiously look about you, for I am your God. I will strengthen you, surely I will help you, surely I will uphold you with my righteous right hand" (Isaiah 41:10, NASB).

Sometimes people intentionally do not read the Bible because they fear it will bring conviction about things in their lives they need to change. They also do not realize God's Word brings conviction of sin. However, it also contains God's wisdom to help us know what to do about the sin in our life. It has the solution to every trial in life. People must conquer the fear of the unknown so they can have joy in the Lord. Jesus was speaking to the disciples, explaining to them why he must go away. This was difficult for the disciples to understand.

> But I will send you the Counselor—the Spirit of truth. He will come to you from the Father and will tell you all about me.
>
> John 15:26 (NLT)

And when he comes, he will convince the world of its sin, and of God's righteousness, and of the coming judgment. The world's sin is unbelief in me. Righteousness is available because I go to the Father, and you will see me no more. Judgment will come because the prince of this world has already been judged.

> John 16:8–11 (NLT)

I have told you these things, so that in me you may have peace. In this world you will have trouble. But take heart! I have overcome the world.

> John 16:33 (NIV)

Jesus was concerned for his disciples, so he prayed to the Father for them: "Now this is eternal life: that they may know you, the only true God, and Jesus Christ, whom you have sent" (John 17:3, NIV).

There needs to be no fear, because we are offered eternal life through Jesus's death on the cross for our sins.

What is your greatest fear in life today?

Where do you go for comfort?

Have you ever feared something you knew very little about, but when you attempted to do it or confront whatever it was, you found it really was nothing to fear? What was it and where did you get your confidence to overcome that fear?

Why Did God Create Me?

Growing up, and even as an adult, I had such great examples of what a true follower of the Lord was to be. My dad, mom, and grandmother (Mama Cordie) lived lives worthy of being imitated by others. They loved the Lord with all their heart, soul, and mind. They sought the Lord daily through prayer and the study of his Word.

A young lady I know in Oklahoma City radiates with the love of the Lord. Her whole countenance is one of a humble spirit, a deep love and concern for others, and certainly not centered on self. She has a way of making others feel at ease with her. When you are talking to her, you know her thoughts are centered on you because of the way she responds. She loves the Lord with her whole heart and has such a desire to serve him. She serves with great humility: "Are there any of you who are wise and understanding? You are to prove it by your good life, by your good deeds performed with humility and wisdom" (James 3:13, GNT). My young friend exhibits great humility and wisdom in all she does. She gives all glory and honor to the Lord for who and what she is today.

Jesus Christ is a great example of one who showed great humility. My greatest desire in life is to imitate the life of Jesus Christ. The Bible tells us we are to have the same mind, the same attitude as Jesus: "Let this same attitude and purpose and [humble] mind be in you which was in Christ Jesus: [Let him be your example of humility:]" (Philippians 2:5, AMP).

As a believer, I am to have the same attitude, purpose, and humble spirit that Jesus had. I am to think more highly of others than of myself and be more concerned about their needs than of my own. Jesus Christ did not think of his equality with God to be something he would cling to, but was willing to humble himself and come to earth in human form. He was not thinking of himself, but the needs of others. He was willing to give his life so others might have everlasting life. He took upon himself the sin burden of the world. What greater example could we have of true humility?

Believers are to exhibit the same love and compassion Jesus showed for others.

> Jesus traveled through all the cities and villages of that area, teaching in the synagogues and announcing the good news about the kingdom. And wherever he went, he healed people of every sort of disease and illness. He felt great pity for the crowds that came, because their problems were so great and they didn't know where to go for help. They were like sheep without a shepherd.
>
> Matthew 9:35–36 (NLT)

When Jesus saw people's physical and spiritual needs, his spirit burned within him. He had a desire for others to know the source of their strength. Jesus taught his disciples a very important lesson all of us need to hear: "He said to his disciples, 'The harvest is so great, but the workers are so few. So pray to the Lord who is in charge of the harvest; ask him to send out more workers for his fields'" (Matthew 9:37–38, NLT).

How long has it been since your heart was so stirred about the lostness of our world, that tears came to your eyes and you wept over what you saw? Jesus continually shared the good news (the gospel) with others so they could know where to find help. How long has it been since you shared the gospel with another person?

The people Jesus showed compassion to were people who appeared as sheep without a shepherd. I am continually reminded of the book by Phillip Keller, *A Shepherd Looks At Psalm 23*. I love the way he compares the life of a person to that of sheep. A good shepherd watches his flock very carefully. If he sees a sheep has wandered off, he will immediately go look for the sheep. If he does not, the sheep can easily get into trouble. Sheep get tangled in the bushes or sometimes fall over in the mud of the stream and most likely will not be able to get up. A shepherd who loves his sheep will go, find the sheep, and carry it back to where it is supposed to be. It reminds me of the parable of the lost sheep:

> What man among you, if he has a hundred sheep and has lost one of them, does not leave the ninety-nine in the open pasture, and go after the one which is lost, until he finds it? And when he has found it, he lays it on his shoulders, rejoicing. And when he comes home, he calls together his friends and his neighbors, saying to them, "Rejoice with me, for I have found my sheep which was lost!" I tell you that in the same way, there will be more joy in heaven over one sinner who repents than over ninety-nine righteous persons who need no repentance.
>
> Luke 15:4–7 (NASB)

Just as a shepherd is concerned about one lost sheep, we must be concerned about the many lost people around us. There are many people wandering around like a sheep without a shepherd because they do not know Jesus as Savior. The number increases daily as many come from foreign lands to our United States. The fields are so ripe for harvest, but few are those who go to labor in those fields, cultivating the ground, planting the seeds, and caring for the plants as they grow. Once this is done the harvest can be reaped.

May God quicken our hearts and stir within us the burning desire to see a great awakening take place in our world today. The only way this will happen is for God's people to fervently pray for lost people to be saved. We must be diligent in our prayer life, put feet to our prayers and share the good news of Jesus Christ with the lost. I was commenting to a friend the other day about people here in the United States complaining about so many people coming from other countries to live in our country. I told her if we would look at it from Jesus's perspective, he is bringing a mission field to us, dropping it right on our doorstep. It could be said, if we will not go to the mission field, God will bring the mission field to us.

When others see you, do they see a witness for the Lord in the things you do and say? My mother always said to me, "Your actions speak louder than words." My prayer is for others to see Jesus in me and I pray this is also the prayer of your heart.

Are you willing to go the extra mile and do whatever God calls you to do? Do you spend time before the Lord waiting for him to speak to you? What do you hear God saying to you? What is your answer?

Do you imitate the loving compassion and humility displayed by my young friend in Oklahoma City and the great example of Jesus? What are some changes you need to make in your life to be more like Jesus?

The Infestation of Crickets

Nothing is more annoying than the sound of a cricket hidden somewhere within the walls of your home. I understand from brief research that only the male cricket makes the annoying sound. They stay in sheltered places during the day and come out at night to find food. The past few weeks we have been overrun with crickets. Many are very small, so we know they are hatching here in the house. The other morning as I was studying and having my time with the Lord, one dropped from somewhere above onto my desk. We walk down our hall and they are hopping about. We are hoping they will soon starve to death. They are not as fast as the normal cricket, and many times we can stomp them. Sometimes it sounds like we are having a stomping contest as we have carpet throughout our house. The thought of an insect of any kind being in one's house is aggravating. We hope as the season of the year is changing and cooler weather is coming, they will disappear. Even though the crickets are annoying, they remind me of the exodus of the Israelites.

The Israelites were slaves in the land of Egypt. Moses was pasturing the flock of Jethro, his father-in-law, in the area of Mount Horeb. Moses had an unbelievable experience with God in this place. The angel of the Lord appeared to Moses in a burning bush. The amazing thing is the bush did not burn up. When Moses turned aside to look at the bush, God spoke to Moses: "When the Lord saw that he had caught Moses' attention, God called to him from the bush, 'Moses! Moses!' 'Here I am!' Moses replied. 'Do not come any closer,' God told him. 'Take off your sandals, for you are standing on holy ground'" (Exodus 3:4–6, NLT).

Moses had an unusual experience as God spoke to him from the burning bush. God was very much aware of the oppression of the Israelites in Egypt. Their hardships were increasing day by day. "'Now go, for I am sending you to Pharaoh. You will lead my people, the Israelites, out of Egypt.' 'But who am I to appear before Pharaoh?' Moses asked God. 'How can you expect me to lead the Israelites out of Egypt?' Then God told him, 'I will be with you'" (Exodus 3:10–12a, NLT).

Moses was to be the one to lead the Israelites from Egypt out of Pharaoh's bondage. Moses questioned the Lord concerning his own personal ability to do this, but the Lord let it be known it would not be in Moses' power, but by God's power. Because of Moses' feelings of inadequacy, God agreed to allow his brother, Aaron, to go with him and speak for him. God gave Moses certain signs to perform to show the Egyptians and Pharaoh the power of the Lord. Moses and Aaron did as God said, but Pharaoh's magicians and sorcerers of Pharaoh could perform the same acts. Pharaoh's heart was hardened, and he would not let the children of Israel go. He simply made their labor harder.

God gave Pharaoh many warnings about what would happen, but he did not heed the warnings. Finally, God allowed Pharaoh to live in his own misery because he continually resisted God's warnings. Do you think God does the same with a person today whose heart is stirred many times to give up their old sinful life, believe in him, and receive eternal life, but yet they refuse to accept him? This person is pictured in the parable of the sower.

The sower went out to sow his seed; and as he sowed, some fell beside the road; and it was trampled under foot, and the birds of the air ate it up. Now the parable is this: the seed is the word of God. And those beside the road are those who have heard; then the devil comes and takes away the word from their heart, so that they may not believe and be saved.

Luke 8:5, 11–12 (NASB)

Many people die and go to hell because they allow the devil to rule their life and they refuse to accept Jesus as Savior. Like Pharaoh, their hearts become hardened just as Pharaoh's heart was hardened. Because of Pharaoh's persistent refusal to allow the children of Israel to leave the land of Egypt, God sent ten plagues upon the Egyptians. We think we have been infested with crickets, but it is nothing compared to what happened to Pharaoh and his people. "Now the Lord says, 'You are going to find out that I am the Lord. Look! I will hit the water of the Nile with this staff, and the river will turn to blood. The fish in it will die, and the river will stink. The Egyptians will not be able to drink any water from the Nile'" (Exodus 7:17–18, NLT). If you have ever been on a pond or riverbank where someone has left a dead fish and smelled the stench of the rotting fish, you can imagine the smell along the Nile River. It can be compared to the foul smell coming from a person who allows Satan to rule their life and continues to live a life infested with the sins of this world.

God then sent a plague of frogs upon the land.

> This is what the Lord says: Let my people go, so they can worship me. If you refuse, then listen carefully to this: I will send vast hordes of frogs across your entire land from one border to the other. The Nile River will swarm with them. They will come up out of the river and into your houses, even into your bedrooms and onto your beds! Every home in Egypt will be filled with them. They will fill even your ovens and your kneading bowls.
>
> Exodus 8:1b–3 (NLT)

I can just imagine reaching for a bowl in my cabinet and it being filled with dead frogs because of the lack of food and air. The other day I drove into our garage and did not realize there was a dead frog on the floor. I squashed it with the tire of our car. My! What a horrible stink! I quickly got water and a broom and proceeded to wash the tire and floor to get rid of the horrible odor. Still, Pharaoh's heart was hardened even after the plague of frogs.

God sent the plagues of insects (like gnats or lice), flies, and pestilence that brought death on the Egyptian's livestock. There were boils on people and animals alike. Crops, people, animals, and anything outside was destroyed by hail, and locusts devoured every living plant and tree the hail had not destroyed. A deep darkness covered their land, so dark they could not see to move. Finally, God sent the plague of the death of the firstborn sons of Pharaoh, the Egyptians, and even the firstborn of animals. The Israelites were given instruction as to what to do with the blood of the lamb so the death angel would pass over their homes, and their firstborn sons would not die. Pharaoh finally agreed to let the children of Israel leave: "Pharaoh sent for Moses and Aaron during the night. 'Leave us!' he cried. 'Go away, all of you! Go and serve the Lord as you have requested'" (Exodus 12:31, NLT).

After the Israelites left Egypt, Pharaoh began to think about what had happened. He realized they no longer had the Israelites to serve them. God hardened his heart once again and Pharaoh and his army pursued the Israelites. In the process, Pharaoh and his army lost their lives.

What happened here is what happens many times in the heart of one who has accepted the Lord as Savior. We allow our heart to move from focusing on the Lord to the things of the world. Suddenly, our hearts become hardened. Satan gets a foothold in our life and things begin to go wrong. When God finally gets our attention, we must confess our sin to the Lord and change our ways. "If we confess our sins, he is faithful and righteous to forgive us our sins and to cleanse us from all unrighteousness" (1 John 1:9, NASB). We must allow God to control our life.

The heart of a person, who refuses again and again to accept Jesus as Savior, becomes hardened toward things of the Lord.

They do not want anyone to speak to them about Jesus Christ. They wallow in the muck and mire of sinfulness, and just like a pen full of hogs wallowing in the mud, they begin to have a very distasteful odor about them. What is our responsibility as a believer concerning these people?

> But you, dear friends, must continue to build your lives on the foundation of your holy faith. And continue to pray as you are directed by the Holy Spirit. Live in such a way that God's love can bless you as you wait for the eternal life that our LORD Jesus Christ in his mercy is going to give you.
>
> Jude 20–22 (NLT)

What is the condition of your heart today? Is your heart infested with sin? If so, confess your sin to the Lord and seek his forgiveness. If you do not know the Jesus as Savior, cry out to him, asking him to save you.

Time Out: Need to Regroup

Thinking of time out, I remember a young man on our high school football team in Heavener, Oklahoma, who was great at faking an injury so our team could have a time out. He was famous for doing this near the end of the game when the score might be tied, and we were out of time outs. He would fake being injured for the team to have time to regroup and call a play to possibly win the game. Without this time, it was almost certain we would lose the game. This is not a good reputation to have, but it makes good application of what I want us to think about today.

As a believer, if we do not take time out to be alone with God in prayer, we fail to develop a strong, cohesive relationship with our Father. What is prayer? According to the Bible dictionary, it involves the dialogue between God and people, especially his covenant partners. It is a desire for a relationship with our Father. Prayer is extremely important in a believer's life. It is as important as food and air are for our physical survival. Martin Luther said, "As a shoemaker makes a shoe, and a tailor makes a coat, so ought a Christian to pray. Prayer is the daily business of a Christian." Without the daily practice of communing with the Father through prayer, the flow of the daily nourishment from the Lord is blocked. The excitement, the joy of the Lord, is lost in a believer's life.

Jesus set the greatest example regarding the need of prayer in one's life. Jesus had been baptized by John the Baptist in the Jordan River. As Jesus came up out of the water an amazing thing happened: " ... and a voice came out of the heavens: 'Thou art my beloved Son, in thee I am well-pleased'" (Mark 1:11, NASB).

Jesus immediately was compelled by the Spirit to go into the wilderness where he experienced temptations by Satan. Later, Jesus came into Galilee preaching the gospel. He began choosing his disciples. He went about the work of healing those who were sick. Jesus had healed some with diseases and cast demons from others. I believe Jesus considered what he did next to be the most important activity of his life: "And in the early morning, while it was still dark, he arose and went out and departed to a lonely place, and was praying there" (Mark 1:35, NASB).

If prayer was so important in the life of Jesus, why should it not be important in our life?

Many events took place after this time of prayer. Jesus went to his hometown of Nazareth where he taught in the synagogue. The people would not believe his teaching and no miracles were performed there. He sent the twelve out to teach and minister in his name. John the Baptist was beheaded by King Herod. Jesus taught the five thousand men, many women and children on the mountainside. He performed the miracle of feeding the five thousand. What did Jesus do after that? "And after bidding them farewell, he departed to the mountain to pray. And when it was evening, the boat was in the midst of the sea, and he was alone on the land" (Mark 6:46–47, NASB).

Jesus always took time to pray to his Father for strength to do what God had sent him to do. He knew the success of his ministry here on earth depended on Him keeping his lifeline open to his Father.

As more and more people heard about Jesus and the miracles he was performing, his following grew larger and larger. "But he himself would often slip away to the wilderness and pray" (Luke 5:16, NASB).

Did you notice a very important word in this verse? I believe one of the most important words there is "often." Jesus did not have a spasmodic prayer life, praying only when he could find time, but the scripture said he would slip away "often" to pray. According to the dictionary, often means many times, frequently. Is your prayer life a priority in your life? Do you slip away frequently throughout the day to pray? If you cannot slip away by yourself, do you pause frequently to pray throughout the day?

Before Jesus chose the twelve apostles, he spent all night in prayer. "And it was at this time that he went off to the mountain to pray, and he spent the whole night in prayer to God" (Luke 6:12, NASB).

Communion with his Father was more important to Jesus than physical rest. I personally do not know anyone today who spends all night in prayer. What an example for you and me to imitate!

One of my favorite examples of the real need for prayer in my life is that of Jesus in the garden of Gethsemane. He knew the events ahead were going to be very difficult. He did not desire to die, but knew this was why his Father had sent him in human form to the earth. Jesus took Peter, James, and John with him into the inner section of the garden, but went aside from them to pray:

> ... Saying "Father, if thou art willing, remove this cup from me; yet not my will, but thine be done." Now an angel from heaven appeared to him, strengthening him. And being in agony he was praying very fervently; and his sweat became like drops of blood, falling down upon the ground.
>
> Luke 22:42–44 (NASB)

What agony our Lord went through knowing what was ahead. If at all possible, he did not want to experience the agony of death on the cross or being separated from his Father. But, he was willing to do whatever his Father desired. How long has it been since you agonized in prayer over a lost person or a person who had strayed away from the Lord? How long has it been since you agonized over the sin in your life? To agonize means to suffer, to struggle, to be in anguish or extreme pain because of something. We cannot even fathom the agony Jesus felt because of what he was required to do for our sin. Prayer was extremely important to Jesus.

Jesus knew the scriptures, and he used them to rebuke Satan. It is a must for you and me to spend significant time in the Word of God so we are knowledgeable of the promises in his Word. Our faith is strengthened as we spend time in God's Word. "Let the word of Christ dwell in you richly as you teach and admonish one another with all wisdom, and as you sing psalms, hymns and spiritual songs with gratitude in your hearts to God" (Colossians 3:16, NIV).

We must spend much time reading and meditating on what God's Word is saying to us and allowing it to sink in our hearts and minds if we are going to grow in him. "Jesus answered, 'It is written: Man does not live on bread alone, but on every word that comes from the mouth of God'" (Matthew 4:4, NIV).

God's Word is our foundation for a powerful prayer life. We learn from it what God desires and how to pray according to his will.

The young man I referred to earlier faked being injured so the football team could have a timeout. Do you take a "timeout" for the Lord? Prayer is an action we can practice silently or out loud. It can be practiced morning, noon, and night and throughout the day. It is your lifeline to the Lord. I can think of many times in my life when I was afraid and praying to God brought peace to my heart. As we have served in foreign lands doing mission work, I know how I was strengthened because other believers were lifting me up in prayer. Prayer is a powerful tool given to us by God.

Think of a time in your life when you felt the need to take a "timeout—need to regroup." What did you do during this "timeout?"

When you pray, do you practice a time of praise, thanksgiving, and worship, a time of confession and repentance, a time of petition and supplication, a time of intercession, and a time of meditation? Stop what you are doing and spend time in prayer using each of these types of prayer. Listen to what God is saying to you.

What's in the Water?

Through the years, I have heard preachers refer to church baptism as the stirring of the waters. In obedience to the command of our Lord, when a person comes to know Jesus as Savior, they are baptized and brought into the fellowship of the church. Baptism symbolizes the death, burial, and resurrection of Jesus. It also symbolizes burying our old way of life or dying to self, our sinful life, and walking afresh and anew with Jesus, allowing him to control our life. I am reminded of a baptismal service we attended in Malawi. No ordained preacher had come to the village since the church had been organized and there were fifteen people to be baptized. When our translator, an ordained minister, came to baptize the chief's wife, he struggled to get her under the water. First of all, the place we were baptizing looked like it could be infested with snakes and maybe crocodiles. Secondly, the woman was very afraid of water. As he tried to get her completely submerged under the water, she strongly resisted. Finally, Charles got everything, but her nose under the water. We had to believe this would be acceptable to God as baptism by immersion. It was truly a sight to behold. There was no saving power in this water, but people were simply following the command of our Lord and demonstrating to others what had taken place in their lives.

God demonstrated many different things using water. When Pharaoh allowed the children of Israel to leave Egypt to go and worship their God, he realized they no longer had the Israelites to serve as their slaves. He and his army pursued them in their chariots. God gave Moses instruction as to what he was to do:

Then Moses stretched out his hand over the sea; and the
LORD swept the sea back by a strong east wind all night,
and turned the sea into dry land, so the waters were divided.
And the sons of Israel went through the midst of the sea
on the dry land, and the waters were like a wall to them
on their right hand and on their left. Then the Egyptians
took up the pursuit, and all Pharaoh's horses, his chariots
and his horsemen went in after them into the midst of the
sea. Then the LORD said to Moses, "Stretch out your hand
over the sea so that the waters may come back over the
Egyptians, over their chariots and their horsemen."

Exodus 14:21–24, 26 (NASB)

God performed an amazing miracle at just the right time with
the waters of the Red Sea. He demonstrated to the children of
Israel his power over his creation and his great love for them. I
am sure as the children of Israel looked at the Red Sea in front of
them they knew it was impossible for them to cross. God had the
power to make the waters serve as a wall on the right and left of the
Israelites. He also dried the floor of the sea with the wind through
the night. It was impossible for man, but with God all things were
possible and this is what he wanted them to realize.

God used the water of the Jordan River to cleanse Naaman, the
captain of the army of the king of Aram, of his leprosy. The Bible
tells us Naaman was a great warrior, but he was also a leper. A young
Israelite girl who had been taken captive was serving Naaman's wife.
The girl told his wife he needed to go see the prophet in Samaria.

So Naaman came with his horses and his chariots, and stood
at the doorway of the house of Elisha. And Elisha sent
a messenger to him, saying, "Go and wash in the Jordan
seven times, and your flesh shall be restored to you and you
shall be clean." But Naaman was furious and went away

and said, "Behold, I thought, 'He will surely come out to me, and stand and call on the name of the LORD his God, and wave his hand over the place, and cure the leper.'"

2 Kings 5:9–11 (NASB)

Naaman was angered by the healing process suggested by Elisha because he felt he should receive more attention from Elisha than he did. It was such a simple thing to go wash seven times in the river, but it angered him because it was the small and dirty Jordan River. It would not have been so bad if it had been some famous body of water that was clean and sparkling. He refused to do what Elisha said and went away angry. In order to be healed, he needed to be obedient to the Lord and humble himself. Naaman's pride was an obstacle to his healing. "So he went down and dipped himself seven times in the Jordan, according to the word of the man of God; and his flesh was restored like the flesh of a little child, and he was clean" (2 Kings 5:14, NASB).

Was there healing power in the waters of the Jordan River? No, it came from a humble heart and being willing to do what God commanded Elisha to tell him. How many times do we miss the blessings of the Lord because we are not willing to submit ourselves in obedience to his simple command?

God became disturbed by the actions of the children of Israel. He had sent them into a land filled with many good fruits, lush green grass, trees, and plants. They had gone into the land and literally polluted it. The priests, religious leaders, and rulers defied God. They began chasing empty dreams and different kinds of schemes far away from what God had taught them. God was bringing charges against them and he called Jeremiah to deliver this message to them. "My people have committed a compound sin: they've walked out on me, the fountain of fresh flowing waters, and then dug cisterns—cisterns that leak, cisterns that are no better than sieves" (Jeremiah 2:13, MSG).

In several translations, it refers to the water as living water, referring to God himself. The people had rejected God and his teachings. They had dug cisterns for themselves and turned to worshiping idols. The idols were broken and empty and would not respond to the people in any way. God had been faithful to go with them through the wilderness and into the promised land. He listened to their cries and their praises. He responded to them and did miraculous things no idol could do, but yet they had forsaken their God for idols. There was no hope for them as long as they sought to worship things other than God. God offered them life in him. "O Lord, the hope of Israel, all who turn away from you will be disgraced and shamed. They will be buried in a dry and dusty grave, for they have forsaken the Lord, the fountain of living water" (Jeremiah 17:13, NLT).

When Jesus stopped by Jacob's well in Samaria, he visited with the Samaritan woman when she came to draw water. He explained to her the difference in ordinary drinking water and the living water he offered her: "Jesus replied, 'People soon become thirsty again after drinking this water. But the water I give them takes away thirst altogether. It becomes a perpetual spring within them, giving them eternal life'" (John 4:13–14, NLT).

Once we come and partake of the living water Jesus offers us, we receive eternal life because we have placed our faith and trust in him. No one can take that from us. Sheep, at times, stray away from their shepherd who is caring for them and he must search for them and return them to the fold. Sometimes we stray away from the Lord and our fellowship with him is broken, but we do not lose our salvation, our hope of spending eternity with God our Father in heaven. "My sheep hear my voice, and I know them, and they follow me; and I give eternal life to them, and they shall never perish; and no one shall snatch them out of my hand" (John 10:27–28, NASB). Once we accept Jesus as Savior and Lord, no one can snatch us out of the Father's hand. We recognize the Father's voice and we follow him.

The waters of the river in Malawi held no saving power, but the people were obeying the command of our Lord, demonstrating to others what God had done in their lives. The waters of the Jordan River had no healing power; it was simply Naaman's act of obedience that healed him from his leprosy. The children of Israel were reprimanded by God because they had turned from the fountain of living water—God—worshiping idols. Jesus offered the woman of Samaria living water, eternal life, where she would never thirst again. What's in the water? Ordinary water is nothing special, but in the fountain of living water there is the promise of eternal life.

Do you trust in the Lord or in something you have set up as your idol?

If you do not know Jesus, why not ask him to forgive you of your sin and be your Savior and Lord?

My Most Preposterous, Absurd, Nonsensical Decision

The other day I was preparing for the Trunk-or-Treat we have at our church for the children on Halloween. I made cards on the computer with bright-colored pumpkins and sheaves of grain and typed the following scripture on the card: "For God so loved the world, that he gave his only begotten Son, that whoever believes in him should not perish, but have eternal life" (John 3:16, NASB). I also wrote a note inviting people to come to our church. Then I glued a piece of candy on the card. The first mistake I made was selecting a piece of candy that was too heavy to stay glued to the card. The next afternoon, I put the cards in a box and put it in the trunk of our car. Since it was Wednesday, I then went to church for an early afternoon prayer meeting. Afterwards, I hurried home and decided to transfer the cards to another box. As I did, the candy fell off twenty-five of the cards. Frustrated, I hurriedly came in the house to fix the cards because I had to be back in town within an hour. I laid the cards on the dining room table and proceeded to glue candy on them. Now, let me acquaint you with the most preposterous, absurd, nonsensical decision I made. Since the Elmer's glue had not held the heavy candy, I decided to use contact cement. Unlike what I normally would do, I did not put paper between my cards and the table. This proved to be an extremely preposterous decision. This time because they were lighter in weight, I decided to put bite size pieces of snickers on the cards. I checked one or two of the cards to be sure the glue was not coming through. As I reflect back, I think as the cement began to set up, it became very warm, and in seventeen places it melted the finish on our table. When I picked up the cards, my heart sank to the bottom of my feet. Oh my! What a bad decision! I ended up throwing the cards away because they smelled like contact cement. Just for your information, Doyal did not get angry or threaten to divorce me. Of course, what I had done was not brilliant, but he was very kind, and we still love one another. How can we apply this to our life?

The most preposterous, absurd, nonsensical decision a person can make in life is to refuse to accept Jesus as Savior. There are many excuses people give as to why they refuse to follow Jesus. Consider the rich young ruler who came to question Jesus: "As Jesus started on his way, a man ran up to him and fell on his knees before him. 'Good teacher,' he asked, 'what must I do to inherit eternal life?'" (Mark 10:17, NIV).

Jesus first corrected the man who had called him good by telling him no one was good except God. He then talked about keeping the commandments of God. The rich young ruler said he had kept all these since he was a boy. Jesus then told him what he needed to give up to follow him completely. "Jesus looked at him and loved him. 'One thing you lack,' he said. 'Go, sell everything you have and give to the poor, and you will have treasure in heaven. Then come, follow me.' At this the man's face fell. He went away sad, because he had great wealth" (Mark 10:21–22, NIV).

He placed his faith in his great wealth and not in Jesus. He did not realize it was more important to store up riches in heaven than here on earth. Earthly riches cannot be taken to heaven when we die. He went away saddened by Jesus's request, but was unwilling to do what Jesus said. Being wealthy is not a sin, but anything we choose to trust in for life rather than in the Lord is a sin.

Many people reject Jesus's invitation to come join him for the great feast because it is inconvenient at the time.

Jesus replied with this illustration: "A man prepared a great feast and sent out many invitations. When all was ready, he sent his servant around to notify the guests that it was time for them to come. But they all began making excuses. One said he had just bought a field and wanted to inspect it, so he asked to be excused. Another said he had just bought five pair of oxen and wanted to try them out. Another had just been married, so he said he couldn't come."

Luke 14:16–20 (NLT)

One never knows when he or she refuses to come at Jesus's invitation if it might be his or her last time to hear the Lord extend an invitation to him or her. He or she might not have another day of life where he or she could accept Jesus. Some refused because of business, some because of getting married, and still others because of what they had purchased with the wealth God had given to them.

These people had even witnessed the many miracles Jesus performed while on earth and they still rejected him. They were without excuse and were destined for hell because of the sin in their lives. They had been exposed to what happened to people when they placed their faith and trust in the Lord. People who have heard the message of salvation know what they must do to receive eternal life. Many choose to continue walking in the sin rather than giving up their sinful way of life and walking with Jesus as his children.

Paul was writing to the church at Rome and he expressed his conviction about the gospel of Jesus Christ.

For I am not ashamed of this good news about Christ. It is the power of God at work, saving everyone who believes— Jews first and also Gentiles. This good news tells us how God makes us right in his sight. This is accomplished from start to finish by faith. As the Scriptures say, "It is through faith that a righteous person has life."

Romans 1:16–17 (NLT)

A person must accept the gospel of Jesus Christ by faith in order to be saved. He must be willing to turn from his sin (repent), change his way of living, and come to accept Jesus Christ as his Savior and Lord. "Whoever believes in the Son has eternal life, but whoever rejects the Son will not see life, for God's wrath remains on him" (John 3:36, NIV).

One who believes in Jesus receives life, but one who rejects him will experience the wrath, the anger, of God the Father.

> But God shows his anger from heaven against all sinful, wicked people who push the truth away from themselves. For the truth about God is known to them instinctively. God has put this knowledge in their hearts. From the time the world was created, people have seen the earth and sky and all that God made. They can clearly see his invisible qualities—his eternal power and divine nature. So they have no excuse whatsoever for not knowing God.
>
> Romans 1:18–20 (NLT)

Even though people throughout the world are aware there is a God, this does not excuse us as believers from going to share with them how they can come to know Jesus as Savior. God without Jesus is not the God of the Bible. Jesus was God in the flesh so without knowing him we can't know God. Being aware there is a God is not enough; they must come to know him personally as their Savior, the one who has the power to save them from their sin. If they reject this message and do not follow Jesus, they are destined to burn in the everlasting fire of hell. No excuse will be accepted for the condition of their life.

I made a terrible mistake in not preparing our table with papers to keep the glue from affecting the finish of the table. Until we get the table refinished, I will see the evidence of my decision. One right decision I made when I was eight years old was to accept Jesus as my Savior. Oh, I still make mistakes daily, but I am provided the opportunity to confess those sins to the Lord and he promises to forgive me. In this way, my fellowship with him remains open, and I continue to grow in him daily.

Are you making the mistake of rejecting the gospel, the good news about Jesus? Admit you are a sinner in need of God. Believe that Jesus died and rose again for your sins. Confess Jesus as Lord of your life.

The Ups and Downs of Life

Friday and Saturday of this week, we will have our fall retreat for the women of our church at our Baptist campgrounds in Talihina, Oklahoma. It is always an enjoyable time of fellowship as our women come away from the busyness of life and spend time reflecting on what the Word of God is saying to them concerning their lives. We pray they will be more aware of all God has done in their lives by the time they leave the retreat. Each member of our women's ministry team has been asked to decorate a table in the dining area so it tells the story of our life. We are to share our past and how God walked with us through the ups and downs of life. Some of our women really groaned as they thought about looking back at their past. It brought back memories of things in their past they were not proud of. The question on their heart was whether they wanted to reveal that part of their life to others. Compared to some of them, I have led a protected and sheltered life. All of us have sinned and have things in our life we are ashamed of, but the glorious thing about our Lord is when we confess those sins to him, he forgives us. "On the other hand, if we admit our sins—make a clean breast of them—he won't let us down; he'll be true to himself. He'll forgive our sins and purge us of all wrongdoing" (1 John 1:9, MSG).

We can each learn from the mistakes others have made in life. How many times have we tried to instruct our children about how they should live and they turn a deaf ear to us? They think they have the right to live as they please. Later years, they may say, "Mom, Dad, I sure wish I had listened to the advice you tried to give me."

The Book of Joel was written by the prophet Joel to warn the people of Judah of God's impending judgment if they did not turn from their sin. It reminds me so much of what is taking place in

America today. The people in Jesus's time had become prosperous
and they had become complacent about their service to the Lord.
They were centered on themselves, on worshipping things other
than God, and on living a life monopolized by sin. Does this remind
you of the condition of our world today? God's punishment for sin
can be so overwhelming and dreadful it is almost unbearable. Joel
used the devastation brought on by a plague of locusts to explain to
the people of Judah what would happen. He also instructed them
to tell their children about what had happened so they might walk
in the ways of the Lord rather than on the road to sin.

> After the cutting locusts finished eating the crops, the
> swarming locusts took what was left! After them came the
> hopping locusts, and then the stripping locusts, too! Wake
> up, you drunkards, and weep! All the grapes are ruined,
> and all your new wine is gone! A vast army of locusts has
> invaded my land"
>
> (Joel 1:4–6a, NLT).

What one group of locusts did not destroy, the one coming behind
would. Warren Wiersbe writes in his commentary on Joel:

> Joel wanted the people of Judah to understand what God was
> saying to them through the plague and the drought. In our own
> times, the nations of the world are experiencing severe droughts
> and famines, frightening epidemics, unexpected earthquakes,
> devastating floods, and other "natural disasters," all of which have
> greatly affected the national and global economy, yet very few
> people have asked, "What is God saying to us?"

> When they interviewed different people after 9/11, I did not
> hear one person say, "I wonder what God is trying to show us or
> what he is saying to us?" Just as in the days of Joel, it takes major

disasters to get people's attention and make them realize they need a relationship with Jesus Christ.

One of the sins addressed was drunkenness. The locusts had destroyed the vineyards and there would be no wine for the drunkard to drink. "Sober up, you drunks! Get in touch with reality—and weep! Your supply of booze is cut off. You're on the wagon, like it or not" (Joel 1:5, MSG).

Not only did it affect those who drank the wine and became drunk, but wine and bread was considered as a main part of a meal. It was an economic disaster for the people because they had no income from the crops. Yet, the people refused to turn from their sin. There was no wine or grain to bring to the temple of the Lord and the priests were mourning because there were no offerings. The devastation in the land affected all people. Joel told the people what they must do.

> Dress yourselves in sackcloth, you priests! Wail, you who serve before the altar! Come, spend the night in sackcloth, you ministers of my God! There is no grain or wine to offer at the temple of your God. Announce a time of fasting; call the people together for a solemn meeting. Bring the leaders and all the people into the temple of the LORD your God, and cry out to him there.
>
> Joel 1:13–14 (NLT)

Joel called the people to prayer. They must come with a humble heart and cry out to God. There needed to be a time of repentance.

Solomon had finished building the temple of the Lord and he prayed, dedicating the temple to the Lord. When he had finished, the Lord appeared to him with a message.

> When I shut up the heavens so that there is no rain, or command locusts to devour the land or send a plague among my people, if my people, who are called by my name, will

humble themselves and pray and seek my face and turn from their wicked ways, then will I hear from heaven and will forgive their sin and will heal their land.

2 Chronicles 7:13–14 (NIV)

God was relating to Solomon what must happen when the people stray from him and begin to give their attention to things causing them to sin. I believe the same message God gave to Solomon and the message God gave Joel contains a definite message for us today. When we allow Satan to invade our life and lead us astray, we must fall to our knees confessing our sin to the Lord and cry out to him for mercy. "But I confess my sins; I am deeply sorry for what I have done. Do not abandon me, Lord. Do not stand at a distance, my God. Come quickly to help me, O Lord my savior" (Psalm 38:18, 21–22, NLT).

David realized his sin caused broken fellowship with God. He cried out to God to not abandon him, but to come and help him. Jesus's prayer in the garden of Gethsemane is a great example. Jesus did not want to die, but the main thing that grieved Jesus was taking the burden of our sin because he would be separated from his Father. Sin separates us from fellowship with our God and Father who created us.

Commentators differ on whether the plagues actually took place or whether the illustration was used to show what would happen when the invading armies came to destroy their land. We know drought and insects come from time to time destroying crops, so we know either thought could be true. One thing we know, we must turn from our sin and follow God.

As we prepared our tables for the retreat, we looked back at our lives and at the "ups and downs of life" that have brought us to where we are today. It was good to look at the "up" times of our life, but possibly painful to look at the "down" times of life. But, we saw how God has led us through those bad times of life and made us what we are today.

Are there unconfessed sins in your life today you need to confess to God? Why not pause and pray, confessing those sins to the Lord? You want to consistently do this so your fellowship with the Lord will not be broken.

What do you think God is saying to people of all nations with the different disasters we are experiencing?

God Was There!

The women of our church have just returned from our yearly fall retreat at Kiamichi Baptist Assembly. God blessed us this year with unbelievable presenters; neither of the two knew or had heard of the other. They blended in such a fashion that the Holy Spirit's working was so prevalent. The theme for our retreat was "Journey of a Lifetime." Carolyn Teague spoke about looking inward at the condition and circumstances of our personal life, looking up to Jesus from whom we receive the power through Holy Spirit that was needed for us to serve him, and then looking outward to the world around us and being a witness in lifestyle evangelism. Jaxie Ochsner led the music worship in preparation for the message God had for us. She also spoke on the wilderness journey we encounter when we take our eyes off of Jesus and become critical and disgruntled with people and things around us, losing sight of God's will for our life. You could feel the very presence of the Lord throughout our time there. It was a mountaintop experience as the Holy Spirit stirred within our hearts the need to be a lifestyle witness for the Lord.

What are some encounters throughout Scripture where people experienced the presence of God? Isaac called Jacob to him to bless him and then told him to go to the house of Bethuel, his mother's father, and to take a wife from the daughters of Laban, his mother's brother. Jacob started his journey to Haran and on the way he spent the night in the area of Luz. As the sun set, he took a stone, put it under his head and lay down to rest. During the night something very special happened.

And he had a dream, and behold, a ladder was set on the earth with its top reaching to heaven; and behold, the angels of God were ascending and descending on it. And behold, the LORD stood above it and said, "I am the LORD, the God of your father Abraham and the God of Isaac; the land on which you lie, I will give it to you and your descendants. Your descendants shall also be like the dust of the earth, and you shall spread out to the west and to the east and to the north and to the south; and in you and in your descendants shall all the families of the earth be blessed. And behold, I am with you and will keep you wherever you go, and will bring you back to this land; for I will not leave you until I have done what I have promised you.

Genesis 28:12–15 (NASB)

Jacob had an encounter with God through a dream. He saw the Lord and the Lord assured him of his presence with him. The Lord told him that he would never leave him until he had accomplished what he promised to Jacob. "Then Jacob woke up and said, 'Surely the Lord is in this place, and I wasn't even aware of it.' He was afraid and said, 'What an awesome place this is! It is none other than the house of God—the gateway to heaven!'" (Genesis 28:16–17, NLT).

Just as Jacob had an encounter with God, so our women had an encounter with God as we prayed, sang, and experienced God through the teaching of the two presenters. The Holy Spirit stirred our hearts and spoke to us in that place.

Moses led the children of Israel out of Egypt as God had instructed him to do. Because of their sinfulness, they were made to wander in the wilderness for forty years. Finally, God told Moses to lead the people into and possess the promised land (the land of Canaan.) God made a statement that disturbed Moses: "Go up to a land flowing with milk and honey; for I will not go up in your midst, because you are an obstinate people, lest I destroy you on the way" (Exodus 33:3, NASB).

The people went into a time of mourning when they heard from Moses what God had said. Moses pitched a tent outside of their camp and all who sought the Lord would go to this place and cry out to God. When Moses would go to the tent, the scripture says a cloud would come and stand over the entrance and God would speak to Moses at that time. "When all the people saw the pillar of cloud standing at the entrance of the tent, all the people would arise and worship, each at the entrance of his tent. Thus the Lord used to speak to Moses face to face, just as a man speaks to his friend" (Exodus 33:10–11a, NASB).

Moses had a definite encounter with God as he entreated the Lord to show him what he had in mind for him and what God intended for his people. "And the Lord replied, 'I will personally go with you, Moses. I will give you rest—everything will be fine for you'" (Exodus 33:14, NLT).

Moses continued to speak to the Lord about his concerns and asked the Lord that if he was not going to go with them, to please not send them out. Moses wondered how the people of the land would know they were the Lord's special people if he was not with them. "Then Moses had one more request. 'Please let me see your glorious presence,' he said" (Exodus 33:18, NLT).

Moses was not permitted to look on the Lord's face for any who did would die, but God promised to put him in the cleft of the rock and cover him with his hand as he passed by. When God removed his hand, Moses would be able to see him from behind. Moses would know the Lord was with him. We knew God was at the retreat as we got away from the busyness of life and spent time with the Lord in his Word.

Many of us told about times in our lives when we had gone through trials, but had felt God's presence. Throughout his Word he promises to be with us and carry us through those trials. One scripture I have come to love is found in Isaiah: "I have called you by name; you are mine! When you pass through the waters, I will be with you; and through the rivers, they will not overflow you. When you walk through the fire, you will not be scorched, nor will the flame burn you. For I am the Lord your God" (Isaiah 43:1b–3a, NASB).

He has been so faithful and always carried me through the trials I have encountered. His presence is so prevalent in my life.

The women of First Baptist Church, Wilburton, Oklahoma, truly encountered the Lord at Kiamichi Baptist Assembly. God worked through presenters to help us see the Lord in every avenue of our lives. What a journey we took as we received the "abundant blessings of our Lord!"

Think of a time in your life when you encountered some difficulty and felt God's presence.

Pray and thank God for his provision of his grace in your life.

What promise of God did you claim during difficult times?

Cry Out to God

I will never forget going to the hospital to have my first son. Of course I had never experienced anything of this sort before, so I was rather apprehensive about the whole situation. In the delivery room next to me was a woman who continually hollered and screamed about her pain. This made me rather uneasy since I had not the slightest inkling what was going to happen. She hollered, "Help! Somebody help me!" She yelled so much the nurses almost turned a deaf ear to her. We often fear the unknown, and that was my position. She made me a lot more nervous about going through the delivery process to have my baby. With God's help I had a bouncing baby boy who was beautiful in my eyes. This lady cried out for help and so do the lost people of this land. They appear to not want to hear, but I firmly believe they are crying for help.

I have just returned from the Baptist General Convention of Oklahoma. The major emphasis of the convention was the urgency of praying for the lost of Oklahoma and our world. What an awesome experience, as we joined our hearts in small groups during the meetings to pray for the lost. The final evening was a time of worship and praise to our Lord and a crying out by God's people to him for the salvation of the lost. What a blessed time, as people were gathered in small groups crying out to God for cleansing for our churches and nation.

We must personally go before the Lord for a time of cleansing before we can offer petitions for the lostness of others. We must first have a time of confession and repentance of the sin in our life. "If my people, who are called by my name, shall humble themselves, pray, seek, crave, and require of necessity my face and turn from their wicked ways, then will I hear from heaven, forgive their sin, and heal their land" (2 Chronicles 7:14, AMP).

We must come humbly before the Lord confessing the sin in our own life and seeking his forgiveness. God will not hear our prayer for the lost if we are harboring sin in our heart. "I acknowledged my sin to thee, and my iniquity I did not hide; I said, 'I will confess my transgressions to the Lord;' and thou didst forgive the guilt of my sin" (Psalm 32:5, NASB).

David did not hide his sin from the Lord, but came before him in humility confessing his sin and God forgave him and removed the guilt of sin. "He who covers his transgressions will not prosper, but whoever confesses and forsakes his sins will obtain mercy" (Proverbs 28:13, AMP).

When our life is in order and we are walking with the Lord, we can come to the Lord in prayer for spiritual awakening in our land. "For the eyes of the Lord are upon the righteous, and his ears attend to their prayer, but the face of the Lord is against those who do evil" (1 Peter 3:12, NASB).

Before a great spiritual awakening can take place, those who claim to be God's children must experience revival in their own heart and in the church. God promises to hear the prayers of his children as they come to him confessing their sin and calling out to him on behalf of the lost of this world. " ... But sanctify Christ as Lord in your hearts, always being ready to make a defense to everyone who asks you to give an account for the hope that is in you, yet with gentleness and reverence" (1 Peter 3:15, NASB).

In 1734, Jonathan Edwards, a pastor in Northampton, Massachusetts, began praying for those in his congregation and those throughout North America who did not know Jesus as Savior. He had a passion for God to be glorified and for the lost to be saved. It was as if a fire swept over the people of his church and people who knew Jesus were revived and lost people were saved. It spread from Maine to Georgia. Very few people in Northampton were unaffected by the revival. People would come to his church to see what was happening and their hearts would be stirred. They would return to their own towns with convicted hearts and revival would spread. God's people humbled themselves, prayed, sought his face, cried out to God on behalf of the lost of the world and a great awakening took place. In the next seven years, records indicate around one-third of the American colonies experienced salvation.

Are you really concerned about your neighbor who lives next door who does not know Jesus? Do you call out the name of this person to the Lord each day asking God to use you as a witness to them about salvation? Do you have such a burden on your heart for this person and others who are lost to literally weep for them before the Lord? Jesus's heart was broken over the condition of the people of Jerusalem: "O Jerusalem, Jerusalem, the city that kills the prophets and stones God's messengers! How often I have wanted to gather your children together as a hen protects her chicks beneath her wings, but you wouldn't let me. And now look, your house is left to you, empty and desolate" (Matthew 23:37–38, NLT).

As Jesus lamented over the city of Jerusalem, he was expressing his love and grief because they had refused the opportunities he had given them for salvation. The nation had rejected and many times killed God's messengers. Still, Jesus wanted to gather his people to him and save them. God would not force salvation on them and so many refused to come to him: "Yet you refuse to come to me so that I can give you this eternal life" (John 5:40, NLT).

May our hearts be broken over the lost of Oklahoma, the USA, and the world. May we petition God on behalf of those who have no hope.

During our mission's celebration at the convention, we heard from Carrie McDonnall, the sole survivor in a group of five missionaries who were attacked by terrorists in Iraq on March 15, 2004. Carrie's husband, David, was among the four missionaries killed. In spite of all that happened, Carrie still has a deep love for the people of Iraq. She describes the common people of Iraq as a loving people, and she is very offended when people in the USA ask her how she feels towards "those people." When she looks at the people of Iraq, she sees people in need of Jesus. Even though she was shot many times, hit by much shrapnel, had many broken bones, and lost her husband in the attack, she still loves the people and desires for them to come to know Jesus. Listening to Carrie McDonnall speak, I believe she would say the same thing about the people of Iraq and even the terrorists as Stephen did about the Jewish leaders. Even in the midst of suffering for Jesus, we are to have a yearning for all people to know him. In the Bible, Stephen was speaking before the Jewish council, and they became infuriated with his message. As he looked up into heaven, he claimed to see the Son of Man standing in the place of honor at God's right hand. They dragged Stephen out of the city and began to stone him: "And they went on stoning Stephen as he called upon the Lord and said, 'Lord Jesus, receive my spirit!' And falling on his knees, he cried out with a loud voice, 'Lord, do not hold this sin against them!' And having said this, he fell asleep" (Acts 7:59–60, NASB).

If you have unconfessed sin in your life, I ask you to stop what you are doing, bow your head, confess your sin to the Lord and ask him to cleanse you. Pray God will cause you to weep over the lost of this world. Ask God to help you be the witness you need to be.

Write the names of those you will pray for and seek an opportunity to witness to about the saving grace of Jesus.

I Am Confident of this One Thing

My husband, Doyal, has been doing concrete work since 1958. In my opinion, he is an excellent concrete man. He is dependable and does the very best job possible for people. He has confidence in his ability. Why? He began doing this when he was in his early twenties for a company in California. He learned quickly and soon became a foreman. He always tried to do the best job possible. He formed his own company in 1969. He has always been confident in his ability to do the work and has always strived for excellence. In the last thirty-three years, he has come to realize where his ability and confidence comes from. When confronted with things on the job he is not sure about, he goes to his truck, sits quietly, and allows God to show him what he must do. He has confidence in his ability, but that's because he's aware God is in control and will show him what to do.

> "For I know the plans I have for you," declares the Lord, "plans to prosper you and not to harm you, plans to give you hope and a future. Then you will call upon me and come and pray to me, and I will listen to you. You will seek me and find me when you seek me with all your heart."
>
> Jeremiah 29:11–13 (NIV)

This morning, with the Lord in his Word and in prayer, I was thinking about different scriptures relating to being bold in my witness for the Lord and in my prayer life. We must be bold when we approach the Lord in prayer for the salvation of our world and in our prayers for the needs of others and our own concerns. "This is the confidence we have in approaching God: that if we ask anything according to his will, he hears us—whatever we ask—we know that we have what we asked of him" (1 John 5:14–15, NIV).

We must be sure that the things we ask for are in accordance with God's will. How do we know this? We saturate our minds and hearts with God's Word, so we will know what he desires. When we know his desires, we can come boldly before him asking him to hear and answer our prayer. Yesterday, I wrote a devotional about crying out to God for a great spiritual awakening in our land. The only way we can experience a great spiritual awakening is through fervent, determined, intentional prayer for God to bring this about. We can approach the throne of the Lord with confidence because we know this is what God desires.

God's message of salvation is for all people. It is for Jew and Gentile alike. Paul said God had revealed it by the Holy Spirit to his holy apostles and prophets.

> And this is the secret plan: The Gentiles have an equal share with the Jews in all the riches inherited by God's children. Both groups have believed the good news, and both are part of the same body and enjoy together the promise of blessings through Christ Jesus. By God's special favor and mighty power, I have been given the wonderful privilege of serving him by spreading this good news. Just think! Though I did nothing to deserve it, and though I am the least deserving Christian there is, I was chosen for this special joy of telling the Gentiles about the endless treasures available to them in Christ. I was chosen to explain to everyone this plan that God, the Creator of all things, had kept secret from the beginning.
>
> Ephesians 3:6–9 (NLT)

This plan was carried out through Jesus Christ. The good news, the gospel, is for all people. Every person has the opportunity to come to know Jesus as Savior. Paul was bold in his witness for the Lord even though he suffered because of his boldness.

Jesus used the parable of the lost sheep to teach about his concern for mankind. He spoke of a shepherd who had one hundred sheep. If one sheep wandered away from the flock, he would leave the ninety-nine and go searching for the one sheep. He used this picture so his disciples could understand that there should be more concern about the one lost person than the ninety-nine people in the church who knew him. Jesus told us to seek lost people and share with them the message of salvation. Those who know Jesus as Savior have the assurance of spending eternity with the Lord in heaven. Those who do not know him are destined to the everlasting fire of hell. There is rejoicing in heaven when a lost sheep, a person, is found or comes to know Jesus. "Just so it is not the will of my Father who is in heaven that one of these little ones should be lost and perish" (Matthew 18:14, AMP).

How bold are you in your witness for the Lord? Are you willing to go the extra mile and befriend people who do not know Jesus and come to know them personally so you might have the opportunity to share the love of Jesus with them? Do you have confidence in the message God has given you, and will you boldly approach the Lord asking him to save these people?

Lottie Moon was a very dedicated Southern Baptist missionary who began serving among the Chinese people in the late 1800s. Lottie rebelled against Christianity until she was eighteen years old. At that time, she came to know Jesus as Savior. She sailed to China when she was thirty-two years old to fulfill the call God had placed on her life to serve as a missionary to the Chinese people. She was from a wealthy family and was very well educated. She was somewhat out of her position in life, but she served a God that did not do things in a typical fashion. He had gripped her heart with a burden for the lostness of China. She labored in China for thirty-nine years and people actually feared and rejected her, but she refused to leave. She began baking Chinese teacakes and the sweet aroma of her cookies drew the people to her house. She wore traditional Chinese dress and learned the language and customs. Eventually, many accepted Jesus as Savior because of her witness to them as they came to her home to partake of the cookies. She literally gave her life for them. In 1912, there was war and a famine followed. The people were starving and this wore heavy upon Lottie's heart. Rather than eating, she would give her food to the hungry. Her greatest desire was for them to come to know Jesus and she took every opportunity to share the message of Jesus Christ with them. She displayed the ultimate sign of love for the Chinese; she literally gave her life for them. She became so malnourished and physically ill because of her sacrifice that she died on a ship on Christmas Eve as she was returning to the United States. She gave her all for the cause of Christ.

> And so, dear brothers and sisters, I plead with you to give your bodies to God. Let them be a living and holy sacrifice—the kind he will accept. When you think of what he has done for you, is this too much to ask? Don't copy the behavior and customs of this world, but let God transform you into a new person by changing the way you think. Then you will know what God wants you to do, and you will know how good and pleasing and perfect his will really is.
>
> Romans 12:1–2 (NLT)

Lottie Moon surrendered her heart, mind, and body to the Lord for his service. God changed her rebellious spirit when she accepted Jesus and changed her into a new person with a love for the people of China. She gave her life so they would come to know Jesus. She was confident in the truth of the message she had to deliver to the Chinese people.

Are you willing to come boldly to the throne of grace today, bow before the Lord and ask him what he desires for your life? Will you say yes to whatever he tells you to do and surrender your life to serve him in spite of what it might cost you? Pray daily concerning what God would have you do and ask for strength to fulfill God's call on your life.

Imitating Those we Love

When I was young, one of my favorite meals my mom cooked was brown beans, fried potatoes, fried okra, and cornbread. Down through the years, I have tried to imitate my mother's cooking. As far as this meal is concerned, I can cook brown beans, cornbread, and fried potatoes to perfection, at least in the eyes of my husband and children. The one thing I have not been able to do is to fry okra the same way as my mom. When my mom was with us, I would have her stand right beside me and tell me exactly what to do; the correct heat, the length of time to fry it, and still it was not the same. It never tasted like Mom's okra. Sometimes it is a struggle to completely imitate those we love.

The people in the church of Corinth had some division among them. Paul wrote a letter to them concerning the condition of their spiritual lives. He said he should be able to write to them as mature Christians, but he still had to feed them milk rather than solid food because they were not growing in their knowledge of God and his Word.

> I had to feed you with milk and not with solid food, because you couldn't handle anything stronger. And you still aren't ready, for you are still controlled by your own sinful desires. You are jealous of one another and quarrel with each other. Doesn't that prove you are controlled by your own desires? You are acting like people who don't belong to the LORD. When one of you says, "I am a follower of Paul," and another says, "I prefer Apollos," aren't you acting like those who are not Christians?
>
> 1 Corinthians 3:2–4 (NLT)

Paul explained that they were simply mere men used as God's servants. His job was to plant the seed, but Apollos watered the ground. God was the one who caused the seed to germinate and produce fruit. Paul and Apollos were partners working together for the cause of God.

Paul brought up a very important point: "Don't you realize that all of you together are the temple of God and that the Spirit of God lives in you? God will bring ruin upon anyone who ruins this temple. For God's temple is holy, and you Christians are that temple" (1 Corinthians 3:16–17, NLT).

When we come to know Jesus as Savior, Holy Spirit comes to live in our hearts. We are to keep our heart, mind and body clean and pure in the eyes of the Lord. "How can a young man keep his way pure? By keeping it according to thy word. With all my heart I have sought thee; do not let me wander from thy commandments. Thy word I have treasured in my heart, that I may not sin against thee" (Psalm 119:9–11, NASB).

We need to saturate our lives with the Word of God, coming to know more and more about him with each passing day. We are to strive to live by his standards, imitating Jesus Christ, not man. Paul said we are not to take pride in following any specific leader because we belong to Christ and Christ belongs to God. Paul told them to look at him and Apollos as mere servants of Christ who have been put in charge of explaining the secrets of God.

Paul continued to counsel the Corinthian believers about being judgmental of those who served them:

For I am conscious of nothing against myself, yet I am not by this acquitted; but the one who examines me is the LORD. Therefore do not go on passing judgment before the time, but wait until the LORD comes who will both bring to light the things hidden in the darkness and disclose the

NEVER THE SAME AGAIN

motives of men's hearts; and then each man's praise will
come to him from God.

1 Corinthians 4:4–5 (NASB)

We are not to be judgmental of other Christians as to whether they
are living the life God desires. This is between them and the Lord.
We are to focus on our own life and whether or not our life is
glorifying the Lord. The Corinthians had split into various cliques
with some following Apollos and others following Paul. Each group
felt as if they were the only ones who knew the truth, but they had
become spiritually proud. Paul cautioned them about their beliefs.
He mentioned how all who served the Lord and taught the Word
of God had at times suffered in order to do this:

> To this very hour we go hungry and thirsty, we are in rags,
> we are brutally treated, we are homeless. We work hard
> with our own hands. When we are cursed, we bless; when
> we are persecuted, we endure it; when we are slandered,
> we answer kindly. Up to this moment we have become the
> scum of the earth, the refuse of the world.

1 Corinthians 4:11–13 (NIV)

Paul taught the people at Corinth, instructing them in the ways
of the Lord. Many came to follow Jesus Christ as Savior and
Lord. Paul questioned them as to why they had strayed from the
teaching in the past, since he was like their father. No servant takes
a position above his master. Jesus was Paul's master teacher. Many
will claim they are teaching in the name of Christ, but they are not
true followers of him. "For if you were to have countless tutors in
Christ, yet you would not have many fathers; for in Christ Jesus I
became your father through the gospel. I exhort you therefore, be
imitators of me" (1 Corinthians 4:15–16, NASB).

Paul was telling them to imitate those aspects of his life that
followed Christ's life. In doing so, they would not only imitate Paul,

but in essence they would be imitating Christ because he was Paul's master teacher. "Therefore be imitators of God, as beloved children; and walk in love, just as Christ also loved you, and gave himself up for us, an offering and a sacrifice to God as a fragrant aroma" (Ephesians 5:1–2, NASB).

If we walk in love, showing others the love Christ showed us, we will not be critical and judgmental of others. This expression of love will give off a sweet, fragrant aroma of Jesus Christ.

In order to please my family with the food I served, I tried to imitate the cooking of my mother. She was my example and the one I imitated. As believers, we are to imitate the life of Jesus Christ. If we truly love the Lord with all our heart, soul, mind, and strength, we will offer a good example for others to follow. "And you shall love the Lord your God with all your heart and with all your soul and with all your might" (Deuteronomy 6:5, NASB).

Who are you imitating in your daily living? This includes your speech, your thoughts, and your actions.

What are some changes you need to make in order to imitate Jesus Christ in your daily life?

Where do you go to get instruction for living? What verse from the Bible can you claim to help you walk with the Lord?

Honor God with a Thankful Heart

Today is Thanksgiving and we are reminded to be thankful for God's blessings. We had Thanksgiving dinner early with our children because it was the only time they could come home. I am reminded this day to be thankful to God for all he has done in my life. I am thankful that even before I was conceived in my mother's womb, he knew exactly what I would be doing today. "My frame was not hidden from thee, when I was made in secret, and skillfully wrought in the depths of the earth. Thine eyes have seen my unformed substance; and in thy book they were all written, the days that were ordained for me, when as yet there was not one of them" (Psalm 139:15–16, NASB).

I am thankful God gave me good Christian parents, who loved me and taught me about the Lord.

> And you shall love the LORD your God with all your heart and with all your soul and with all your might. And these words, which I am commanding you today, shall be on your heart; and you shall teach them diligently to your sons and shall talk of them when you sit in your house and when you walk by the way and when you lie down and when you rise up. And you shall bind them as a sign on your hand and they shall be as frontals on your forehead. And you shall write them on the doorposts of your house and on your gates.
>
> Deuteronomy 6:5–9 (NASB)

I am thankful my parents took seriously the instruction of God to teach me to love the Lord with all my heart. They diligently taught me the Bible and lived out the Word of God in their lives.

I am so thankful God saw fit to save me when I was eight years old. The whole salvation message can be found in one simple verse: "For God loved the world in this way: He gave his one and only Son, so that everyone who believes in him will not perish but have eternal life" (John 3:16, HCSB).

I am thankful that the Holy Spirit came to live in my heart when I came to know Jesus as Savior. He helps me to know right from wrong. "Whether you turn to the right or to the left, your ears will hear a voice behind you, saying, 'This is the way; walk in it'" (Isaiah 30:21, NIV).

The Spirit of God lives in us and we must be quiet and listen for his voice of instruction. He instructs us how we are to live in our world today. We are to be the example of Almighty God. "Or do you not know that your body is a temple of the Holy Spirit who is in you, whom you have from God, and that you are not your own? For you have been bought with a price: therefore glorify God in your body" (1 Corinthians 6:19–20, NASB). We have a responsibility to live for God, so others will see the difference he makes in a person's life.

I am thankful for the joy I have because of my relationship to Jesus Christ. The definition of joy in one of my Bibles is the happy feeling of being right with God and other people. When we abide in the Lord, our reservoir of joy will be filled to overflowing because our relationship with him is alive and we produce fruit for him. "These things I have spoken to you, that my joy may be in you, and that your joy may be made full" (John 15:11, NASB).

I am thankful for the opportunities of service God has given to Doyal and me. We have been privileged to represent the Lord not only here at home, but many times by being on mission for him overseas. What a joy it is to be counted worthy to serve the Lord in this fashion! " …But you shall receive power when the Holy Spirit has come upon you; and you shall be my witnesses both in Jerusalem, and in all Judea and Samaria, and even to the remotest part of the earth" (Acts 1:8, NASB).

We are to be witnesses for our Lord whether we are here at home, in other parts of the United States, or overseas. We have a responsibility to the Lord to proclaim his Word wherever we are.

> But how can they call on him to save them unless they believe in him? And how can they believe in him if they have never heard about him? And how can they hear about him unless someone tells them? And how will anyone go and tell them without being sent? That is what the Scriptures mean when they say, "How beautiful are the feet of those who bring good news!"
>
> Romans 10:14–15 (NLT)

I am thankful for my family. God has given me a strong Christian husband who loves me and provides for me in every way imaginable. Because of his great love for me, it stirs within my heart the desire to be pleasing to him and to God. "Charm is deceptive, and beauty does not last; but a woman who fears the Lord will be greatly praised. Reward her for all she has done. Let her deeds publicly declare her praise" (Proverbs 31:30–31, NLT).

My desire is to walk with the Lord in order to bring honor to him, but also to Doyal because of the great love God has given me for him. I thank God for our children. "Behold, children are a gift of the Lord; the fruit of the womb is a reward. Like arrows in the hand of a warrior, so are the children of one's youth. How blessed is the man whose quiver is full of them" (Psalm 127:3–5a, NASB).

I am thankful for my church family. The word church is defined in one of my Bible dictionaries as a group of Christians. All people who have come to know Jesus as Savior make up the church. "For the husband is the head of the wife as Christ is the head of the church, his body, of which he is the Savior" (Ephesians 5:23, NIV). It offers great assurance to a believer to know he or she has a group of believers who are supporting them, encouraging them, and praying for them.

The list could go on and on for what I am thankful for. God has blessed me in so many ways and I never want to forget to thank him and praise him for all that he has done. "Enter his gates with thanksgiving; go into his courts with praise. Give thanks to him and bless his name" (Psalm 100:4, NLT).

How thankful are you for all that God has done for you in your life? List some things in your life you are thankful for.

What is the one thing you are most thankful for? Offer to God a prayer of thanksgiving.

The Frigid Bite of Cold

All of a sudden, old man winter has made it evident that winter is at hand. The early morning temperatures this week have been in the high 20s and low 30s. It brings to mind a parsonage we lived in when I was in fifth and sixth grade in northwestern Oklahoma in the wheat-farming community of Driftwood. The house we lived in had two stories. There was absolutely no insulation in the house. The bedrooms for us three girls were upstairs and there was no heater on the second floor. As the frigid winter winds would blow across the wheat fields, it felt like the wind was blowing right through our rooms. We would put so many heavy quilts on our bed to keep out the cold that we could hardly turn over.

Imagine how God feels when our heart grows cold towards him. He became upset even with the church at Laodicea because they were neither cold nor hot: "I know all the things you do, that you are neither hot nor cold. I wish you were one or the other! But since you are like lukewarm water, I will spit you out of my mouth! I am the one who corrects and disciplines everyone I love. Be diligent and turn from your indifference" (Revelation 3:15–16, 19, NLT). God was very upset with the church at Laodicea because they would not listen to his advice. They thought they were rich and did not need a thing. God told them they were wretched, miserable, poor, blind, and naked. They were distasteful to God because of their indifference, which had brought about idleness on their part. They were more interested in material wealth on earth than having a living, growing relationship with the Lord. He wanted them to have a deep, passionate love for him and to be clean and pure vessels for his use in a lost world. If they did not turn from their indifference, God would discipline them because they were complacent and not attentive to him. "Look! Here I stand at the door and knock. If you hear me calling and open the door, I will come in, and we will share a meal as friends" (Revelation 3:20, NLT). They did not hear when he knocked at the door of their hearts because they were so entangled in their materialism. Their hearts were lukewarm.

How do you think God feels about churches today? Many are intent on having big, beautiful buildings with exquisite stained glass windows. They must have padded pews to get the people to come and sit for an hour. Many give a lot of attention to music and very little attention to the Word of God. They are performance oriented. People have allowed their jobs, homes, weekend outings to fish, hunt, hike, ride motorcycles, and many other things to become their god. They give very little, if any, allegiance to God Almighty. They only come to worship God when it is convenient or benefits them in some way. People's hearts have become lukewarm or even cold toward the Lord. They have pushed to the back of their mind what the Scripture says:

> For the word of God is full of living power. It is sharper than the sharpest knife, cutting deep into our innermost thoughts and desires. It exposes us for what we really are. Nothing in all creation can hide from him. Everything is naked and exposed before his eyes. This is the God to whom we must explain all that we have done.
>
> Hebrews 4:12–13 (NLT)

When we think about this scripture, it is rather frightening. God's Word is so powerful it cuts deep into our mind and heart, revealing our thoughts and innermost feelings. God knows everything about us. He knows any hidden thing in our life we have not confessed to him. Many are fooling themselves when they say they are a believer, but they do not show evidence of change in their lives.

But whenever anyone turns to the LORD, then the veil is taken away. Now, the LORD is the Spirit, and wherever the Spirit of the LORD is, he gives freedom. And all of us have had that veil removed so that we can be mirrors that brightly reflect the glory of the LORD. And as the Spirit of the LORD works within us, we become more and more like him and reflect his glory even more.

2 Corinthians 3:16–18 (NLT)

If we have had a sincere salvation experience, our life will show evidence of change for good. Those who do not show change and continue reverting back to their old ways will be surprised when they stand before the judgment seat of the Lord.

Again, the kingdom of heaven is like a fishing net that is thrown into the water and gathers fish of every kind. When the net is full, they drag it up onto the shore, sit down, sort the good fish into crates, and throw the bad ones away. That is the way it will be at the end of the world. The angels will come and separate the wicked people from the godly, throwing the wicked into the fire. There will be weeping and gnashing of teeth.

Matthew 13:47–50 (NLT)

Pastors, evangelists, teachers, and every witness for the Lord must proclaim the truth of God's Word to all people. "Do your best to present yourself to God as one approved, a workman who does not need to be ashamed and who correctly handles the word of truth" (2 Timothy 2:15, NIV). We have a responsibility to know what the Bible says and to give the Holy Spirit freedom to lead us to teach the truth. "The sum of thy word is truth, and every one of thy righteous ordinances is everlasting" (Psalm 119:160, NASB).

When the Word of God is proclaimed in truth, it will convict the hearts of the people who hear. The Scriptures tell us that an angel of the Lord spoke to Philip and told him to go south on the road toward Gaza. Philip obeyed and he saw an Ethiopian eunuch who was returning from worshiping in Jerusalem. He was sitting in his chariot reading from the Book of Isaiah. The Scripture was from Isaiah 53 where Isaiah spoke about one being led as a sheep to the slaughter. The Spirit of the Lord told Philip to approach the chariot. "And when Philip had run up, he heard him reading Isaiah the prophet, and said, 'Do you understand what you are reading?' And he said, 'Well, how could I, unless someone guides me?' And he invited Philip to come up and sit with him" (Acts 8:30–31, NASB).

> And the eunuch answered Philip and said, "Please tell me, of whom does the prophet say this? Of himself, or of someone else?" And Philip opened his mouth, and beginning from this scripture he preached Jesus to him. And as they went along the road they came to some water; and the eunuch said, "Look! Water! What prevents me from being baptized?" [And Philip said, "If you believe with all your heart, you may." And he answered and said, "I believe that Jesus Christ is the Son of God."]
>
> Acts 8:34–37 (NASB)

When the truth of God's Word is revealed, it brings conviction to a person's heart. Philip explained to the eunuch what he was reading and he was changed because of the convicting power of Scripture.

It is time for Christians to wake up and realize they cannot be lukewarm or cold concerning their relationship with the Lord. We must come out of the stupor of complacency and realize the urgency of the hour. People are lost and going to hell because they do not hear and understand the Bible. They do not see the Scriptures lived out in the lives of people who claim to be believers in the Lord Jesus Christ. Believers must know the Word of God and allow it to change their lives. "Your words are what sustain me. They bring me great joy and are my heart's delight, for I bear your name, O Lord God Almighty" (Jeremiah 15:16, NLT).

When God's Word changes our heart and our life, we will be a witness to the lost people of our world.

What is the condition of your heart today? Is your heart cold, lukewarm, or hot? If it is cold or lukewarm, what has made it that way?

Do you think God is pleased with your spiritual condition? If not, why not?

What will you do to change the condition of your spiritual life?

Willingness to Go and Share the Love of Jesus

I think about people who are willing to go and share the good news of Jesus Christ with others in spite of what it may cost them. I think of David and Carrie McDonnall, Karen Watson, and Larry and Jean Elliott. They were in Iraq giving humanitarian aid to people who were displaced by the war. They sought to provide aid in the area of food and clean water. All of these missionaries, except Carrie, lost their lives as terrorists attacked their vehicle in Iraq. It was a miracle she survived because her body was riddled with shrapnel and bullet wounds. I think about Martha Myers, Bill Koehn, and Kathy Gariety, who were killed by a Yemeni man in a hospital in Jibla, Yemen, while giving medical aid to the people of Yemen. I think of those that go and share in areas where they cannot be known as missionaries because it would endanger their lives. They must enter the country under different titles and cannot be outspoken about the Lord. They live out the love of Jesus amongst the people and can share with others about their Lord when they are asked questions, but still very cautious about what they say. I remember missionaries we have served with who give up the comforts of American living to go and teach people about Jesus Christ. They, many times, are away from their children because they must go to another country to be educated. They are away from their parents and their own siblings. Daily they may experience electricity going off or water turned off at certain times each day. They must buy certain food items when they first see them on the shelf because the next time they shop the item will be sold out. They cannot travel after dark because of the danger of someone attacking their car. These have taken the Great Commission very seriously and are willing to do whatever it takes to lead people to Jesus. "Go therefore and make disciples of all the nations, baptizing them in the name of the Father and the Son and the Holy Spirit, teaching them to observe all that I commanded you; and lo, I am with you always, even to the end of the age" (Matthew 28:19–20, NASB). What are you and I willing to give up so we can share Jesus with a lost and dying world?

Stephen was one of the seven men selected by the apostles to help in ministering to the widows and others in need. The Bible says Stephen was full of the Holy Spirit and had great wisdom. He went about performing great wonders among the people of Jerusalem. Men who were members of the synagogue of the freedmen objected to his teaching. They stirred up the people, elders, and scribes against him. They dragged him before the council. Stephen stood before them and gave his defense for what he was doing. Stephen really hit a tender spot with the council when he began to speak about what they were doing:

> You stubborn people! You are heathen at heart and deaf to the truth. Must you forever resist the Holy Spirit? But your ancestors did, and so do you! Name one prophet your ancestors didn't persecute! They even killed the ones who predicted the coming of the Righteous One—the Messiah whom you betrayed and murdered. You deliberately disobeyed God's law, though you received it from the hands of angels.
>
> Acts 7:51–53 (NLT)

The Jewish leaders were infuriated by the accusations Stephen brought against them:

> They dragged him out of the city and began to stone him. The official witnesses took off their coats and laid them at the feet of a young man named Saul. And as they stoned him, Stephen prayed, "LORD Jesus, receive my spirit." And

he fell to his knees, shouting, "LORD, don't charge them with this sin!" And with that, he died.

Acts 7:58–60 (NLT)

Stephen gave his life standing up for what he believed. Even in his death, he asked the Lord to not hold this sin against those who were stoning him to death. Are we willing to die so others may know Jesus?

In Hebrews 11 is a list of people who lived out their faith in the Lord. Some of those were Abel, Enoch, Noah, Abraham, Sarah, Isaac, Jacob, Joseph, Moses, Rahab, Gideon, Barak, Samson, Jephthah, David, Samuel, and the prophets. "And it came about in due time, after Hannah had conceived, that she gave birth to a son; and she named him Samuel, saying, 'Because I have asked him of the Lord'" (1 Samuel 1:20, NASB). Hannah had promised the Lord she would give her son Samuel to serve him all the days of his life. She kept him home until he was a young boy and then took him to the temple to serve Eli the priest. Even as a young boy, Samuel heard the voice of the Lord. He did not realize it at first, but Eli finally realized it was God calling to Samuel: "Then the Lord came and stood and called as at other times, 'Samuel! Samuel!' And Samuel said, 'Speak, for thy servant is listening'" (1 Samuel 3:10, NASB).

As a prophet, Samuel heard from God many times in later years. Often, people did not want to hear Samuel's message from the Lord, but he was willing to do whatever God told him to do. He lived out his faith for the Lord. Are you living out your faith before the people you are with in your home, on your job, as you walk along the street or drive in rush hour traffic?

David was chosen by the Lord to be king as a young boy. He encountered many different obstacles to his becoming king. King Saul was very jealous of David and sought to kill him because God was with him when he went out to war. God protected David from Saul. Later, David committed the sin of sleeping with Bathsheba, who was the wife of Uriah the Hittite. He then had Uriah put on the front line in battle so he would be killed. The son born to Bathsheba, died, bringing great grief to David's heart. Many bad things happened in David's life. David admitted the sin in his life and cried out to God: "Be gracious to me, O God, according to thy loving kindness; according to the greatness of thy compassion blot out transgressions. Wash me thoroughly from my iniquity, and cleanse me from my sin. For I know my transgressions, and my sin is ever before me" (Psalm 51:1–3, NASB).

David cried out to God and God heard his cry. He asked the Lord to create in him a clean heart, to restore his steadfast spirit, and to restore to him the joy of his salvation. In the Scriptures we are told Jesus Christ descended from King David.

This is the record of the ancestors of Jesus the Messiah, a descendant of King David and of Abraham:

Matthew 1:1 (NLT)

For a child is born to us, a son is given to us. And the government will rest on his shoulders. These will be his royal titles: Wonderful Counselor, Mighty God, Everlasting Father, Prince of Peace. His ever expanding, peaceful government will never end. He will rule forever with fairness and justice from the throne of his ancestor David. The passionate commitment of the LORD Almighty will guarantee this!

Isaiah 9:6–7 (NLT)

Even though he sinned, he served the Lord well. David was counted amongst the great people of faith.

When you enter heaven's gates, do you think you will hear, "Well done, my good and faithful servant"?

Do you consider sharing the gospel of salvation with lost people to be your responsibility?

Pray about your response and what God would have you do. We are called by God to go and share the good news of Jesus Christ with the lost of this world. We are held accountable by God for what we do for him. What is your response to God's call? "Lord, I'll go! Send me!" (Isaiah 6:8b, NLT).

Slipping and Sliding Without a Firm Foundation

We live on Ash Creek Road, north of Wilburton, Oklahoma. We received a lot of rain during June and July of 2007. The tinhorn at Rough Hollow began washing out. The county came in and built a bypass on the low side of the road for us to drive on while they constructed a new bridge. It is really a dangerous bypass, as it makes a very sharp curve downward and then a sharp curve upward on the other end. Large trucks with trailers have a difficult time making the turn and some have got crosswise in the road. Saturday night and all day yesterday, we had a light rain that fell. Usually at the top of the turn, we go to the right so cars getting ready to go down the bypass can come down the left side. Approaching the right side, Doyal could feel the tires begin to spin. The layer of gravel they had placed on the road had been pressed down deep in the dirt and was now mud. This time we had to go to the left because it was not quite so steep and still had a firm foundation. In order to give us a firm foundation to drive on, they will need to come in and grade the road and put more gravel on it.

What happens in a Christian's life when he or she gets away from the firm foundation of the teachings of the Lord and begins to walk in the ways of the world? In the Old Testament, we read about the children of Israel and how they allowed themselves to be drawn away from the Lord and began worshiping idols. In the third month after the children of Israel had left Egypt, Moses went up on Mount Sinai to meet with God. After God spoke with Moses, he told him to go down and warn the children of Israel not to come up to Mount Sinai. Moses went back and warned them again about coming up on the mountain, but he also told them what the Lord spoke to him. We want to think about two things God spoke to him while on the mountain. "You shall have no other gods before me. You shall not make for yourself an idol, or any likeness of what is in heaven above or on the earth beneath or in the water under the earth" (Exodus 20:3–4, NASB). God gave instruction for them not to give allegiance to any other person or thing. He was the Lord their God and they were to worship him alone. It seems the Israelites were much like us, for they were easily enticed by things that were not of God. How many times do we put material goods, activities, or our jobs ahead of the Lord? We say we cannot come to worship the Lord on Sunday because we must work, be with our family at the lake or some amusement park, or Sunday is the only day we have for ourselves. We have made these things our god rather than worshiping the one and only true God. God gave Moses further instruction: "Now the Lord said to Moses, 'Come up to me on the mountain and remain there, and I will give you the stone tablets with the law and the commandment which I have written for their instruction'" (Exodus 24:12, NASB).

The Bible says Moses was on Mount Sinai for forty days and forty nights. The children of Israel began to allow their thoughts to stray once again from the Lord. They allowed their minds to be filled with wrong thoughts.

> Now when the people saw that Moses delayed to come down from the mountain, the people assembled about Aaron, and said to him, "Come, make us a god who will go before us; as for this Moses, the man who brought us up from the land of Egypt, we do not know what has become of him."
>
> Exodus 32:1 (NASB)

The Israelites had seen the invisible God in action throughout their journey, but still, they were easily led away from following him.

They wanted a god they could see. Moses had asked God to send Aaron to speak for him, but Aaron was not a strong leader like Moses. He was swayed by the people's demands and told them to gather all the gold rings from the ears of the women and bring them to him. He melted down the gold and formed an idol for them to worship.

> Then Aaron took the gold, melted it down, and molded and tooled it into the shape of a calf. The people exclaimed, "O Israel, these are the gods who brought you out of Egypt." When Aaron saw how excited the people were about it, he built an altar in front of the calf and announced, "Tomorrow there will be a festival to the Lord!"
>
> Exodus 32:4–5 (NLT)

Aaron and the children of Israel did everything wrong in the sight of the Lord. They sacrificed burnt offerings and peace offerings to the golden calf. They celebrated with feasting and much drinking. They began to indulge in sexual immorality. They were in a downward spiral away from the Lord's teachings that Moses had taught them.

> Then the Lord told Moses, "Quick! Go down the mountain! The people you brought from Egypt have defiled themselves. They have already turned from the way I commanded them to live. They have made an idol shaped like a calf, and they have worshiped and sacrificed to it. They are saying, 'These are your gods, O Israel, who brought you out of Egypt.'"
>
> Exodus 32:7–8 (NLT)

God was very angry with the Israelites and threatened to allow his anger to blaze against them and destroy them. Moses once again pleaded with the Lord concerning God's own people. He reminded

God about what the Egyptians would say and also about the covenants he had made with Abraham, Isaac, and Jacob. The Lord withdrew his threat to destroy them.

I believe we need to look at the Israelites situation in comparison with what is happening in our world today. The United States of America in the past has been known as "one nation under God." We are so far away from this distinction today it is very frightening. The USA is made up of a multitude of different nationalities from many different countries. As the people from other lands have come to live on American soil, they have brought their gods with them and many Americans have adopted their gods.

> Fear the LORD your God, serve him only and take your oaths in his name. Do not follow other gods, the gods of the peoples around you; for the LORD your God, who is among you, is a jealous god and his anger will burn against you, and he will destroy you from the face of the land.
>
> Deuteronomy 6:13–15 (NIV)

I firmly believe what God said to Israel he is saying to us as believers in the United States of America. We are not to adopt the gods of other nations. We are to worship the one true God on which the principles of our nation was built. When we follow other gods, our God becomes very angry, for he is a jealous god. We are to stand on the firm foundation of the teachings of God's Word because the Bible is the word of truth.

Wake up, America! Look around and see what is happening in our nation. We are so far from the Lord that attendance in churches is falling off drastically. People do not want to take time out of their busy lives to worship the God who created them. May we listen to the word God has for us. "God is spirit, and those who worship him must worship in spirit and truth" (John 4:24, NASB).

Our God is a living God. His Spirit lives within our hearts and helps us to know right from wrong. We worship the one true God who speaks to us each and every day, if we will spend time with him in his Word and in prayer, taking time to listen to him. We must repent of our sin and turn back to him. We must stop slipping and sliding around because we do not have a firm foundation. Get into the Word of God and allow him to build a firm foundation in your life.

What is the condition of your life and your beliefs? Are you on a downward spiral or are you reaching upward to the Lord for help? Ask God to bring healing to the people of our world.

To Tell the Truth

In the 1960s and early 70s, I watched a TV show called "To Tell the Truth." This show began running in 1956 and was on television for forty-five years. A team of celebrity panelists tried to determine which of three contestants were telling the truth concerning their identity. The catch phrase used was "Will the real John Doe please stand up?" A story was told each time and only one of the three contestants was actually the person in the story. The host would tell about this person and it might be funny, sad, or inspirational. They might talk about the person's professional career, his or her political activity, or some cause he or she was actively involved in. Each of the four celebrity panelists would take turns asking questions of each of the people. At the end, they each voted for the person they thought was the real John Doe. Each incorrect vote by the panelists increased the amount of money the contestant received. The maximum amount won by the contestant was $1,000.

We do not need to question who the real Jesus is, because the Bible states it very clearly. "Therefore the Lord himself will give you a sign: The virgin will be with child and will give birth to a son, and will call him Immanuel" (Isaiah 7:14, NIV). This event actually took place and is recorded in the New Testament in the Book of Matthew: "The virgin will be with child and will give birth to a son, and they will call him Immanuel"—which means, 'God with us'" (Matthew 1:23, NIV).

God sent Jesus in human form to earth. He came as a baby, born to Mary, a virgin. The child was conceived in Mary by the Holy Spirit. "Now the birth of Jesus Christ was as follows. When his mother Mary had been betrothed to Joseph, before they came

together she was found to be with child by the Holy Spirit"
(Matthew 1:18, NASB).

His earthly father was Joseph. Jesus was sent to earth with a
purpose. "And we have beheld and bear witness that the Father
has sent the Son to be the Savior of the world" (1 John 4:14, NASB).
Savior means "One who saves."

> For the Son of Man has come to seek and to save that
> which was lost.
>
> Luke 19:10 (NASB)

> For God did not send the Son into the world to judge the
> world, but that the world should be saved through him.
>
> John 3:17 (NASB)

> And there is salvation in no one else; for there is no other
> name under heaven that has been given among men, by
> which we must be saved.
>
> Acts 4:12 (NASB)

John the Baptist talked about Jesus's coming: "And he was preaching
and saying, 'After me one is coming who is mightier than I, and
I am not fit to stoop down and untie the thong of his sandals. I
baptized you with water; but he will baptize you with the Holy
Spirit'" (Mark 1:7–8, NASB).

He was preparing the way for Jesus, who would come after
him. John the Baptist baptized with water as a witness of a person's
repentance of sin. Jesus would come baptizing with the Holy Spirit.
"Peter replied, 'Repent and be baptized, every one of you, in the
name of Jesus Christ for the forgiveness of your sins. And you will
receive the gift of the Holy Spirit'" (Acts 2:38, NIV).

Repentance brings about salvation. When one is baptized with water, it is the outward sign of repentance and forgiveness of sins. We receive forgiveness through placing our faith in Christ, not through baptism. The Holy Spirit is the gift we receive when we believe and accept Jesus as Savior.

Jesus came as a humble servant. "For even the Son of Man did not come to be served, but to serve, and to give his life as a ransom for many" (Mark 10:45, NIV). Jesus was our supreme example of a servant. Wherever he went, he was always serving others making the lame to walk, the blind to see, the deaf to hear and the sick well. He gave a good example of servanthood at the Last Supper with his disciples: " ...so he got up from the meal, took off his outer clothing, and wrapped a towel around his waist. After that, he poured water into a basin and began to wash his disciples' feet, drying them with the towel that was wrapped around him" (John 13:4–5, NIV). He demonstrated to the disciples what they must be willing to do.

> When he had finished washing their feet, he put on his clothes and returned to his place. "Do you understand what I have done for you?" he asked them. "You call me 'teacher' and 'LORD,' and rightly so, for that is what I am. Now that I, your LORD and teacher, have washed your feet, you also should wash one another's feet. I have set you an example that you should do as I have done for you."
>
> John 13:12–15 (NIV)

These verses not only applied to his disciples, but they apply to you and me. We are to be willing to humble ourselves and serve others; willing to do whatever it requires of us. Jesus was a servant up to the very end of his life as he died on the cross for our sin.

Jesus is a friend to all people. "I command you to love each other in the same way that I love you. And here is how to measure it—the greatest love is shown when people lay down their lives for their friends. You are my friends if you obey me" (John 15:12–14, NLT). When we love one another and live in obedience to the commands of the Lord, Jesus tells us we will be his friends. Jesus befriended all people even though he was criticized because of those he associated with. "And I, the Son of Man, feast and drink, and you say, 'He's a glutton and a drunkard, and a friend of the worst sort of sinners!' But wisdom is shown to be right by what results from it" (Matthew 11:19, NLT).

Jesus was criticized no matter what he did. When he befriended Zaccheus and went to his home to eat, he was criticized. Because of his friendship, Zaccheus became a follower of Jesus. Jesus befriended Mary Magdalene, and because of his friendship, she believed in him and followed him on his journeys, serving him and helping to support him. There are many examples in the Bible concerning Jesus's friendship with others that brought about salvation, such as the woman of Samaria. The Jews hated her because she was a Samaritan. Many people came to believe in Jesus because Jesus befriended this woman.

Jesus continually taught his disciples and others. His disciples were disturbed by the things Jesus taught concerning what would happen in the future. He told them to not be troubled because he was going to prepare a place for them in his Father's house. One day he would come again and take them to be with him because where he was they would be there also. Thomas told Jesus they did not know where he was going and wondered how they would know the way. Jesus voiced a very important statement for all people: "Jesus said to him, 'I am the way, and the truth, and the life; no one comes to the Father, but through me'" (John 14:6, NASB).

Only through Jesus can a person be saved. I like what the Life Application Bible says concerning this verse: "As the way, he is our path to the Father. As the Truth, he is the reality of God's promises. As the life, he joins his divine life to ours, both now and eternally." Jesus is everything we need.

Why not trust him today as Savior if you do not know him?

Can you say without hesitation that you know the truth about Jesus? If so, write your testimony about when you came to know Jesus (the truth) as Savior.

What evidence can you give, if questioned, as to who Jesus is?

What's That You Say?

All of us have failed to respond to our parent's call at some time in our life. We have heard our parents call us to supper or to come clean our room, but we have pretended we did not hear. Our parents have called us over and over, and with each call they became a little more irritated because we were not heeding their call. Finally, when we responded, we were probably in trouble because of our failure to obey. I can remember many times calling our younger boys to get out of bed and get ready for breakfast. If they hopped right out of bed, all was fine, but if they continued to lie there, the more I had to call out to them, the more irritated I became. I wanted their immediate obedience to my call. I am afraid our boys failed to read the command of our Lord in "You children must always obey your parents, for this is what pleases the Lord" (Colossians 3:20, NLT). I imagine, growing up, each of us could identify with this type of disobedience.

Think with me how God must feel when he calls us to be on mission for him, but we ignore his call and continue to do what we desire. Perhaps God speaks to us and tells us to do a particular thing for him and we begin to make excuses or we give reasons why we should or should not do what he says.

> The word of the LORD came to Jonah son of Amittai: "Go to the great city of Nineveh and preach against it, because its wickedness has come up before me." But Jonah ran away from the LORD and headed for Tarshish. He went down to Joppa, where he found a ship bound for that port. After paying the fare, he went aboard and sailed for Tarshish to flee from the LORD.
>
> Jonah 1:1–3 (NIV)

When God told Jonah to go the city of Ninevah, the capital of the Assyrian Empire, Jonah did not want to go. His people had suffered terrible things at the hands of the Assyrians. What Jonah did not realize was he could not flee from the presence of the Lord. God is in all places at all times. We may refuse to go where he wants to send us, but we cannot run away from his correction. We all know the story about Jonah boarding the ship to go to Tarshish, and while they were sailing, a violent storm came. Jonah was on the lower deck asleep. The captain woke him and told him to cry out to his God to save them. Jonah said he was the reason for their trouble and told them to throw him overboard. Jonah was swallowed by a big fish and spent three nights in its belly. Jonah began to pray and pledged to keep his vows to the Lord by not worshiping any other god and acknowledging God as the god of his salvation. God ordered the big fish to vomit him onto dry ground. "Then the word of the Lord came to Jonah a second time: 'Go to the great city of Nineveh and proclaim to it the message I give you.' Jonah obeyed the word of the Lord and went to Nineveh" (Jonah 3:1–3a, NIV).

Jonah finally obeyed the call of the Lord to go and deliver his message to the people. The message from God caused them to turn from their evil ways. Jonah still was not in complete obedience to the Lord because he became angry when the people repented of their sin and God forgave them. He began to pout and God had to set his thinking straight. There are times God has had to do the same with you and me. We forget God is sovereign and that he is the Creator of all things. It is God's right to do whatever he desires to do. We are simply created by God to be his vessel.

Think with me about a command our Lord gave to Hosea. In my mind, this command would have caused utter confusion for Hosea.

When the LORD first began speaking to Israel through Hosea, he said to him, "Go and marry a prostitute, so some of her children will be born to you from other men. This will illustrate the way my people have been untrue to me, openly committing adultery against the LORD by worshiping other gods."

Hosea 1:2–3 (NLT)

I don't know about you, but if God told me to go marry a man who had relations with many women, I think I would say, "What's that you say?" I would think I had misunderstood what God was saying to me. I would probably question God about his reasoning. Gomer was the prostitute Hosea married. God told Hosea she would be unfaithful to him after they were married. God told Hosea some of the children she would have during their marriage would be by other men. Now, I believe I would really take a step backward and take another look at the situation if God said this to me. I would wonder if I had heard him correctly. But, Hosea stepped forward in obedience and did exactly what God told him to do. God had been faithful in his covenant with Israel, but Israel had not been faithful to God. They went away from worshiping him alone, to worshiping false gods. They sought military help from Assyria and Egypt rather than turning to God for help and protection. Hosea was warning Judah not to follow Israel's example. Even after Gomer had relations with other men, God told Hosea to go and bring her back. "Then the Lord said to me, 'Go and get your wife again. Bring her back to you and love her, even though she loves adultery. For the Lord still loves Israel even though the people have turned to other gods, offering them choice gifts'" (Hosea 3:1, NLT).

Even though Israel had sinned, God continually sent prophets to deliver his message concerning the repentance of sin and their return to him. Obedience in Hosea's case was a difficult choice, but he obeyed because God told him to do it. Our God is a god of restoration and the desire of his heart is to restore his relationship with his children.

Charles Haddon Spurgeon was considered to be England's best-known preacher for most of the second half of the nineteenth century. By the age of twenty-one, he was the most popular preacher in London. During his early years, even though he received religious training, he was very rebellious. The period of his life from the ages of ten to sixteen was a very difficult time for Charles. The following is a quote from Spurgeon:

> *"I must confess," he says, "that I never would have been saved if I could have helped it. As long as ever I could, I rebelled, and revolted, and struggled against God. When he would have me pray, I would not pray, and when he would have me listen to the sound of the ministry, I would not. And when I heard, and the tear rolled down my cheek, I wiped it away and defied him to melt my soul. But long before I began with Christ, he began with me."*

Spurgeon gives his mother the credit for arousing in him a concern for his soul as she prayed and exhorted him to walk with the Lord. "And all things you ask in prayer, believing, you shall receive" (Matthew 21:22, NASB). Spurgeon's mother prayed fervently for him and the other children in the family. Every Sunday evening Mrs. Spurgeon would gather her children around the table, read the Scripture to them and explain it to them verse by verse. I quote from an article about Spurgeon:

> *Then she prayed, and her son declares that some of the words of her prayers her children never forgot. Once she said, "Now, Lord, if my children go on in their sins, it will not be from ignorance they perish, and my soul must bear swift witness against them at the day of judgment if they lay not hold of Christ." That was not at all in the modern vein, but it was the arrow that reached the boy's soul. "The thought of a mother bearing swift witness against me pierced my*

conscience and stirred my heart." His father recalled that his wife once said to him, speaking of their eldest son, "What a mercy that boy was converted when he was young."

Spurgeon admitted when he preached his first sermon that he was once a very sinful child who did not listen to the wise counsel of his parents. But, his mother was faithful in praying for him, and because of her faithfulness he stood to preach to his congregation every Sunday. Charles Spurgeon ran from God, but became one of the greatest preachers ever known. "The time is fulfilled, and the kingdom of God is at hand; repent and believe in the gospel" (Mark 1:15, NASB).

Are you listening to God today? Are you responding to his call or are you acting like you do not hear by saying, "What's that you say?"

What things do you need to rid your life of in order to obediently answer the call of the Lord? What do you believe God is calling you to do?

The Rhythm of the Beat of a Healthy Heart

Dow Morris, a member of our church and a close friend, recently had heart bypass surgery. Last night, we stopped by to visit for a few minutes. We were talking about how this type of surgery is very difficult and it really takes a lot of time for the person to recover. I had been acquainted with this in the past as my dad and one of my sisters had bypass surgery. Cecilia, his wife, was explaining to us how a heart and lung pump is used to keep the person alive while they do the bypasses. It is an amazing thing what modern medicine can do. His chest looks to me like he has a railroad track running down it. He calls it a zipper. Once they have repaired the arteries, they hook everything back up and whether the doctors realize it or not, through the power of our Lord, the heart begins beating again. This will happen if the surgery was successful and all went as they had planned.

Is your heart beating for the Lord today? What is the desire of the Lord for the heart of a believer? "A cheerful heart is good medicine, but a broken spirit saps a person's strength" (Proverbs 17:22, NLT). There should be no greater joy in the heart of any person than in the heart of a child of God. We all know when we enter a store or an office with a smile on our face, more than likely we will be greeted with a smile in return. The true joy of the Lord in a person's heart is contagious. We are given instruction in the Word of God as to how we are to respond to the Lord. "Always be full of joy in the Lord. I say it again—rejoice!" (Philippians 4:4, NLT). This joy comes from a believer having his heart and life in right relationship with the Lord.

God desires for us to have a heart for him. "For the eyes of the

Lord range throughout the earth to strengthen those whose hearts are fully committed to him" (2 Chronicles 16:9a, NIV).

Webster's Dictionary's definition of commit is to put in charge or trust. We are to allow God to be in charge of our hearts. We are to entrust our life to him knowing he will bring about what is best. When we walk with him in obedience, he gives us strength to accomplish whatever he sends us to do. The Lord found a person such as this in David. "After Saul had ruled forty years, God removed him from office and put King David in his place, with this commendation: 'I've searched the land, and found this David, a son of Jesse. He's a man whose heart beats to my heart, a man who will do what I tell him'" (Acts 13:21b–22, MSG).

Wouldn't it be exciting if God could say this about you and me? Just think about the possibility of our heart beating to the same rhythm as God's heart and living in obedience to him in all things. I don't know about you, but the thought really is exciting to me. I want to hear God say, "She is a woman whose heart beats to my heart, a woman who will do what I tell her."

God desires our heart to be soft, moldable and responsive to him. "I'll give you a new heart, put a new spirit in you. I'll remove the stone heart from your body and replace it with a heart that's God-willed, not self-willed. I'll put my Spirit in you and make it possible for you to do what I tell you and live by my commands" (Ezekiel 36:26–27, MSG).

When God calls to you and you do not respond, do you think he considers you to have a heart of stone or a heart of flesh? You may be able to think of a time in your life when you knew God was speaking to you, but you turned a deaf ear to him because your heart was hardened. You had no desire to do what God said. The Bible gives clear instruction to us concerning the hardening of our heart.

Be careful then, dear brothers and sisters. Make sure that your own hearts are not evil and unbelieving, turning you away from the living God. You must warn each other every day, as long as it is called "today," so that none of you will be deceived by sin and hardened against God.

Hebrews 3:12–13 (NLT)

Mel Trotter was born in 1870 to William and Emily Lorch Trotter. His father was a bartender, and he and his two brothers helped their father tend bar. His mother, to no avail, prayed for him and encouraged him to live a Christian life. Finally, he set off on his own, determined to do what he wanted and worked as a barber. He married Lottie Fisher in 1891. He began to drink heavily and had difficulty holding a job. He became an alcoholic and committed petty crimes to buy liquor. He was away from his wife and baby for long periods of time because of his trouble with the law and drunkenness. One day he came home after one such period and found his baby boy dead. In 1897, he was in Chicago and had sold his shoes to buy alcohol. He spent all the money he had and was utterly destitute. He stumbled into a rescue mission in the city, Pacific Garden Mission. He was so drunk it took them three days to get him sober. He did not want to hear any sermons from anyone. The director of the mission did not preach to him, but told him he could stay there as long as he needed. They silently showed him love and concern. A week later, he heard a message by the superintendent of the mission and he committed his life to Christ. He established more than sixty-seven rescue missions in his lifetime, and became one of the world's great evangelists. His heart was hardened towards the Lord, but the kindness shown to him by those at the mission and the convicting power of God's Word changed his life.

When we walk with the Lord and allow his Word to change our lives, we will walk in the rhythm of the beat of a healthy heart. Dow's heart was not healthy and the beat was not correct when the arteries were blocked. Because of his bypass surgery, hopefully, he will truly have the rhythm of the beat of a healthy heart.

If God were to do a heart check, what would be the condition of your heart today? Would he find a joyful heart, a heart of flesh, a heart of stone, or would he find a heart that is controlled by the Holy Spirit, completely committed to him and beating with the same rhythm as his heart? How is the beat of your heart today?

The Plus of Technical Training

We purchased a new ceramic cooktop from Sears, and they sent two young men to deliver and install it yesterday. As they came through the door, I sensed they really were not knowledgeable of their job. You could tell by their appearance they were not too concerned about doing a top rate job. Don't get me wrong, they were very congenial and cordial to me and removed the old cooktop with no problem. When they placed the new cooktop in the hole, it was loose. They began to get a puzzled look on their faces. They voiced their bewilderment as to how they were going to make it stationary. I suggested it might be good for them to read the instruction booklet, which they did. They found a couple of braces to install, but then there was a large space between the bottom of the cooktop and the bottom of the brace. Once again, they were puzzled. They had very few tools, so I had to get them the proper tools to use. I asked them if Sears provided any technical training for them before they started the job of installing appliances and they said, "No, none at all." I was simply amazed at this since they were working with 220 electric. In a sense, it rather unnerved me because they were working on our home and electric fires could cause so much damage. Let me give you a comparison of them and the electrician I had come later in the day to work on some of our light fixtures. He had gone to school and he was working with a licensed electrician. He received the proper training for his job. The gentleman came fully prepared with tools and knowledge. He had the gauges to check the amount of electricity flowing through the wiring. He was a quality electrician and there was all the difference in the world in his work than that of the two young men. I had him check over their work to be sure we were safe. There is a real plus in people obtaining the technical training they need for their particular job.

People need to have the skill required to complete the job they are given. God chose Aaron and his sons to minister as priests to him. God gave instructions as to the garments they were to wear. "Make special clothing for Aaron to show his separation to God— beautiful garments that will lend dignity to his work. Instruct all those who have special skills as tailors to make the garments that will set Aaron apart from everyone else, so he may serve me as a priest" (Exodus 28:2–3, NLT). God gave special instruction as to how each piece was to be made. The different pieces were the chest piece, an ephod, a robe, an embroidered tunic, a turban and a sash. There were also to be special garments made for his sons when they would serve as priests before the Lord. The Lord instructed Moses about the material to use for each piece. It was important to the Lord for the men making these garments to be skilled craftsmen.

God then gave Moses instructions concerning the items to be placed in the tabernacle.

> The LORD also said to Moses, "Look, I have chosen Bezalel son of Uri, grandson of Hur, of the tribe of Judah. I have filled him with the Spirit of God, giving him great wisdom, intelligence, and skill in all kinds of crafts. He is able to create beautiful objects from gold, and silver, and bronze. He is skilled in cutting and setting gemstones and in carving wood. Yes, he is a master at every craft."
>
> Exodus 31:1–5 (NLT)

God wanted everything in the tabernacle to be just as he had instructed. God continued to give instructions and stated that he had given special skill to the naturally talented craftsmen He had chosen. They were to do the tabernacle, the ark of the covenant, the cover for the ark, the place of atonement and all the furnishings of the tabernacle. God did not have unskilled craftsmen working on the tabernacle. Work of the best quality was important to God. Don't you think God would be pleased if we were particular about how we displayed his temple today? As believers, we are the temples of the Holy Spirit. When people look at us do they see a temple worthy of Jesus Christ?

When Solomon was building the temple, he sent for skilled craftsmen:

> Now King Solomon sent and brought Hiram from Tyre. He was a widow's son from the tribe of Naphtali, and his father was a man of Tyre, a worker in bronze; and he was filled with wisdom and understanding and skill for doing any work in bronze. So he came to King Solomon and performed all his work.
>
> 1 Kings 7:13–14 (NASB)

He constructed all types of pillars, figurines to go on the pillars, and designs all around the temple. All the utensils to be used in worship were molded by him. He did quality work and King Solomon was very pleased. When the Lord charged Solomon with the task of building the temple he gave him careful instructions as to what type of work was to be done.

> Now behold, with great pains I have prepared for the house of the LORD 100,000 talents of gold and 1,000,000 talents of silver, and bronze and iron beyond weight, for they are in great quantity; also timber and stone I have prepared, and you may add to them. Moreover, there are many workmen with you, stonecutters and masons of stone and carpenters, and all men who are skillful in every kind of work.
>
> 1 Chronicles 22:14–15 (NASB)

God wanted his temple to be the very best. "Now set your heart and your soul to seek the Lord your God; arise, therefore, and build the sanctuary of the Lord God, so that you may bring the ark of the covenant of the Lord, and the holy vessels of God into the house that is to be built for the name of the Lord" (1 Chronicles 22:19, NASB). The work performed was a representation of the name of the Lord.

When we went to Russia on a mission trip, we were amazed at the massive, exquisite structures created by skilled craftsmen. There were steeples and domes made of solid gold. The artwork inside a large Russian Orthodox church we visited was unbelievable. The top of the building was a dome structure and all around the inside of the dome were scenes from different Bible stories. Everything was done in the very best of taste. The Hermitage was an amazing sight to behold with its eight or nine hundred rooms. They were all filled with quality artwork. The outside of many of the buildings in Russia display fine art work in the rock laying, the sculptures, and the different designs on the buildings. Truly, many of the buildings were the work of extremely skilled craftsmen.

"Thus says the Lord, your Redeemer, and the one who formed you from the womb, 'I, the Lord, am the maker of all things, stretching out the heavens by myself, and spreading out the earth all alone" (Isaiah 44:24, NASB). No craftsmen at any time in history can compare to Almighty God. He intricately wove the very structure of our body together in our mother's womb. Most of us were blessed with fingers, toes, eyes and ears. He constructed the brain so we could think for ourselves. He placed organs within our bodies to perform the necessary functions. He was the creator of the heavens and the earth. Our God is the master craftsman!

When you do work for our Lord, are you particular about the type of work you do so you will represent God well? Think of an example of something you have done and share it with a special friend.

What work is God calling you to do today? Are you listening and responding to him?

High Expectations

When I was born in 1944, life was simple, and it took little to satisfy a child. Times were hard and we expected very little. My dad enjoyed doing special things for us when possible. We had Kress' and TG&Y stores in the larger towns. You could buy warm Spanish peanuts, hot popcorn, and there was fresh candy where you could select the pieces you wanted. When we went to town, we hoped we would get something special. The dictionary tells us hope is "desire accompanied by expectation of fulfillment." My favorite treat was the warm peanuts, and I lived with high expectation of getting some on our trips to town.

I attended college in California, and I came home once a year. When the time approached for me to return to Oklahoma, I would get excited and have high expectations of being home with my parents. I knew my mom would fix all the special foods I enjoyed. My dad would plan outings to the lake where we would fish and cook a meal over an open fire. I had the hope of all my expectations being fulfilled.

As a believer in the Lord, hope has come to have new meaning. Hope is the confident assurance of future glory and blessing.

Praise be to the God and Father of our Lord Jesus Christ! In his great mercy he has given us new birth into a living hope through the resurrection of Jesus Christ from the dead, and into an inheritance that can never perish, spoil or fade—kept in heaven for you, who through faith are shielded by God's power until the coming of the salvation that is ready to be revealed in the last time.

1 Peter 1:3–5 (NIV)

We live, encountering trials from time to time, but knowing when Jesus comes again our salvation will be made complete. "For I am confident of this very thing, that he who began a good work in you will perfect it until the day of Christ Jesus" (Philippians 1:6, NASB). Our salvation is secure from the moment we are saved. However, God's work is completed in our life when Jesus comes again and we go to heaven to live with the Lord forever.

The many trials we encounter in life are used by God to grow us to maturity. "You rejoice in this, though now for a short time you have had to be distressed by various trials so that the genuineness of your faith—more valuable than gold, which perished though refined by fire—may result in praise, glory, and honor at the revelation of Jesus Christ" (1 Peter 1:6–7, HCSB). Our faith in Jesus Christ becomes stronger as we endure times of testing. James, the brother of Jesus, stated it well in the Book of James: "Consider it pure joy, my brothers, whenever you face trials of many kinds, because you know that the testing of your faith develops perseverance. Perseverance must finish its work so that you may be mature and complete, not lacking anything" (James 1:2–4, NIV). I am afraid few of us are joyful about trials we encounter, but when we look back, we can see the Lord was working in our life.

While we are here on earth, we are to be storing up treasures in heaven, not precious jewels and gold like a pirate thinks of treasure. The treasure we as believers store in heaven is the fruit we are producing for the Lord each day. One of the ways we do this is by sharing Jesus with a lost person and helping him or her understand how they can accept Jesus as Savior and Lord. The Lord expects other things from us. We express the love of Jesus to others in many different ways. Jesus told his disciples about the time he was hungry and they gave him something to eat; he was thirsty and they gave him a drink; he was a stranger and they invited him into their home, and he was naked and they gave him clothes. The disciples did not understand what Jesus was saying for they knew they had not done this for him. They began to question the Lord about when this happened. "And the King will tell them, 'I assure you, when you did it to one of the least of these my brothers and sisters, you were doing it to me!'" (Matthew 25:40, NLT).

What we do for others in the name of Jesus is producing fruit for him. When we show kindness to a child who has lost his way, we are bearing fruit. We may have elderly parents living with us or a parent who is dependent on us, and we are patient with them as they become feeble; this is demonstrating the fruit Jesus desires to see in us. We are producing fruit for the Lord when we show mercy to a person injured in a car wreck as they wait for the ambulance to come. We may kneel down beside him or her and pray for him or her as they wait. As we grow in the Lord, we will produce more and more fruit for him because our hope and trust is in him.

Warren Wiersbe states in his commentary on 1 Peter that we are not to be complacent on the battlefield of life: "Hope is not a sedative; it is a shot of adrenaline, a blood transfusion." When a person in a weakened condition receives a blood transfusion, it is as if they have received a shot of adrenaline. They perk right up and usually become much stronger. " ... Christ lives in you, and this is your assurance that you will share in his glory" (Colossians 1:27b, NLT). A believer has this hope in the Lord. Holy Spirit lives within us giving us the assurance we will one day share in the glory of the Lord.

> So brace up your minds; be sober (circumspect, morally alert); set your hope wholly and unchangeably on the grace (divine favor) that is coming to you when Jesus Christ (the Messiah) is revealed. [Live] as children of obedience [to God]; do not conform yourselves to the evil desires [that governed you] in your former ignorance [when you did not know the requirements of the Gospel]. But as the one who called you is holy, you yourselves also be holy in all your

conduct and manner of living. For it is written. You shall be holy, for I am holy.

1 Peter 1:13–16 (AMP)

We are to set our sights on the Lord and not allow things to deter us. Our hope is built on knowing Jesus is coming again and will take us to heaven to live with him. We are to live our life in obedience, not reverting back to our old way of life. Jesus lived a holy life and we are to imitate him. We should say, without any hesitation whatsoever, as David said, "And now, Lord, what do I wait for and expect? My hope and expectation are in you" (Psalm 39:7, AMP).

Growing up, I hoped to get warm peanuts when I went to town. When I went home from college, I hoped Mom would cook my favorite foods and Dad would have fishing trips and cookouts planned. As I grew in my faith, I realized there was a lot more to hope. I look forward with confident assurance of future glory and blessing when Jesus returns.

Do you expect great things from the Lord? If not, why not?

"Now glory be to God! By his mighty power at work within us, he is able to accomplish infinitely more than we would ever dare to ask or hope" (Ephesians 3:20, NLT). When God's power is at work within us, we can expect great things to happen. Think of a verse that expresses the hope you have in Jesus Christ.

Proclaimed Faithful

This is a very simple example of being faithful. Most mama cows are excellent mothers and very protective of their calf. They usually have their calf far off in the pasture or even up in the woods behind our house. If you come within fifty feet of them, they get up and begin to look at you with great suspicion. If you continue to walk towards them, they will begin pacing back and forth in front of their calf. The closer you get to them, the more upset they become. There are those who will charge you, thinking you are a danger to their calf. It is extremely difficult to get close enough to check the calf and be sure it is okay. One could proclaim them to be faithful as a mama to their calf because of the protection they offer to them.

God our Father is far more faithful to protect his children.

> He found him in a desolate land, in a barren, howling wilderness; he surrounded him, cared for him, and guarded him as the pupil of his eye. He watches over his nest like an eagle and hovers over his young; he spreads his wings, catches him, and lifts him up on his pinions. The LORD alone led him, with no help from a foreign god. He made him ride on the heights of the land and eat the produce of the field. He nourished him with honey from the rock and oil from flint-like rock, cream from the herd and milk from the flock, with the fat of lambs, rams from Bashan, and goats, with the choicest grains of wheat; you drank wine from the finest grapes. Then Jeshurum became fat and reveled—you became fat, bloated, and gorged. He abandoned the God who made him and scorned the rock of his salvation.

Deuteronomy 32:10–15 (HCSB)

Jeshurum refers to the nation of Israel, and the Lord was protective of his children, the Israelites. As long as they were being obedient, he gave them the very best fertile fields to grow their crops, honey from the rock, and even olive trees grew from the flint-like rock, producing olives with which they could make oil. They were well fed with plenty of milk to drink and meat to eat. As they became prosperous and were growing fat from the abundance of food, they forsook the God who loved them, provided for them, and was faithful to them in every situation. Do you see any similarities between the children of Israel and the people of today? God has abundantly blessed us as citizens of the United States compared to other nations. Yet, we have strayed so far from the Lord. I am sure it brings great grief to our Father. Looking at your own life, do you think you would be proclaimed faithful to the Lord?

Nehemiah went to Jerusalem to lead the people to repair the wall around the city. When he arrived, he found the broken wall around the city and people with broken lives. He gathered the people together to hear the reading of God's law by Ezra the priest. As the people listened, they begin to weep for they knew they were not obeying the Law. Later, they returned to have the seven-day feast of tabernacles. They confessed their own sins and the sins of their ancestors: "The Book of Law of the Lord their God was read aloud to them for about three hours. Then for three more hours they took turns confessing their sins and worshipping the Lord their God" (Nehemiah 9:3, NLT).

How many of us would set for three hours to hear the Bible read aloud and then spend three more hours in a time of confession and worshiping the Lord our God? I truly believe this is what Greg Frizzell is talking about in his book *Iceberg Dead Ahead!* Until believers have a hunger and thirst for the Word of God and his presence in our life, and we are undeniably repentant of our sin, we will never see spiritual awakening in our land. When we allow sin to be prevalent in our lives, we are stumbling blocks to those who do not know Jesus. Others should be able to look at us and see Jesus Christ in our words and actions. David called out to God for cleansing from his sin:

> Wash me thoroughly from my iniquity, and cleanse me from my sin. For I know my transgressions, and my sin is ever before me. Against thee, thee only, I have sinned, and done what is evil in thy sight, so that thou art justified when thou dost speak, and blameless when thou dost judge.
>
> Psalm 51:2–4 (NASB)

As children of God we must fall to our knees in humble submission and cry out to the Lord for the forgiveness of our sin! Nehemiah and Ezra were faithful in serving the Lord and leading God's people to serve him. When people speak of you and me, would the same thing be said about us?

The children of Israel were given thorough instructions as they were preparing to go and inhabit the promised land: "Hear, O Israel! The Lord is our God, the Lord is one! And you shall love the Lord your God with all your heart and with all your soul and with all your might. And the words, which I am commanding you today, shall be on your heart" (Deuteronomy 6:4–6, NASB).

Moses talked to them about having things they had not had and living in houses that were full of things they did not put there. They would have vineyards and olive trees to eat from that they did not plant. They would be able to eat until they were full. Moses issued a warning of caution so they would not forget the Lord their God who had brought them out of Egypt and through the wilderness. They were instructed to worship the Lord their God only. "For you are a holy people to the Lord your God; the Lord your God has chosen you to be a people for his own possession out of all the peoples who are on the face of the earth" (Deuteronomy 7:6, NASB). The children of Israel had been set apart to be a holy people for the

Lord had chosen them as his very own possession. He gave them a warning as to what would happen if they were not obedient to him:

> It was simply because the LORD loves you, and because he was keeping the oath he had sworn to your ancestors. That is why the LORD rescued you with such amazing power from your slavery under Pharaoh in Egypt. Understand, therefore, that the LORD your God is indeed God. He is the faithful God who keeps his covenant for a thousand generations and constantly loves those who love him and obey his commands. But he does not hesitate to punish and destroy those who hate him.
>
> Deuteronomy 7:8–10 (NLT)

God had led the children of Israel through many different circumstances in their wilderness journey. He had put up with their grumbling and complaining. He had performed miracles before their eyes, yet in time, they forgot what God had done. They were easily led astray to worship other gods. He very clearly stated to them if they would love him and obey his commandments, he would be faithful to them. He warned them he would not hesitate to punish all who hate him. One paraphrase of this scripture gives the idea that those who hate him will be publicly punished and destroyed. He would deal with them face to face. Does this situation in any way convict your heart about the condition of our world today, particularly America? Are you faithful enough to our Lord to spend long periods of time in deliberate, intentional, and purposeful prayer concerning the condition of America?

Think of people in your life who have been faithful to pray for you, cry with you, laugh with you, and teach you about the Lord.

If you were standing before God right now, would you be counted as the Lord's faithful servant? If not, why? If you feel you would be found faithful, what would be your reasoning?

The Bread of Life

One of the staple foods of most people's lives is bread. We have eaten many kinds of breads on our mission trips to different countries. What amazes me about eating bread in Brazil, Russia, Estonia, and Malawi is it is always served cold. I loved going by my mom's when I would get off work, and as I walked into her home, I would smell homemade bread baking. One of my fondest memories is when we would sit down to eat with her and she served hot bread that would be oozing with butter. My mom was a connoisseur of scrumptious homemade bread. My sister, Ann, is the only one of us four girls who bakes delicious yeast bread. I bake a lot of biscuits and cornbread, but baking yeast bread is not an art I have accomplished. Americans love to have hot bread served at a meal whether it is yeast bread, biscuits, or cornbread. Many people feel a meal is not complete without hot bread.

Jesus stated he was the bread of life: "Jesus said to them, "'I am the bread of life; he who comes to me shall not hunger, and he who believes in me shall never thirst'" (John 6:35, NASB). Jesus, in referring to himself as the bread of life, was not offering us bread like we eat each day at a meal. He was saying he was the source of everlasting life. If we would come to him, accept him as Savior, we would have eternal life and would never hunger again.

> Truly, truly, I say to you, he who believes has eternal life. I am the bread of life. Your fathers ate the manna in the wilderness, and they died. This is the bread which comes down out of heaven, so that one may eat of it and not die. I am the living bread that came down out of heaven; if anyone eats of this bread, he shall live forever; and the bread also which I shall give for the life of the world is my flesh.
>
> John 6:47–51 (NASB)

When we are united with Jesus Christ, we receive the bread of life.

Passover was seven days set aside by God for Israel to celebrate their deliverance from slavery to the Egyptians. It was to remind them of what God had done. The annual feast of the Passover was to celebrate the night the death angel passed over the homes of the Israelites because they had done as the Lord said. Any firstborn son of the Israelites would be killed if they did not have the blood of a lamb on the doorpost of their home. All firstborn sons of the Egyptians would be killed. The Israelites were given specific instructions as to what they were to eat during this seven-day period. One instruction concerned the bread they ate. They were to use no yeast or leaven in baking bread: "You must eat unleavened bread for seven days. On the first day you must remove yeast from your houses. Whoever eats what is leavened from the first day through the seventh day must be cut off from Israel" (Exodus 12:15, HCSB).

Bread was used as an offering to the Lord.

> If you bring a grain offering baked in an oven, it is to consist of fine flour: cakes made without yeast and mixed with oil, or wafers made without yeast and spread with oil. Bring the grain offering made of these things to the LORD; present it to the priest, who shall take it to the altar. He shall take out the memorial portion from the grain offering and burn it on the altar as an offering made by fire, an aroma pleasing to the LORD.
>
> Leviticus 2:4, 8–9 (NIV)

The bread left from the offering would be given to Aaron and his sons, who served as priests, for their food.

Bread was used in the tabernacle and the temple to symbolize the presence of God. Before the holy of holies was built, God gave Moses specific instructions as to what was to be on the table. The bread of presence, or shewbread, was to be kept on the table at all times. The bread was to be baked in a special way.

Take fine flour and bake twelve loaves of bread, using two-tenths of an ephah for each loaf. Set them in two rows, six in each row, on the table of pure gold before the LORD. Along each row put some pure incense as a memorial portion to represent the bread and to be an offering made to the LORD by fire. This bread is to be set out before the LORD regularly, Sabbath after Sabbath, on behalf of the Israelites, as a lasting covenant.

Leviticus 24:5–8 (NIV)

This memorial offering, made by fire, was done in memory of the everlasting covenant God had made with the Israelites.

Bread was also used in the Old Testament to represent an enemy who would be conquered. "Only do not rebel against the Lord, nor fear the people of the land, for they are our bread; their protection has departed from them, and the Lord is with us. Do not fear them" (Numbers 14:9, NKJV).

Bread was used to symbolize hospitality as Lot invited the angels of the Lord to enter his house to spend the night and eat with them: "Yet he urged them strongly, so they turned aside to him and entered his house; and he prepared a feast for them, and baked unleavened bread, and they ate" (Genesis 19:3, NASB).

Bread symbolized wisdom in the Book of Proverbs: "Whoever is simple (easily led astray and wavering), let him turn in here! As for him who lacks understanding, [God's] wisdom says to him, come, eat of my bread and drink of the [spiritual] wine which I have mixed" (Proverbs 9:4–5, AMP).

God provides us the opportunity to partake of the bread and drink he offers to us. If we will ask, he will give us the wisdom to understand situations in life and the food he desires us to glean from his Word.

As we previously read in John 6:35, bread symbolizes Jesus Christ.

Then Jesus declared, "I am the bread of life. He who comes to me will never go hungry, and he who believes in me will never be thirsty. But as I told you, you have seen me and still you do not believe. All that the Father gives me will come to me, and whoever comes to me I will never drive away. For I have come down from heaven not to do my will but to do the will of him who sent me."

John 6:35–38 (NIV)

God promises he will not reject any who come to him in simple faith. They must believe Jesus is his Son; he died for their sin and was raised from the grave, so they might have everlasting life.

Bread also symbolizes the body of Jesus Christ: "For I received from the Lord that which I also delivered to you, that the Lord Jesus in the night in which he was betrayed took bread; and when he had given thanks, he broke it, and said, 'This is my body, which is for you; do this in remembrance of me'" (1 Corinthians 11:23–24 NASB). The bread Jesus broke for them to eat at the Last Supper represented his body offered on the cross for our sin.

The bread also symbolizes the unity of the church: "Since there is one bread, we who are many are one body; for we all partake of the one bread" (1 Corinthians 10:17, NASB). The one bread pictures the unity of believers in the body of Christ. We are one in Christ Jesus because of our relationship with him.

The hot, delicious loaf of bread my mom served had such a sweet aroma and would certainly tickle your taste buds. If I had to choose between her bread and the bread of life, I would choose the bread of life, the Lord Jesus Christ.

What about you? What does the term "bread of life" mean to you? Have you feasted on the words Jesus spoke, "I am the bread of life"? He offers you life everlasting if you accept him as Savior. If you do not know him, pray and ask him for the forgiveness of the sin in your life and ask him to be your Savior and Lord. Write down the date and place you made this decision.

Our physical bodies cannot live without food but neither can our spirit. Read the Word of God and meditate on it, asking God to speak to your heart from the Word.

The Light of the World

If Mom and Dad went to bed before I came home in the evening, they would have the porch light on and one in the living room. It was comforting to me to have the lights on. In essence, they were saying, "Come on in, we are ready for you." I remember as a young adult if I was going to be gone from home after dark, I would leave one light on in the house so I could see as I entered. We always had a light outside to light up the yard. We have been in Malawi many times serving in missions and I have learned to sleep with a flashlight beside our bed because there are no outside lights. If I did not have the flashlight to light my way, I would bump into the furniture in the room. When we went outside after dark, we always took a light of some sort because of the possibility of poisonous snakes. I thank God we never saw one in our yard. Something about a light brings assurance and lessens the fear of darkness. Being able to see where we are going helps us to be more surefooted and aware of all that is around us.

Jesus was confronted by the scribes and the Pharisees concerning the woman caught in adultery. They told Jesus the Law of Moses said the woman was to be stoned to death. I am sure these men were shocked when Jesus knelt down and wrote with his finger on the ground. He then stood and spoke to them, "He who is without sin among you, let him be the first to throw a stone at her" (John 8:7b, NASB).

Again, Jesus stooped down and wrote on the ground. When Jesus got up, none of the men were there. They all left, one by one. Possibly, they realized none of them had the right to condemn her. Jesus told her he did not condemn her either and she was to go and not continue sinning. Jesus then made a very important statement:

"Again therefore Jesus spoke to them saying, 'I am the light of the world; he who follows me shall not walk in the darkness, but shall have the light of life'" (John 8:12, NASB).

When a person follows Jesus Christ, believing and trusting in him, he will experience life that enables him to walk in the light. He will no longer walk in darkness because he has found the source of light. Jesus Christ, the Son, is the center and the source of everlasting life to a believer. "In him was life, and the life was the light of men" (John 1:4, NASB).

The light referred to in this verse was eternal life. The word darkness is used to describe the sin in one's life. "Your eye is a lamp for your body. A pure eye lets sunshine into your soul. But an evil eye shuts out the light and plunges you into darkness. If the light you think you have is really darkness, how deep that darkness will be!" (Matthew 6:22–23, NLT).

When our thoughts are on things of the world and not the Lord, Satan makes great strides in pulling us away from the Lord and into a life of sin, a life of darkness. The prophet Isaiah prophesied about the child who would be born and would turn darkness into light.

The people who walk in darkness will see a great light; those who live in a dark land, the light will shine on them. For a child will be born to us, a son will be given to us; and the government will rest on his shoulders; and his name will be called Wonderful Counselor, Mighty God, Eternal Father, Prince of Peace.

Isaiah 9:2, 6 (NASB)

Isaiah was prophesying about the coming of the Messiah, the anointed one. His purpose would be to free a sinful people from the bondage of sin and give them opportunity to have eternal life in Christ Jesus. We know this event took place because it is recorded in the New Testament.

Now the birth of Jesus Christ was as follows. When his mother Mary had been betrothed to Joseph, before they came together she was found to be with child by the Holy Spirit. "And she will bear a son; and you shall call his name Jesus, for it is he who will save his people from their sins."

Matthew 1:18, 21 (NASB)

Jesus Christ was born in Bethlehem in a manger and he brought light into a world full of darkness.

Another time Jesus referred to light was when he was speaking to his disciples concerning his upcoming death. He was describing to them the type of death he would suffer. "And I, if I be lifted up from the earth, will draw all men to myself" (John 12:32, NASB).

The disciples questioned him as to how he could say the Son of Man must be lifted up. They asked him who this Son of Man was. "Jesus therefore said to them, 'For a little while longer the light is among you. Walk while you have the light, that darkness may not overtake you; he who walks in the darkness does not know where he goes. While you have the light, believe in the light, in order that you may become sons of light'" (John 12:35–36, NASB).

Jesus would be with them just a little while longer in bodily form, but it was difficult for the disciples to understand this. They were to take advantage of his presence with them and learn from him so when he was gone, their lives would shine with his light in a dark world.

John the Baptist was the forerunner of Jesus. He came to bear witness of the light: "He came for a witness, that he might bear witness of the light that all might believe through him. He was not the light, but came that he might bear witness of the light. There was the true light which, coming into the world, enlightens every man" (John 1:7–9, NASB).

John the Baptist was referring to Jesus as the light. He was the only true light and would give light to everyone who believed.

"God is light and there is no darkness in him at all. But if we are living in the light of God's presence, just as Christ is, then we have fellowship with each other, and the blood of Jesus, his Son, cleanses us from every sin" (1 John 1:5b, 7, NLT).

God brings light and there is no darkness or evil in him. As a believer, we are to be living examples of God's presence in our life.

Jesus was teaching the disciples and explaining the responsibility they would have to the people of the world. "You are the light of the world. A city set on a hill cannot be hidden. Let your light shine before men in such a way that they may see your good works, and glorify your Father who is in heaven" (Matthew 5:14, 16, NASB). Jesus would not always be on earth amongst them. It was very important for them to realize they were to be a light to all people. The things they did were to be done to the glory of God the Father. They would be living lights in a world of darkness. The disciples would point others to Jesus. We are given the same challenge today to be lights in a dark world because we have the light of Jesus in our life. Jesus used the example of not covering a light in our home with a basket, but leaving it uncovered, so it would light the whole house. We must not be timid in our witness. We must be a light shining brightly for the Lord, so many will be saved. "For God did not give us a spirit of timidity, but a spirit of power, of love and of self-discipline. So do not be ashamed to testify about our Lord, or ashamed of me his prisoner. But join with me in suffering for the gospel, by the power of God" (2 Timothy 1:7–8, NIV).

Let us all proclaim with boldness, "Jesus Christ is the Light of the World and desires to be the light of your life."

How long has it been since you shared the light, Jesus Christ, with someone? If you were to give a witness for the Lord today, what would you say?

Do you have the light of Jesus in your life? If you are not sure, read again the verses given in this devotional and decide what it means to have the light of Jesus.

The Gate

According to the dictionary, a gate is an opening for passage in a wall or fence; a city or castle entrance often with defensive structures. Each gate usually has a specific purpose and there are many different types of gates. When I married Doyal, I learned about a gap gate. This is often a temporary gate in a barbwire fence through which one can enter a pasture. It consists of the four or five strands of barbwire tied to a stationary post. At the end where you open the gate there is usually a wooden post attached. You put the top and bottom of the post through a loop at the top and bottom of another stationary post. Sometimes they are very difficult to close once you take them down because the barbwire is hard to stretch tight. This was true of the gap gate going into our pasture by the pond where I fish. I entered the pasture between the strands of barbwire on the gate because it was easier than trying to get the gap gate back in place. The gap gate served to keep the cattle in the pasture and not allow them to wander towards the road.

In biblical times, there were gates in the protective walls around the cities. The city of Jericho was surrounded by a wall with a strong gate for people to enter. At night, the gate would be closed for their protection. Joshua had sent two spies across the Jordan River to check out the situation of the promised land, especially the city of Jericho. They came to Rahab's inn to spend the night. Someone told the king of Jericho there were two men from Israel who had come to search out the land. Rahab was ordered to bring the two men out who had entered her house.

But the woman had taken the two men and hidden them, and she said, "Yes, the men came to me, but I did not know where they were from. And it came about when it was time to shut the gate, at dark, that the men went out; I do not know where the men went. Pursue them quickly, for you will overtake them."

Joshua 2:4–5 (NASB)

Rahab said they left before the gate was closed at dark.

Jesus used the story of the shepherd and his flock to illustrate his description of a gate to the people:

I tell you the truth, the man who does not enter the sheep pen by the gate, but climbs in by some other way, is a thief and a robber. The man who enters by the gate is the shepherd of his sheep. The watchman opens the gate for him, and the sheep listen to his voice. He calls his own sheep by name and leads them out. When he has brought out all his own, he goes on ahead of them, and his sheep follow him because they know his voice.

John 10:1–4 (NIV)

We know this is so because a flock of sheep recognize the voice of their shepherd and will follow him as he leads them to water or greener pastures. Jesus made the point about sheep not following a stranger's voice. They really did not understand what Jesus was telling them.

Therefore Jesus said again, "I tell you the truth, I am the gate for the sheep. All who ever came before me were thieves and robbers, but the sheep did not listen to them. I am the gate; whoever enters through me will be saved. He will come in and go out, and find pasture. The thief comes only to steal and kill and destroy; I have come that they may have life, and have it to the full."

John 10:7–10 (NIV)

Several translations refer to the gate as the door, but it means the same thing.

Anyone who is the true shepherd of a flock will have been called and sent by God. When a preacher stands and proclaims the Word of God, the sheep will hear what he says and they will not be afraid to follow his leading. This is so in our church because our pastor is a student of the Word of God. He understands the Greek and the Hebrew, which gives him greater understanding, but most of all, he is an anointed, called out man of God. He functions under the leadership of the Holy Spirit. Therefore, we, the sheep, are willing to follow the shepherd God has given to lead us.

"I am the door; anyone who enters in through me will be saved (will live). He will come in and he will go out [freely], and will find pasture" (John 10:9, AMP). Those who enter in through Jesus, the door or gate, and place their faith and trust in him will become a sheep belonging to his flock. Only through Jesus Christ can a person be saved: "And there is salvation in no one else; for there is no other name under heaven that has been given among men, by which we must be saved" (Acts 4:12, NASB).

Jesus delivers sinners from the bondage of sin. He leads them into freedom because they are saved. According to Wiersbe, "saved" means "delivered safe and sound." The sheep are now safe in the arms of Jesus. They cannot lose their salvation even though they may go through times when their fellowship with the Lord is not as it should be because of sin in their life. " ...And I give eternal life to them, and they shall never perish; and no one shall snatch them out of my hand. My Father, who has given them to me, is greater than all; and no one is able to snatch them out of the Father's hand" (John 10:28–29, NASB).

Jesus, the shepherd, not only leads people out of the bondage of sin, but he leads them into what we refer to as the church. According to Jesus' teaching, born again believers are the church of God.

It is expedient for us to share the message of salvation with urgency. "You can enter God's Kingdom only through the narrow gate. The highway to hell is broad, and its gate is wide for the many who choose the easy way. But the gateway to life is small, and the road is narrow, and only a few ever find it" (Matthew 7:13–14, NLT).

Many people desire what they think is the easy way of life, the way of sin. A multitude of people walk this broad road that has a wide gate because they do not believe it leads to hell, where they will suffer for eternity. They have led themselves to believe the life of sin is a happy life. They think they will be restricted by walking through the narrow gate leading to life everlasting, a joyous life. If only they would realize the narrow gate leads to freedom from the bondage of sin. Believers have the responsibility to go and share Jesus with people not only here at home, but in every nation.

Have you walked through "the narrow gate" leading to salvation? If you have not and you realize you are in need of salvation, admit to the Lord right now that you are a sinner. Confess your sin to the Lord and ask him to forgive you. Pray and ask God to be your Savior and Lord. He will change your life forever and you will no longer want to live a life of sin. You will desire to become more and more like Jesus. Write down the date and time of your decision. Place it in a prominent place to remind you of what happened to you on this special day. In your own words, describe what Jesus meant when he said, "I am the gate."

The Good Shepherd

Thinking about the good shepherd brought to mind a phrase from an old hymn: "Savior, like a shepherd lead us, much we need thy tender care." I thought of my mother caring for my grandmother, Mama Cordie, after she became bedfast. My grandmother was walking across Mom's living room and without stumbling over anything she fell. Severe osteoporosis caused the pelvic bone to fracture, causing her to fall to the floor. My grandmother never walked again. Mom's new home had large bedrooms, so she had a hospital bed brought in to properly care for my grandmother. For some time, my grandmother was aware of things around her and could carry on a conversation, but gradually she lost that ability. Soon, she could not care for herself in any way, so Mom cared for her around the clock. Mom finally got some help a few hours through the week so she could have some relief. During the evening and night Mom would turn my grandmother to prevent bedsores, trying to keep her as comfortable as possible. Mom would get up several times during the night to do whatever was needed for her mother. Mom showed tender compassion as she cared for her mother. I believe this is the type of compassion Jesus, the good shepherd, shows towards us.

One of the statements Jesus made about himself was: "I am the good shepherd; the good shepherd lays down his life for the sheep" (John 10:11, NASB). Jesus not only said he was the good shepherd, but he was willing to give his life for his sheep. Jesus walked the road to Calvary carrying the cross he would be crucified on. This is so vividly illustrated in the way an actual shepherd cares for his sheep. When a man shepherds a flock, he watches over them from morning to night, aware of the needs of his sheep. Each morning, he gets up early to look over his flock to be sure all the sheep are in good condition. If there is something wrong, he gives them immediate care. Throughout the day, he continually looks over his flock to be sure all is well. During the night, it is as if he sleeps "with one eye and both ears open," so he can get up quickly to take care of any problem. This is how Jesus Christ cares for us as his children: aware, at all times, of what is going on in our life. "He will not let you stumble and fall; the one who watches over you will not sleep. Indeed, he who watches over Israel never tires and never sleeps. The Lord himself watches over you! The Lord stands beside you as your protective shade" (Psalm 121:3–5, NLT).

Jesus is pictured as a gentle shepherd. "He will feed his flock like a shepherd: He will gather the lambs in his arm, he will carry them in his bosom and will gently lead those that have their young" (Isaiah 40:11, AMP).

When times get tough and we do not know which way to turn, we have the assurance our good shepherd will gently take us in his arms and carry us. It will be an intimate time with our Lord because of his great love for us.

Jesus is also portrayed as the great shepherd:

Now may the God of peace who brought up our LORD Jesus from the dead, that great shepherd of the sheep, through the blood of the everlasting covenant, make you complete in every good work to do his will, working in you what is well pleasing in his sight, through Jesus Christ, to whom be glory forever and ever. Amen.

Hebrews 13:20–21 (NKJV)

Jesus Christ will work in our life to produce the type of person pleasing to him. The Lord wants us to be in the center of his will and he will equip us for the work he has called us to do.

Jesus was referred to as the shepherd and guardian of our souls. One translation calls him the shepherd and overseer of our souls.

A guardian or overseer is one who takes care of the safety and well-being of a person or property. Another translation calls Jesus the shepherd and bishop of our souls. "He himself bore our sins in his body on the tree, so that we might die to sins and live for righteousness; by his wounds you have been healed. For you were like sheep going astray, but now you have returned to the shepherd and overseer of your souls" (1 Peter 2:24–25, NIV).

Jesus took all our sin on himself and died so we might have salvation. He suffered upon the cross for us, and we must be willing to suffer for the cause of Christ so others might hear the message of salvation. Jesus is always concerned about our well-being and watches over us continually. He has already encountered everything we will confront in our life. He is always with us, walking right beside us.

> Your unfailing love is better to me than life itself; how I praise you! I will honor you as long as I live, lifting up my hands to you in prayer. You satisfy me more than the richest of foods. I will praise you with songs of joy. I lie awake thinking of you, meditating on you through the night. I think how much you have helped me; I sing for joy in the shadow of your protecting wings. I follow close behind you; your strong right hand holds me securely.
>
> Psalm 63:3–8 (NLT)

David wanted the Lord to be his shepherd, his guardian, and his overseer. He had a great hunger and thirst for the Lord. In this psalm, David was in the wilderness of Judah and was searching for the Lord in this dry and parched land. David decided the Lord was all he needed.

Believers, have the assurance, when Jesus returns, we will receive the crown of glory. "And when the chief shepherd appears, you will receive the crown of glory that will never fade away" (1 Peter 5:4, NIV).

Our Lord has made provision for all we will ever need. He not only makes provision here on earth, but in heaven. We will receive our reward for what we have done in the name of Jesus and we will experience a never-ending share of his glory and honor.

My mother had a tender, compassionate love for her mother who became bedfast after her fall. She did whatever was needed to care for her. Jesus Christ has done the same for us as our good shepherd. He cares for his sheep (believers) and knows us by name. Through his great love for us, he gave his life for us. His provision for us is sufficient to meet our every need: "The Lord is my shepherd; I have everything I need" (Psalm 23:1, NLT).

How has Jesus been your good shepherd? Give examples of his provision for you during these times.

What are you doing for Jesus Christ today to show his love and compassion to others?

The Resurrection and the Life

Thinking about Jesus being the resurrection and the life brought to mind the book by Don Piper, *90 Minutes in Heaven*. He relates the story of being involved in an automobile accident. He had just left the conference center called Trinity Pines on the north shore of Lake Livingston near Houston, Texas. It was cold and rainy. The roads were wet and he knew he would need to drive cautiously as he left for his home in Alvin, Texas. The road he took was narrow with no shoulders. There was a bridge he would need to cross that had a very sharp upturn at the other end. It blocked the vision of drivers of oncoming traffic. As he neared the end of the bridge, the steady rain had turned into a cloudburst. There was an eighteen-wheeler driven by a trustee at the Texas Department of Corrections coming towards him. The truck weaved across the centerline and hit Don's car head-on. His car was sandwiched between the bridge railing and the driver's side of the truck. A vehicle with two guards from the correction center was following the truck. They called for medical backup from the prison. When the medical people arrived, they couldn't find Don's pulse and declared he had been killed instantly. Don had no recollection of the wreck or what happened afterward. Standing in heaven was the next thing he remembered. He says he did not see Jesus, but he saw all those who had died before him. He relates his encounter with people he knew. After he met these friends, he looked around and was overwhelmed by the brilliance around him. He said everything glowed with a dazzling intensity. The farther he walked, the brighter the light became. He felt as if he was being ushered into the presence of God. He did not see God, but he said he could feel his presence. It was difficult for him to express what he experienced. He said if he had actually seen God, he doesn't think he would have wanted to ever return to earth again. He believed God had sent the people who had died before him to escort him into heaven. The accident had happened at 11:45 a.m. and there was so much going on they did not try to move him until 1:15 p.m. They checked his pulse and he was still dead. A minister who attended the same conference came upon the accident. He asked the police officer if there was anyone he could pray for. The officer told him the other people involved were okay. He said the man in the car covered with a tarp had been pronounced dead. Dick Onerecker, the minister, insisted on praying for the man in the red car. The officer looked at him strangely and said he had been pronounced dead, but because of Dick's insistence, the officer permitted him to pray. He prayed for the man, sang a hymn, and then prayed again. He did not know this was a man he had met at the conference. When he sang "What a Friend We Have in Jesus," Don began to sing. The two things Don remembers are that he heard his own voice and he was aware someone was clutching his hand. It was an amazing thing when Dick told the EMT that Don was alive. When they checked, it was true. Don spent ninety minutes in heaven and was brought back to life. He did not relate his experience until two years later to anyone. He was afraid people would not believe him.

Jesus made an important statement: "Jesus said to her, 'I am the resurrection and the life; he who believes in me shall live even if he dies, and everyone who lives and believes in me shall never die. Do you believe this?'" (John 11:25–26, NASB).

Jesus arrived at the home of Mary, Martha, and Lazarus and found Lazarus was already dead and had been placed in a tomb. Jesus was visiting with Mary and Martha. Jesus told Martha her brother would rise again from the grave. Martha thought Jesus was talking about the resurrection of the dead when Jesus would come again to take his children to heaven.

For the LORD himself will come down from heaven with a commanding shout, with the call of the archangel, and with the trumpet call of God. First, all the Christians who have died will rise from their graves. Then, together with them, we who are still alive and remain on the earth will be caught up in the clouds to meet the LORD in the air and remain with him forever.

1 Thessalonians 4:16–17 (NLT)

Jesus then referred to himself as the resurrection and the life. With my limited understanding, I believe Jesus was saying he had power over life and death. God raised Jesus from the dead and endowed him with the power to raise people from death. He also offered to people eternal life so when they died physically they would live eternally with him in heaven. "In him was life, and the life was the light of men" (John 1:4, NASB). Because Jesus Christ is the light of the world, we can experience life everlasting when we accept him as Savior.

Paul stood boldly before Felix the governor and proclaimed what he believed.

But I confess this to you: that according to the way, which they call a sect, so I worship my fathers' God, believing all the things that are written in the Law and in the prophets. And I have a hope in God, which these men themselves also accept, that there is going to be a resurrection, both of the righteous and the unrighteous. I always do my best to have a clear conscience toward God and men.

Acts 24:14–16 (HCSB)

Paul was not ashamed or afraid to say he worshiped the one true God and he believed in salvation through faith in Jesus Christ. He believed the Word of God. He believed there would be a resurrection from the dead of both believers and unbelievers. When Jesus comes again, they will be separated as sheep from the goats. The sheep represent the believers and the goats the unbelievers. Those who have lived for the Lord will be taken to heaven and those who have lived in the ways of the world and never accepted Jesus will be cast into the everlasting fire of hell.

> I once thought all these things were so very important, but now I consider them worthless because of what Christ has done. Yes, everything else is worthless when compared with the priceless gain of knowing Christ Jesus my LORD. I have discarded everything else, counting it all as garbage, so that I may have Christ and become one with him. I no longer count on my own goodness or my ability to obey God's law, but I trust Christ to save me. For God's way of making us right with himself depends on faith. As a result, I can really know Christ and experience the mighty power that raised him from the dead. I can learn what it means to suffer with him, sharing in his death.
>
> Philippians 3:7–10 (NLT)

The most valuable asset we have is knowing Jesus as Savior and Lord. We must place our faith and trust in him alone, becoming more like him each day. As we become more mature in the Lord, we understand more clearly about his death, burial, and resurrection. If need be, we must be willing to suffer for the cause of Christ. We must serve the Lord with an obedient heart.

Don Piper had the opportunity to experience heaven for ninety minutes. As he laid suffering, there were times he cried out to God, questioning why he brought him back to life. Things were so much better in heaven than here on earth. When Jesus comes again, the dead in Christ will be raised up to meet him in the air and believers who are still alive will be taken up to be with him. What a day that will be when our Jesus we shall see!

When did you accept Jesus and what does it mean to you to know you have everlasting life?

Are you willing to share the message of salvation with the people of the world?

The Way, the Truth, and the Life

Have you ever gone to a campground, an amusement park, or a town where you became completely disoriented? You lose all sense of direction as to which way you need to turn to get to where you need to be. When we go to Falls Creek, a Baptist camp, this happens to me. It seems my intuition tells me to go the opposite way of what I should go. Sometimes when we go to places such as Silver Dollar City in Branson, Missouri, I feel this way when I get in the midst of all the activities. When I go to Oklahoma City for meetings, I am okay when I go to the one place I most often go, but if you have me go to a different place, I get very turned around. You might say I am directionally challenged. Fortunately, the times we have been in Malawi, Africa, where we had a vehicle, Doyal was always driving. When we would get out of town, particularly off the highway, going up in the mountains or over the planted fields to a far village, I would really lose all sense of direction. I am thankful Doyal was there to keep us going in the right direction. Somehow we always found our way.

Jesus Christ made a very important statement about himself: "Jesus answered, 'I am the way and the truth and the life. No one comes to the Father except through me'" (John 14:6, NIV).

Jesus explained to the disciples he would soon be leaving them. During this time, Jesus demonstrated to them how they were to be servants to all people, giving of themselves to help others. Jesus demonstrated this by kneeling down before each of them and washing their feet. He told them he had set the example and they were to go and do likewise. He told them they would be known as his disciples if they loved one for another. Jesus said they could not follow him where he was going. Peter questioned as to why he could not follow him and said he would lay down his life for him. Jesus then spoke the following words that must have cut to the core of Peter's heart: "Then Jesus answered, 'Will you really lay down your life for me? I tell you the truth, before the rooster crows, you will disown me three times'" (John 13:38, NIV).

Jesus told them he was going to prepare a place for them and he would one day come again and take them to this place to be with him. Jesus then said, "You know the way to the place where I am going" (John 14:4, NIV). Thomas, another of the disciples, told Jesus they did not know where he was going, so how could they know the way. Jesus said, "I am the way." Many people wonder how they can find or know God. The only way to God the Father is through Jesus Christ. "I am the gate; whoever enters through me will be saved. He will come in and go out and find pasture" (John 10:9, NIV).

Only through Jesus Christ do we have access to the Father. We must simply put our faith and trust in him. "For my Father's will is that everyone who looks to the Son and believes in him shall have eternal life, and I will raise him up at the last day" (John 6:40, NIV). When we make this important decision to follow Jesus and trust him for eternal life, we have the hope of living in heaven with him someday.

> Therefore, since we have been made right in God's sight by faith, we have peace with God because of what Jesus Christ our LORD has done for us. Because of our faith, Christ has brought us into this place of highest privilege where we now stand, and we confidently and joyfully look forward to sharing God's glory.
>
> Romans 5:1–2 (NLT)

Jesus also said he was the truth: "The Word became flesh and made his dwelling among us. We have seen his glory, the glory of the one and only, who came from the Father full of grace and truth" (John 1:14, NIV).

Jesus Christ came to the earth in human form when he was born to Mary and Joseph. He walked upon this earth performing all types of miracles, teaching people through parables, and living his life as an example for them to imitate. He came from the Father to be the supreme sacrifice on the cross for the sins of all people. "Jesus therefore was saying to those Jews who had believed him, 'If you abide in my word, then you are truly disciples of mine; and you shall know the truth, and the truth shall make you free.' If therefore the Son shall make you free, you shall be free indeed" (John 8:31–32, 36, NASB).

We learn about the teachings of our Lord from the truth of the Bible. If we hold to the teachings of God's Word and live our life in line with those teachings, we truly are his disciples. We understand Jesus is the truth, the good news (the gospel) for lost people. On the cross, Jesus took upon himself the burden of our sin. We no longer are required to carry that burden. We are set free by the blood of Jesus. We must share this message in the valleys, on the mountaintops, through the desert, and over the plains. Jesus Christ is the only truth we need to know to obtain salvation.

Last of all, Jesus said he was the life. "In him was life, and the life was the light of men" (John 1:4, NASB).

Jesus was talking with Martha at the time of Lazarus's death. "Jesus said to her, 'I am the resurrection and the life. He who believes in me will live, even though he dies; and whoever lives and believes in me will never die. Do you believe this?'" (John 11:25–26, NIV). She made a very important statement after Jesus said these words: "She said to him, 'Yes, Lord; I have believed that you are the Christ, the Son of God, even he who comes into the world'" (John 11:27, NASB).

Jesus Christ came to earth offering us eternal life. How blessed we are to be able to know Jesus Christ who is the way, the truth, and the life! When we know Jesus as Savior and Lord, we have the assurance of going to heaven to be with him when he comes again or when we die.

When I go to places I am not familiar with, it is good for me to have someone with me who can point me in the right direction. The Bible, the inspired Word of God, gives us direction in life. It is our road map, our plumb line and our instruction book. If we were to go through life without any direction, we would not have the promise of eternal life. Because Jesus Christ came to earth, died on the cross, and arose from the grave, we have the opportunity to accept him as Savior. Jesus is the way, the truth, and the life.

Are you living your life according to the way God desires? Think and pray about some things you need to change in order for your life to be pleasing to the Lord.

The Vine

As a teenager, my dad had a rose garden he treasured. I can picture my dad, a Baptist preacher, dressed in his white shirt, trousers, and a tie out in the midst of the rose garden, pruning the dead roses or the unnecessary growth. Right in front of the living room windows was a climbing rose bush. As it grew, my dad would attach the branches to the trellis. The branches would be filled with beautiful roses. What a magnificent display of God's amazing creation! If my dad did not care for this bush and the freestanding rose bushes, they would not produce the beautiful roses they were intended to produce. A rose bush must have the dead roses, dead limbs, and the extra growth trimmed off. The branches must be trimmed with the cut going in the right direction or the limbs will grow on top of or across the other. They must have tender, loving care to yield a bountiful supply of beautiful roses.

Picture with me a grape vineyard and the care required to produce fruit. After grapes are harvested from a vineyard, the caretaker and workers, during the winter months, will cut off what are referred to as canes from the vine. They then cut these canes into pieces referred to as cuttings. They are buried in moist sand and kept in a cool place until early spring. The cuttings grow roots and are replanted in the vineyard at that time. Later, they will build supports for the branches to be attached to by their little curly tendrils. During the dormant time of the year, the vines are pruned and the vineyard appears as just a bunch of dead, slender stumps out in a field. The spring of the year brings on new growth as the branches on the vine grow and begin putting on green leaves. It is an amazing thing to drive through the vineyards in California during these months and see large clusters of grapes hanging on the vines.

Jesus made a very important statement to the disciples and to believers when he said, "I am the true vine." In the scripture, the Lord used the illustration of a grapevine to teach a valuable lesson: "I am the true vine, and my Father is the gardener" (John 15:1, NIV).

When we think of a vine, we usually think of something running along the ground, intertwined in a trellis or growing up a tree. The vine is the stump. Those things running along the ground or growing on a trellis or a tree are the branches. The vine is the source of strength and nourishment needed by the branches to produce fruit. Jesus told his disciples he was the source of strength. He referred to God the Father as the vinedresser. The vinedresser is the one who cares for the vineyard. He makes sure the extra growth is cut off so it will not hinder the branches from producing bountiful clusters of grapes. "He cuts off every branch in me that bears no fruit, while every branch that does bear fruit he prunes so that it will be even more fruitful" (John 15:2, NIV).

We may claim to be a child of God, yet we are not doing good works for the kingdom. The fruits of the Spirit are not evident in our life. We are not sharing Jesus with others. We have no desire to help others because our heart is not filled with the love of Jesus. If we are unproductive for the Lord, the Father begins to cut away things that keep us from making him our first priority. He wants us to accomplish his purpose for our life. "And let our people also learn to engage in good deeds to meet pressing needs, that they may not be unfruitful" (Titus 3:14, NASB).

Jesus's followers are to do good deeds in the name of Jesus. In doing so, when others see the love of Jesus in us, they see the need for a relationship with him. "Abide in me, and I in you. As the branch cannot bear fruit of itself, unless it abides in the vine, so neither can you, unless you abide in me" (John 15:4, NASB).

When a branch is broken from the vine, it will be of no use because it will dry up. It is no longer connected to the vine, its source of strength and nourishment. Its lifeline has been severed. It is the same way in the life of a child of God. If we do not keep our life in tune with the Lord by spending time in his Word and in prayer, we will shrivel up and become nonproductive for the Lord. Our lifeline has been severed and it is impossible for us to produce fruit. A grape detached from the cluster of grapes will shrivel up; so will believers who allow things of the world to affect our fellowship with the Lord. We forget why God created us: "For we are his workmanship, created in Christ Jesus for good works, which God prepared beforehand, that we should walk in them" (Ephesians 2:10, NASB).

Jesus Christ wants us to daily partake of the food he has prepared for us, so we may grow in him. He is our source of nourishment. "And he will be like a tree firmly planted by streams of water, which yields its fruit in its season, and its leaf does not wither; and in whatever he does, he prospers" (Psalm 1:3, NASB).

God has given us his Word to feast upon so we will grow in him. "If you remain in me and my words remain in you, ask whatever you wish, and it will be given you. This is to my Father's glory, that you bear much fruit, showing yourselves to be my disciples" (John 15:7–8 NIV).

Producing fruit for the Lord is not a problem, but a joy in our life. Others will see the fruits of the Spirit, which are love, joy, peace, patience, kindness, goodness, faithfulness, gentleness, and self-control in us. "You did not choose me, but I chose you and appointed you to go and bear fruit—fruit that will last. Then the Father will give you whatever you ask in my name" (John 15:16, NIV).

Next time you see a grape vineyard, think about Jesus Christ being the vine or trunk. "I am the vine; you are the branches. If a man remains in me and I in him, he will bear much fruit; apart from me you can do nothing" (John 15:5, NIV).

Are you trying to produce fruit for the Lord on your own or are you drawing nourishment from Jesus daily? Through what avenues are you receiving this nourishment from the Lord?

Are you willing to be used by the Lord to produce much fruit for him? Pray and ask God to show you some ways he wants to use you to produce much fruit for him.

I Promise

The dictionary states that a promise is a pledge to do or not to do something specified. We are in the midst of the month of December and all of us who have children can remember them asking for specific things at Christmas time. If it was within our means, we probably said, "I promise I will try to get it for you." We might say, "I will get it for you if you promise to keep your room clean or if you will keep the trash carried out." They may say, "I promise to be good and to do whatever you ask me to do, if you will get it for me." When boys and girls are teenagers, they promise one another they will not date anyone else, so they begin "going steady." They exchange a class ring or maybe a letterman's jacket. This is their way of pledging or promising to do as they agreed. When we marry our mate, in the marriage ceremony the minister asks the question, "Do you promise to love and obey in sickness or in health, in poverty or in wealth, until death does you part?" When we answer the question, we are promising to stick with the person through whatever happens. We pledge ourselves to each other for life. When we make a verbal or written promise to a person, it is to be binding. We are saying we will not do anything to break our promise.

The Bible is overflowing with promises God made to us if we will live our life in obedience to him. He desires to shower us with his blessings. "Trust in the Lord and do good. Then you will live safely in the land and prosper. Take delight in the Lord, and he will give you your heart's desires. Commit everything you do to the Lord. Trust him, and he will help you" (Psalm 37:3–5, NLT). The Lord promises to protect us and help us to prosper when we trust, lean on, rely on, or place our confidence in the Lord. This does not mean he is promising to make us rich, but he is promising to provide all we need. We are to be committed to him with all our heart, soul, and strength. Everything we do should be for his honor and glory, even a simple act of kindness or mercy shown towards someone. He promises us if we will place our complete, absolute trust in him, he will help us through any situation we face.

God makes many promises to us, but they will not be completed on our timetable. God has his own purpose and plan for our life and we must learn to be patient and wait upon him. As a young boy, David was anointed king, but he had to wait several years before he took his place on the throne. He had to trust God to bring about what he promised. David went through many trials in life. King Saul sought to kill David because he was jealous of the attention David was getting. People praised David for the many he had slain in battle. Absalom, David's son, tried to take the throne away from his father, but he proved to not be a good ruler. David had to show patience through all of this and wait upon the Lord to act. "I waited patiently and expectantly for the Lord; and he inclined to me and heard my cry" (Psalm 40:1, (AMP).

Because David was patient and waited for the Lord's direction, God rewarded his faithfulness. He lifted David out of the pit of despair and set his feet on the solid rock. "He brought me up out of the pit of destruction, out of the miry clay; and he set my feet upon a rock making my footsteps firm" (Psalm 40:2, NASB).

Many of us could testify how the Lord has been faithful when it seemed we had nowhere to turn and we could not see any light at the end of the tunnel. Life seemed hopeless, yet God in his mercy and perfect timing reached down and lifted us out of the mud and the mire and set our feet upon the solid rock where our footing was sure. He gave us new direction in life and restored hope in our heart. We will miss out on the Lord's blessings if we are not patient and wait on him to do as he promised he would do. The Scripture tells us he will put a new song in our heart: "And he put a new song in my mouth, a song of praise to our God; many will see and fear, and will trust in the Lord" (Psalm 40:3, NASB). Did you notice what this verse said? If we put our trust in the Lord, we can rest safe and secure in his arms and know he will be with us through whatever happens.

One of my favorite stories in the Bible is found in the Book of Joshua. The children of Israel had roamed around out in the wilderness for forty years because of their disobedience. Finally, God told Joshua he was going to allow them to cross the Jordan River and go in and possess the promised land. The Israelites began to conquer the land of Canaan. When they came to Jericho, the city was shut up tight and they could not go into the city because of the wall surrounding it. The Lord made a promise to Joshua. "But the Lord said to Joshua, 'I have given you Jericho, its king, and all its mighty warriors'" (Joshua 6:2, NLT).

The Lord gave Joshua instructions as to how he was to do this:

Your entire army is to march around the city once a day for six days. Seven priests will walk ahead of the ark, each carrying a ram's horn. On the seventh day you are to march around the city seven times, with the priests blowing the horns. When you hear the priests give one long blast on the horns, have all the people give a mighty shout. Then the walls of the city will collapse, and the people can charge straight into the city.

Joshua 6:3–5 (NLT)

I can just imagine Joshua standing there with his mouth open and wondering if he heard the Lord correctly. He might have asked, "What did you say, Lord? Did I understand you correctly? We are to march around the city with horns being blown and then shout, and the wall will fall down." Joshua may have been bewildered at what the Lord said, but the scripture does not mention it, nor does it tell us he questioned God. Joshua and the children of Israel did exactly what God said and the wall of Jericho fell. God kept his promise.

My brother-in-law wrote a book about the promises of God. He said there were over 7,487 promises in the Bible. He made a statement I think we all need to heed: "A Christian can only claim as many promises as he knows." How many promises of God do you know? Do you choose to claim at least one promise from the Lord each day? Imagine how victorious we would be as Christians if we would claim a promise from God each day. I challenge you to do a study of the promises of God and see how many you can find in the Bible.

We have all made promises we have failed to keep. When God made a promise, he kept that promise. "Blessed be the Lord, who has given rest to his people Israel, according to all that he promised; not one word has failed of all his good promise, which he promised through Moses his servant" (1 Kings 8:56, NASB).

In his prayer at the dedication of the temple, Solomon prayed and reminded the children of Israel of the Lord's faithfulness. God is just as faithful to you and me as his children as he was to the Israelites. Abraham trusted God to fulfill his promises: " …yet, with respect to the promise of God, he did not waver in unbelief, but grew strong in faith, giving glory to God, and being fully assured that what he had promised, he was able also to perform" (Romans 4:20–21, NASB). Abraham's faith was strong in the Lord. What about you?

A promise is a pledge made to someone to do exactly what we said. It is really a binding agreement. You will more than likely be faithful in keeping your promises to others if you live in accordance with the promises of God. God made many promises to us in the Bible. List as many as you can.

What promise from God do you claim most often?

Breaking Down Barriers: Living Out Your Faith

One of our Southern Baptist missionaries, a single woman working in Mozambique, had been in some villages teaching the Bible to those who would come. All was going well and a few were coming to learn more about the Lord. The chief had shown an interest in attending the Bible study when there were several mosques burned in the area. The rumor began to spread accusing the Baptist missionary of being responsible for the fire. When she would go to the village, the people would not speak to her. In fact, they would move away from her. She found out they had been told if they had anything to do with her, they would be in trouble. There were those in the past who lost their lives when they went against Muslim beliefs. She had to be very careful what she did because of these rumors. Satan has a way of interfering when God is at work in the hearts and minds of the people. The missionary was patient and sought prayer support from Christians around the world. In time, the truth surfaced, proving the missionary had nothing to do with what happened. Because of her faithfulness and willingness to wait on the Lord to act and not try to fix it herself, God honored her faithfulness. She is now able to go back into the village to teach the Word of God. A change is being seen in the people because of God's Word. Our missionaries face many barriers as they strive to be faithful in teaching the Bible to those who have never heard.

"I have called you by name; you are mine! When you pass through the waters, I will be with you; and through the rivers, they will not overflow you. When you walk through the fire, you will not be scorched, nor will the flame burn you. For I am the Lord your God ..." (Isaiah 43:1b–3a, NASB). God certainly carried out the promise in these verses to this missionary.

Before he died, Moses had given the land to two and one half tribes on the east side of the Jordan. Caleb came to Joshua and reminded him about what Moses had said concerning the division of the land. Caleb had gone into the land of Canaan with eleven other spies to check out the lay of the land. They wanted to know whether the land was fertile for growing crops, what was available to them there, what people inhabited the land and how strong they were. When the spies returned, Caleb gave a good report about the land and everything available to them. He knew they could conquer the people there because of what God had said to Moses. "Then the Lord spoke to Moses saying, 'Send out for yourself men so that they may spy out the land of Canaan, which I am going to give to the sons of Israel; you shall send a man from each of their fathers' tribes, every one a leader among them'" (Numbers 13:1–2, NASB).

Ten spies spoke of the richness of the soil and even brought back evidence of the fruit growing there. But they were fearful of the people because of their size and strength. They did not have the faith to believe what God had told Moses earlier. Because of their lack of faith, they wandered in the wilderness for another forty years. Only those twenty years and younger would enter the land. Caleb reminded Joshua about what had happened and because of his faithfulness to the Lord he could have the section of Canaan where he had just been. It would belong to him and his descendants forever. Caleb was forty years old at the time he had gone to spy out the land and now he was eighty-five years old.

I am still as strong today as I was in the day Moses sent me; as my strength was then, so my strength is now, for war and for going out and coming in. Now then, give me this hill country about which the LORD spoke on that day, for you heard on that day that Anakim were there, with great fortified cities; perhaps the LORD will be with me, and I shall drive them out as the LORD has spoken.

Joshua 14:11–12 (NASB)

Caleb's faith was strong in the Lord even though he was now eighty-five years old. He believed God would enable him to conquer all barriers between him and the possession of the land. He was willing to take a bold step of faith to overcome barriers.

The armies of the Moabites, Ammonites, and some of the Meunites declared war on Jehoshaphat. Messengers came to tell Jehoshaphat about the armies who were marching against him. Jehoshaphat called the people to fast and seek the Lord for guidance. The people of Judah came to Jerusalem to seek the Lord. The Spirit of the Lord came upon Jahaziel. He spoke to the people:

> He said, "Listen, King Jehoshaphat! Listen, all you people of Judah and Jerusalem! This is what the LORD says: Do not be afraid! Don't be discouraged by this mighty army, for the battle is not yours, but God's. Tomorrow, march out against them. You will find them coming up through the ascent of Ziz at the end of the valley that opens into the wilderness of Jeruel. But you will not even need to fight. Take your positions; then stand still and watch the LORD's victory. He is with you, O people of Judah and Jerusalem. Do not be afraid or discouraged. Go out there tomorrow, for the LORD is with you."

2 Chronicles 20:15–17 (NLT)

King Jehoshaphat and the people bowed down in humility and worshiped the Lord. As the army of Judah went out the next morning to the wilderness of Tekoa, Jehoshaphat stopped them and said, "Listen to me, all you people of Judah and Jerusalem! Believe in the Lord your God, and you will be able to stand firm. Believe in his prophets, and you will succeed" (2 Chronicles 20:20b, NLT).

Jehoshaphat had faith in the Lord to help them conquer the armies coming against them. He knew with God's help they could break down every barrier. He was living out his faith in leading the army of Judah against the Moabites, Ammonites, and the Meunites.

A couple of weeks ago, the doctor found our younger son has diabetes. Before he knew what was wrong with him, he began to have trouble walking and his equilibrium was off. He had not been sleeping at night for several months. When he went to sleep, he was very difficult to wake up. He could not satisfy his thirst, and his vision had become blurred. He had trouble carrying on a decent conversation because he would fall asleep while talking or lose his train of thought. When the doctors finally found the problem, his blood sugar was 637. The doctor immediately began oral medication and after a few days he added insulin pins. During this time, Stevie became very frustrated and afraid. People all around and his wife began to pray and seek God's help for him in this situation. "He will call upon me, and I will answer him; I will be with him in trouble; I will rescue him, and honor him" (Psalm 91:15, NASB). "I will answer them before they even call to me. While they are still talking to me about their needs, I will go ahead and answer their prayers" (Isaiah 65:24, NLT).

God enabled the doctor to overcome all barriers and find the solution to Stevie's problem that may have been there for some time. He is doing much better and his blood sugar is down in the 100s, but still fluctuating. God restored his sight and he does not fall asleep as much as he did. With God's help, he will be able to break down the barriers between him and a normal life. Stevie must entrust his life to the Lord and live out his faith.

Reflect on things in your life you have been able to overcome because of God working in your life. How did your faith in the Lord grow during these times?

The Menu for a Progressive Dinner

The young adult classes in our church had a progressive dinner for their Christmas party. Doyal and I hosted the group for the main course of the meal: meat and a vegetable. Typically, the group travels from one home to the other, beginning with appetizers at one home and moving to a second home for salad. Next, they go to a home for the main course. Their final home on their celebration is for dessert and a devotional. The group had a good time as they traveled and fellowshipped with one another. It is always good to be able to open your home to friends to celebrate with them the joys of being a child of God. This time we were also celebrating the birth of Jesus Christ.

I want you to think with me about the progression of this dinner in relation to our walk with the Lord. The first course of the dinner is the appetizer. In our relationship with the Lord, this is the planting of seed in a person's life, which causes them to want to know more about Jesus. In the parable of the sower, he was sowing his seed and some fell beside the road and the birds came and ate it. Some seed fell on rocky soil, and as it grew, it withered away because it had a shallow root system. Other seed fell among the thorns, and the thorns grew and choked it out. Then some seed fell on fertile soil and produced a crop one hundred times greater than what was sown. "This is the meaning of the parable: The seed is the word of God" (Luke 8:11, NIV).

The appetizer of the progressive dinner would be the Word of God, the seed, being planted in the heart of a person. Whether or not this seed takes root depends on whether the person has a responsive heart or if the person's heart is hard with no desire to hear about the Lord. It is our responsibility to go and deliver the message found only in the Word of God about the saving grace of Jesus Christ.

> ... That while we were spiritually dead in our disobedience he brought us to life with Christ. It is by God's grace that you have been saved. He did this to demonstrate for all time to come the extraordinary greatness of his grace in the love he showed us in Christ Jesus. For it is by God's grace that you have been saved through faith. It is not the result of your own efforts, but God's gift so that no one can boast about it.
>
> Ephesians 2:5, 7–9 (GNB)

We serve the appetizer to the people as they begin the progressive dinner. Will you do your best to offer to others the appetizer, the seed that is the Word of God, so they might experience God's saving grace?

The second menu item of the progressive dinner is the salad. Now, you have many different salads: a green salad, a Jell-O salad, bean salad, cottage cheese, and fruit or slaw. In life, people are confronted with many different choices of varied beliefs. We know from the Scripture there is only one way to heaven and that is through Jesus Christ: "Jesus said to him, I am the way and the truth and the life; no one comes to the Father except by (through) me" (John 14:6, AMP).

Walking with Jesus will not be easy, because many will try to lead you astray with false doctrine. Satan will try to lead you down the wrong path. It appears to be easier, but it is much harder and is detrimental to one's life. "Enter by the narrow gate; for the gate is wide and the way is broad that leads to destruction, and many are those who enter by it. For the gate is small and the way is narrow that leads to life, and few are those who find it" (Matthew 7:13–14, NASB). Satan places delightful things before us to cause the road of sin to appear enticing. Many choose the broad way and they do not realize their destination is everlasting hell. Matthew 7 tells us there will be false teachers who will appear dressed as sheep but are wolves seeking to devour all they come in contact with. The road to the cross appears narrow, but Jesus specifically told us he is the way, the truth, and the life. He is there to help us walk this road. It will lead us to where we will live eternally with God the Father. As Christians, we must be faithful and bold in our witness to share the gospel of Jesus Christ with a lost and dying world.

The main course of the progressive dinner is the meat, vegetable, and bread. This is the very core of the meal that most people desire. As people come to know the Lord as Savior, they must be presented and instructed in the pure meat of the Word. "All Scripture is inspired by God and is useful to teach us what is true and to make us realize what is wrong in our lives. It straightens us out and teaches us to do what is right. It is God's way of preparing us in every way, fully equipped for every good thing God wants us to do" (2 Timothy 3:16–17, NLT). God's Word is the instruction book for a believer. It helps us to know right from wrong. God sends the Holy Spirit to live in the heart of every person who accepts Jesus as Savior. "Whether you turn to the right or to the left, your ears will hear a voice behind you, saying, 'This is the way; walk in it'" (Isaiah 30:21, NIV).

The Word of God gives instruction in every area of life if we will simply spend time reading and allowing it to speak to our heart. "For you have been born again, not of perishable seed, but of imperishable, through the living enduring word of God. For, 'All men are like grass, and all their glory is like the flowers of the field; the grass withers and the flowers fall, but the word of the Lord stands forever'" (1 Peter 1:23–25, NIV).

A new believer must be taught the truth from the Word of God to be able to stand against the temptations and problems he or she will face.

Finally, we come to the dessert of the progressive dinner, when we partake of those sweet things everyone loves. When we think of this in relation to our walk with the Lord, we might think in terms of the sweet morsels the Lord has to offer us in his Word. "How sweet are thy words to my taste! Yes, sweeter than honey to my mouth!" (Psalm 119:103, NASB). We must develop an insatiable desire for the sweetness of God's Word. In Jeremiah's writings he understood this well: "Thy words were found and I ate them, and thy words became for me a joy and the delight of my heart; for I have been called by thy name, O Lord God of hosts" (Jeremiah 15:16, NASB).

Ezekiel also stated it well as he was commissioned by the Lord to go and speak to the house of Israel: "And he said to me, 'Son of man, feed your stomach and fill your body with this scroll which I am giving you.' Then I ate it, and it was sweet as honey in my mouth" (Ezekiel 3:3, NASB).

Spending time in God's Word is not a burden. It is a joy spending time in his presence, learning from him and eating from the delicious, sweet treats he has for you.

Are you willing to spend time with the Lord so he can speak to you from his Word? What do you need to change to set aside a specific time in your day to feast on his Word?

A progressive dinner offers all the needed foods to fill you to the brim. God's Word offers everything you need to live a life of joy in him. Come! Feast on the riches of his Word!

Destroyer in Action

Six months ago, we purchased a blue heeler puppy we named Daisy. She is an active, over-energized pup. She must get very bored when we are away, because we are constantly finding things around our place she has damaged in some way or the other. When someone is not around to keep her company, I think she searches for something to do. She is a destroyer in action. The other day I threw five pumpkins out in the pasture and she managed to pick them up and bring them all into the yard. It was unbelievable the number of teeth marks on each pumpkin. Somehow, she broke them open and pumpkin seeds were all over the yard. She has a filthy rag she carries from one place to the other, slinging it around in the air. Yesterday, I threw away a two-by-four board that she was chewing up. I found a pull rope in the yard and investigated to see what piece of equipment was without a rope. I found she had chewed the pull rope off of our power mower and then proceeded to chew part of the rubber handle off. She chewed off the rubberized covers on the battery cables of the generator. She also carries cow manure out of the pasture into our front yard and onto our porch. She loves for us to throw the tennis ball and let her retrieve it. When we are not outside, sometimes you see her with the ball in her mouth, slinging it around and going after it. We never know what we will find in our yard from the destroyer in action.

God was very pleased with what he created. God created the heavens and the earth, every kind of tree and flowering plant, every animal, bird, and fish of any sort, and then he created man and woman. "And God saw all that he had made, and behold, it was very good. And there was evening and there was morning, the sixth day" (Genesis 1:31, NASB).

Also in the Book of Genesis, God was very disturbed by the corruption of mankind. They began to commit evil deeds in the sight of God. "Then the Lord saw that the wickedness of man was great on the earth, and that every intent of the thoughts of his heart was only evil continually" (Genesis 6:5, NASB).

There was quite a contrast in how God felt at this time and how he felt at the completion of creation. God decided what he would do concerning the wickedness of man. "And the Lord said, 'I will blot out man whom I have created from the face of the land, from man to animals to creeping things and to the birds of the sky; for I am sorry that I have made them'" (Genesis 6:7, NASB).

There was only one man who was righteous and found favor in the eyes of the Lord. "Noah was a righteous man, blameless in his time; Noah walked with God" (Genesis 6:9b, NASB).

All people who inhabited the earth had become corrupt and were filled with violence. God spoke to Noah concerning what he was going to do: "Then God said to Noah, 'The end of all flesh has come before me; for the earth is filled with violence because of them; and behold, I am about to destroy them with the earth. Make for yourself an ark …'" (Genesis 6:13–14a, NASB).

God was going to spare Noah, his wife, and his three sons and their wives. Noah acted in obedience to the Lord, doing exactly what God told him to do. When the ark was finished, God provided clean animals to be taken on the ark so they would have them for sacrifice. He also selected a male and female of every living animal and creeping thing. God then told Noah how he was going to destroy the land: "For after seven more days, I will send rain on the earth forty days and forty nights; and I will blot out from the face of the land every living thing that I have made" (Genesis 7:4, NASB).

God sent a deluge of rain to destroy all mankind and every creature inhabiting the land. Only Noah's family and the animals in the ark were spared. Noah had built the ark according to God's instruction and God held true to his promise to spare them.

Many of us are familiar with the story of Gideon and how God led him to deliver Israel from Midian. "Again the Israelites did what was evil in the Lord's sight. So the Lord handed them over to the Midianites for seven years" (Judges 6:1, NLT).

Because the Midianites were so cruel to the Israelites, they fled to the mountains and hid in dens and caves. When the Israelites planted their crops, the Midianites would destroy them. They took all of their sheep, oxen, and donkeys, leaving them with no meat to eat.

> When they cried out to the LORD because of Midian, the LORD sent a prophet to the Israelites. He said, "This is what the LORD, the God of Israel, says: I brought you up out of slavery in Egypt and rescued you from the Egyptians and from all who oppressed you. I drove out your enemies and gave you their land. I told you, 'I am the LORD your God. You must not worship the gods of the Amorites, in whose land you now live.' But you have not listened to me."
>
> Judges 6:7–10 (NLT)

The Lord selected a man to come to their rescue. He was the son of Joash from the clan of Abiezer. "The angel of the Lord appeared to him and said, 'Mighty hero, the Lord is with you!' Then the Lord turned to him and said, 'Go with the strength you have and rescue Israel from the Midianites. I am sending you!'" (Judges 6:12, 14, NLT).

Gideon, a member of the weakest clan of the whole tribe of Manasseh, questioned how he was going to accomplish this task. "The Lord said to him, 'I will be with you. And you will destroy the Midianites as if you were fighting against one man'" (Judges 6:16, NLT).

God gave Gideon specific instructions on what to do in preparation for the task. Gideon followed God's instructions. After the preparations were finished, Gideon asked God to give him a sign to prove to him that he was actually going to use him to rescue the nation of Israel. God gave him a sign.

Gideon started out with an army of 32,000 men. God told him there were too many men, so 22,000 who were timid and afraid went home. Gideon was left with 10,000 men. This was still too many men in God's way of thinking. God instructed him to thin them out according to how they drank water from the spring. Finally, three hundred men were selected. "The Lord told Gideon, 'With these three hundred men I will rescue you and give you victory over the Midianites. Send all the others home'" (Judges 7:7, NLT). The Bible tells us Gideon collected all the provisions from the other men along with their ram's horns and sent them home.

The Bible says the armies of Midian, Amalek, and the people of the east were as a swarm of locusts. They had camels too numerous to count. The Lord spoke to Gideon during the night and told him to go to the Midianites camp and listen to what they were saying and he would be encouraged and ready to fight. As Gideon approached the camp, he heard one of the men telling about a dream he had: "I had this dream, and in my dream a loaf of barley bread came tumbling down into the Midianite camp. It hit a tent, turned it over, and knocked it flat" (Judges 7:13b, NLT).

A friend interpreted this dream for him and he said it was evident God had given Gideon victory over all the armies who were there with Midian. When Gideon heard this, he thanked God and returned to his camp. He told the Israelites to get up because God had given them victory over the Midianites.

> He divided the three hundred men into three groups and gave each man a ram's horn and a clay jar with a torch in it. Then he said to them, "Keep your eyes on me. When I come to the edge of the camp, do just as I do. As soon as my group blows the rams' horns, those of you on the other sides of the camp blow your horns and shout, 'For the LORD and for Gideon!'"

Judges 7:16–18 (NLT)

The Midianites ran, crying out as they fled. They were in such panic; they fought one against the other, killing off many of their army. Gideon sent soldiers after the men who fled. God destroyed a huge army made up of several different groups of people with just three hundred men. Gideon placed his trust in the Lord and God brought about victory.

Our young dog is a destroyer in action around our home. God brought about much destruction because of the disobedience of the children of Israel. Their disobedience was very disturbing to God in the way they lived and the gods they worshiped.

What are some things in your life that work at destroying your fellowship with the Lord?

What are some weapons you can use to ward off the destruction Satan desires to bring in your fellowship with the Lord?

Exhibition of God's Amazing Power

Young boys many times look up to their fathers and are amazed by the things they can do. This is particularly so, if boys have a father who will work with them and teach them the things he knows. My husband, Doyal, is able to do many different things. He has always been an example to our boys and they believe nothing is impossible. If you need to remove a nut from a bolt and it will not move, you make a tool to break it loose. If you need to pick up a set of concrete steps, you create a tool you can attach to the bucket of the backhoe to latch onto the steps to pick them up. When we have been in Malawi, Africa, and had very little to do in the evenings, Doyal would sit with a pencil and paper, diagramming a form or a tool he needed back home. We went to Malawi to teach the men how to dig water wells in the villages by hand and concrete them in as they went down. Doyal had to diagram the form to use to pour the concrete and build it himself with the help of a welder in Malawi. I guess one of the most amazing things Doyal has created is the form to pour a concrete cellar in two pieces. The form for the top of the cellar looks like a space ship. All three boys are amazed at how their dad can design any tool he needs for work, at home or wherever, to get the job done. None of them have the God-given ability to do this the way their dad is able to do it. If ever they have a need, they know they can come to him and he will come up with a solution. Does he do these things by his own ability? No, Doyal realizes he is totally dependent on the Lord to give him wisdom to know how to accomplish the task before him. We are all simply amazed at the things he has created. Our family has learned never to say, "It cannot be done."

I want you to think with me about some of the miracles God

performed throughout the Bible. A miracle, according to my Bible dictionary, is "a wonderful thing; a great event which can be done only by God's help." Miracles are special signs to show God's power. Moses was chosen by God to lead the children of Israel out slavery in Egypt to the promised land. This was not going to be an easy task, so God endowed Moses with special abilities. Moses was questioning the Lord concerning what he was to do if they would not believe him or listen to what he said. "And the Lord said to him, 'What is that in your hand?' And he said, 'A staff.' Then he said, 'Throw it on the ground.' So he threw it on the ground, and it became a serpent; and Moses fled from it" (Exodus 4:2–3, NASB).

We all know we could throw a staff on the ground all day long and it would never turn into a serpent. This was simply a miracle performed by Almighty God through Moses, his humble servant. "And the Lord furthermore said to him, 'Now put your hand into your bosom.' So he put his hand into his bosom, and when he took it out, behold, his hand was leprous like snow" (Exodus 4:6, NASB).

The Lord then told Moses to put his hand back in his bosom and when he removed it, his hand was like his other flesh. God can do miraculous things through those who are willing to be used by God. The Lord also demonstrated his power by turning the water of the Nile River into blood. Our God is a god of miracles.

Joshua was preparing to lead the children of Israel across the Jordan River and into the land of Canaan. God gave Joshua specific directions as to what he was to do.

Think of it! The ark of the covenant, which belongs to the LORD of the whole earth, will lead you across the Jordan River! Now choose twelve men, one from each tribe. The priests will be carrying the ark of the LORD, the LORD of all the earth. When their feet touch the water, the flow of water will be cut off upstream, and the river will pile up there in one heap.

Joshua 3:11–13 (NLT)

Some of you may think this is nothing great, but during the harvest season the Jordan River is at flood stage. Those entering the water had faith God would do what he said or the strong current would have swept them away.

> Now it was the harvest season, and the Jordan was overflowing its banks. But as soon as the feet of the priests who were carrying the ark touched the water at the river's edge, the water began piling up at a town upstream called Adam, which is near Zarethan. And the water below that point flowed on to the Dead Sea until the riverbed was dry. Then all the people crossed over near the city of Jericho. Meanwhile, the priests who were carrying the ark of the Lord's covenant stood on dry ground in the middle of the riverbed as the people passed by them. They waited there until everyone had crossed the Jordan on dry ground.
>
> Joshua 3:15–17 (NLT)

Think about what God did. He made the water stand still. The only way you and I can do this is to build a dam to hold the water back. Our God does amazing things through people who believe what he says and act in obedience to his commands.

Manoah's wife was unable to become pregnant. An angel of the Lord appeared to her and told her she was going to give birth to a son. She was given specific instructions as to how to raise this boy. One instruction was for his hair to never be cut. He was to be dedicated to the Lord as a Nazarite from birth. He would be the one who would rescue Israel from the Philistines. When the son was born, they named him Samson. His father and mother did not realize God was at work in his life preparing him to defeat the Philistines and free Israel.

> As Samson and his parents were going down to Timnah, a young lion attacked Samson near the vineyards of Timnah.

At that moment the Spirit of the LORD powerfully took control, and he ripped the lion's jaws apart with his bare hands. He did it as easily as if it were a young goat. But he didn't tell his father or mother about it.

Judges 14:5–6 (NLT)

This was the first evidence of what God was doing in Samson's life. There are many instances in the book of Judges of how God displayed his power through Samson. He slew thirty men by himself, he killed a thousand Philistines with the jawbone of a donkey, and he lifted the gates and the posts of the wall surrounding Gaza out of the ground and carried it to the top of the hill above Hebron. God performed miraculous feats through Samson as long as he obeyed and kept his Nazarite vow of not cutting his hair.

Elisha the prophet did many amazing things through the power of the Lord. The sons of the prophets were a group of men in school, probably at Gilgal, near the Jordan River. Commentators say they followed Elisha to many places so they could receive his instructions, counsel, and prayers. Their number had increased and they needed more room in which to live. They asked Elisha if they could go cut timbers to build a larger place and if he would go with them. He agreed.

When they arrived at the Jordan, they began cutting down trees. But as one of them was chopping, his ax head fell into the river. "Ah, my LORD!" he cried. "It was a borrowed ax!" "Where did it fall?" the man of God asked. When he showed him the place, Elisha cut a stick and threw it into the water. Then the ax head rose to the surface and floated. "Grab it," Elisha said to him. And the man reached out and grabbed it.

2 Kings 6:4–7 (NLT)

All of us know iron will not float. As Elisha threw the stick in the water, it must have been amazing to see the ax head come to the surface and float. No one except God could perform this amazing miracle.

Elisha always knew when the king of Aram was going to attack Israel, and he would tell the king of Israel not to go near that place. The king of Aram thought one of his men was a traitor, but they informed him it was Elisha the prophet telling the king of Israel. The king of Aram sought to kill Elisha. Elisha's servant got up early one morning and saw many soldiers and chariots all around. He went to warn his master.

> "Don't be afraid!" Elisha told him. "For there are more on our side than on theirs!" Then Elisha prayed, "O LORD, open his eyes and let him see!" The LORD opened his servant's eyes, and when he looked up, he saw that the hillside around Elisha was filled with horses and chariots of fire.
>
> 2 Kings 6:16–17 (NLT)

As the Aramean army approached them, Elisha prayed God would make them blind. Elisha led them away from them into Samaria and prayed for God to give them their sight. Only our God could perform miracles such as this.

What is the greatest miracle to ever happen in your life? Who was responsible for this miracle?

From Rags to Riches

I remember as a teenager hearing the story about the pastor who did not appear for the beginning of the service and everyone wondered where he was. They began the regular program of worship according to the bulletin. All of a sudden the back door opened and in walked a very shabbily dressed man. His hair was in disarray, his clothes were dirty, his face was unshaven, and he had somewhat of an odor about him. The people gasped as he walked through the doors of the auditorium. They were not sure what to think and they kept their distance from him. When it came time for the sermon, they wondered where the pastor was. Much to their surprise the shabbily dressed man got up quietly and walked toward the front of the congregation. He stood behind the pulpit and revealed who he was; their pastor then preached a sermon about the way we treat people who are not as well dressed as we are or maybe do not have an education. He spoke about people who are down and out because they have lost their job and are living from meal to meal. He talked about how Jesus treated people from all walks of life. Jesus set the example for us as to how we are to treat others and said, "A new commandment I give to you, that you love one another, even as I have loved you, that you also love one another. By this all men will know that you are my disciples, if you have love for one another" (John 13:34–35, NASB).

The message the pastor preached that day had a great impact on his congregation and changed the hearts of many people. "The rich and the poor have a common bond, the Lord is the maker of them all" (Proverbs 22:2, NASB).

Jesus Christ is certainly the example we are to follow in the way we treat others. He gave up his position with the Father to come to earth as a human being. He gave his all for you and me. "You know how full of love and kindness our Lord Jesus Christ was. Though he was very rich, yet for your sakes he became poor, so that by his poverty he could make you rich" (2 Corinthians 8:9, NLT).

As a human, he was Jesus of Nazareth, a simple carpenter. When Jesus began his ministry of preaching and teaching, he traveled from place to place continually teaching his disciples about life. "And as they were going along the road, someone said to him, 'I will follow you wherever you go.' And Jesus said to him, 'The foxes have holes, and the birds of the air have nests, but the Son of Man has nowhere to lay his head'" (Luke 9:57–58, NASB).

> Do not lay up for yourselves treasures upon earth, where moth and rust destroy, and where thieves break in and steal. But lay up for yourselves treasures in heaven, where neither moth nor rust destroys, and where thieves do not break in or steal; for where your treasure is, there will your heart be also.
>
> Matthew 6:19–21 (NASB)

We are not to worry about the material possessions of this world. If we really want to be rich, our treasures will be laid up in heaven. This will be accomplished by the good deeds we do in the name of Jesus. It will be determined by the fruits of the Spirit in our life. Do we have the love, joy, peace, patience, kindness, faithfulness, gentleness, goodness, and self-control that were present in Jesus's life?

The rich young ruler came to Jesus to question him as to how he could have eternal life. Jesus named off several commandments he must keep and he said he had kept all of them. He wanted to know what he was still lacking. "Jesus said to him, 'If you wish to be complete, go and sell your possessions and give to the poor, and you shall have treasure in heaven; and come, follow me'" (Matthew 19:21, NASB).

This was more than the rich young ruler was willing to do.

According to the scripture, he went away grieved. We must be willing to give up everything to follow Jesus if he asks us to do so. Another way of laying up treasures in heaven is by sharing Jesus with lost people, enlightening them with the Scriptures, and helping them understand what it means to accept Jesus as Savior and Lord. We must be willing to give our all for the cause of Christ.

I have entitled this devotion "From Rags to Riches" for a very special reason. When we think about our life before we accepted Jesus, we really had nothing. Oh, we might have had money in the bank, a nice home, and a brand new car, but in the eyes of the Lord this is nothing.

> Jew and Gentile are the same in this respect. They all have the same LORD, who generously gives his riches to all who ask for them. For "Anyone who calls on the name of the LORD will be saved."
>
> Romans 10:12–13 (NLT)

> So we praise God for the wonderful kindness he has poured out on us because we belong to his dearly loved Son. He is so rich in kindness that he purchased our freedom through the blood of his Son, and our sins are forgiven.
>
> Ephesians 1:6–7 (NLT)

The richest gift we ever receive is salvation. God showed his kindness to people of every race by purchasing our freedom from sin through the blood of Jesus, his Son. When we accept Jesus, our sins are forgiven. If we had all the money in the world, it would not compare in any way to how rich we are in Christ Jesus. We have gone from rags to riches.

In our walk with the Lord, there are times we may need to give up a good job, relinquish the fancy cars we enjoy driving, or move to a distant land. We might have to let go of our pride and be willing to go to those people we have shunned in the past. We may need to let go of all we have in order to learn not to live in our own strength and determination, but to lean on the Lord for his strength and direction. "You're blessed when you're at the end of your rope. With less of you there is more of God and his rule" (Matthew 5:3, MSG). When we relinquish our prideful ways and give God control of our life, we are blessed in abundance with the joy and contentment.

I read a story about a large church in the city that was meeting for Sunday morning worship. Everyone was in their place and dressed in the latest fashions. The worship service had started when the doors at the back of the auditorium opened and in walked a young man barefooted, dressed in shorts, and his hair was in a mess. The deacons were at the back of the church talking among themselves. No one offered to lead him to a seat. He walked down the aisle; finding no place to sit, he seated himself on the floor at the end of the pew at the front of the auditorium. The people gasped at what was happening. They were sure the deacons would do something to correct it. A man in his eighties who was very well to do, walked down the aisle to where the young man was sitting. The people were just sure he would grab him by the arm and lead him out of the church. The most amazing thing happened. Right in front of the whole congregation, he painfully sat himself down on the floor, sitting Indian style, beside the young man. Being as old as he was, this was not an easy thing to do. He demonstrated by his actions the love of Jesus to this young man. "My dear friends, don't let public opinion influence how you live our glorious, Christ-originated faith" (James 2:1, MSG).

What riches are you most concerned about, riches on earth or riches in heaven? Which do you think will really bring you the most happiness in life?

If you were to die today, what do you think the Lord would say about the life you have lived when you enter heaven's gates?

The Hustle and Bustle of Life

It seems Americans are leading busier lives these days. Instead of life slowing down as we grow older, it seems to keep speeding up. I think of all the things I must do in the next three days, and quite seriously, it makes me weary. The Christmas season is a busy time as we add more activities than normal. It is a time for families to gather and enjoy the holiday season. We all enjoy eating together and exchanging gifts. We strive to keep the focus of Christmas on the one it is all about—Jesus. Sometimes it is difficult because everywhere we turn people are trying to sell us something. The stores are packed with people spending money they do not have. Many do not know the true meaning of Christmas these days because they only see the commercial side. They spend their paychecks trying to buy things for their children so they will not feel bad when they go back to school and hear what other children have received for Christmas. We are so caught up in the hustle and bustle of life that we fail to focus on this being the time Jesus was born in Bethlehem. As I was praying this morning, I had instrumental music playing and the song was "Turn Your Eyes Upon Jesus." God spoke to my heart as I listened and stopped to meditate on the message of the words:

> *Turn your eyes upon Jesus,*
> *Look full in his wonderful face*
> *And the things of earth will grow strangely dim*
> *In the light of his glory and grace.*

During the busy days preceding Christmas, the prayer of my heart is to keep my heart, mind, ears, and eyes set on the Lord Jesus and what he has to say to me. There is no greater joy than knowing Jesus and celebrating his birth at this time of year. May we not forget to be thankful for the great sacrifice he made for us by dying on the cross for our sin. He was buried and rose again on the third day so we might have eternal life. What a gift from God our Father!

Jesus's earthly life began in very humble surroundings: "And she gave birth to her first-born son; and she wrapped him in cloths, and laid him in a manger, because there was no room for them in the inn" (Luke 2:7, NASB).

Joseph and Mary were in Bethlehem to register for the census. When they arrived, so many people were in town there were no rooms available. The innkeeper told them they could stay in the stable with the animals. Jesus was born and placed in the manger where they fed hay to the animals. You might say Jesus had a very meager beginning. There were no bright lights or sterile surroundings; everything was very simple.

When Jesus was twelve years old, he went with Joseph and Mary to the feast of the Passover in Jerusalem. The events in the following days made it evident there was something different about Jesus.

> And when he became twelve, they went up there according to the custom of the feast; and as they were returning, after spending the full number of days, the boy Jesus stayed behind in Jerusalem. And his parents were unaware of it, but supposed him to be in the caravan, and went a day's journey; and they began looking for him among their relatives and acquaintances.
>
> Luke 2:42–44 (NASB)

Joseph and Mary did not find him, so they returned to Jerusalem to look for Jesus. It took them a day to return to Jerusalem because they were walking. Life was simple then and getting somewhere fast was not a priority. Do you think we could learn something from the simplicity and quietness of their life? I can just imagine the anxiety of Mary's heart as they walked the long distance back to Jerusalem and then did not find Jesus for three days.

> And it came about that after three days they found him in the temple, sitting in the midst of the teachers, both listening to them, and asking them questions. And all who heard him were amazed at his understanding and his answers. And when they saw him, they were astonished; and his mother said to him, "Son, why have you treated us this way? Behold, Your father and I have been anxiously looking for you." And he said to them, "Why is it that you were looking for me? Did you not know that I had to be in my Father's house?"
>
> Luke 2:46–49 (NASB)

Mary questioned him the same as any parent would question a child if he had wandered off. Anxiety would be present in the heart of every parent who searched for her child for three days. How would you have felt? They were puzzled by Jesus's answer to their questions. They did not realize the important part Jesus would play in the life of all mankind in the future. The Bible tells us Jesus obediently returned with his parents to their home in Nazareth, but Mary pondered these things in her heart. They left the hustle and bustle of Bethlehem, where many had come to register for the census, and returned home to their quiet life in Nazareth.

Thinking about the hustle and bustle of life reminds me of driving through the small towns of Malawi on market day. This is the day everyone has vegetables they have grown, a goat they have butchered, or the flour from the pounding of corn or cassava to sell. Many vendors have cloth, shoes, second-hand clothes, tools, and a varied assortment of things to sell that have been purchased in one of the larger towns. For many who do not grow their own crops, this is their only opportunity for the week to purchase clothes or food they might need. There are so many people at the market; it could be compared to a swarm of bees or a colony of ants. You can hardly drive on the highway because the market is on both sides of the road. It is amazing to see how the quiet, simple life of a Malawian becomes busy with the hustle and bustle of market day. The other six days of the week, the women will be in the fields preparing for the next planting. In some areas, the men will be helping in the fields. The women will walk three or four miles to get water from the river, a well, or a borehole. They will spend time pounding corn or cassava to make flour to use for nsima, their staple food. They will also spend part of their day gathering wood to use in cooking. "Make it your ambition to lead a quiet life, to mind your own business and to work with your hands, just as we told you, so that your daily life may win the respect of outsiders and so that you will not be dependent on anybody" (1 Thessalonians 4:11–12, NIV).

What does your daily schedule look like? Is it a day of hustle and bustle or a quiet, peaceful day? Have you scheduled a time of prayer and meditation on the Scripture?

What is the true meaning of Christmas to you?

Remember When

Last night, as our family gathered to celebrate Christmas, there were twenty-two people in our family room for the evening meal and a time of remembering. Four of our grandchildren were not here. By this time next year we will have a new great grandchild, so we could have twenty-seven people present. Our family is growing, and it was interesting to hear, particularly our four children, tell stories about exciting things from the past. Sometimes the things they tell cause your skin to crawl. They are the kinds of things they seldom share with their parents while growing up. They all enjoy remembering things, particularly their teenage years, which seems to be an exciting time in every child's life. We also played a game they all seemed to enjoy, sang Christmas carols, and read the Christmas story from the Bible. We remembered the great gift God gave us in the person of Jesus Christ. It is always good to remember exciting things in our life as a child, a teenager, and as an adult.

What is the first Christmas you remember? The first Christmas I remember was when I was five years old and we were living in Morris, Oklahoma. It was such a special time when I received from Santa Claus, so I thought at the time, a farm set. It contained a barn, a fence you could put around the barn, and all kinds of farm animals. I think there was even a tractor and trailer that went with it, but since it was fifty-eight years ago, I am not sure. This is one of my fondest memories of Christmas past. When I was eight years old, I received a pink cowgirl jacket made out of vinyl material with fringe all over it. You would have thought I was Annie Oakley. I remember the Christmas my firstborn son was old enough to really enjoy getting presents. It brought joy to my heart to see his expression as he saw all the presents under the tree. It brought great excitement to him as a toddler opening those presents and playing with what he received. These are sweet memories to me.

What is the most exciting thing you can remember that happened to you in the past? My most exciting remembrance is when I came to know Jesus at eight years of age. We lived in a suburb of Longview, Texas, where my dad was a Baptist pastor. My parents always taught me the Bible and took me to church every time the doors opened. They took seriously the instructions found in the Book of Deuteronomy.

> Love the LORD your God with all your heart and with all your soul and with all your strength. These commandments that I give you today are to be upon your hearts. Impress them on your children. Talk about them when you sit at home and when you walk along the road, when you lie down and when you get up.
>
> Deuteronomy 6:5–7 (NIV)

I was taught there was something special about Jesus, who was the Son of God. I learned in my first eight years that God loved me so much he gave his only Son to die for my sin: "For God so loved the world that he gave his one and only Son, that whoever believes in him shall not perish but have eternal life" (John 3:16, NIV).

What a joy it was when I placed my faith and trust in Jesus and accepted him as my Savior and Lord. I did not understand all this meant at the time, but as I grew older I came to understand the real meaning of salvation. It is the sweetest memory I have in life.

What does the Bible say about remembering? When Moses knew his time on earth was coming to an end, he told the children of Israel he knew they would become corrupt, turn from the way he had instructed them to live and do evil in the sight of the Lord, provoking his anger. Moses recited a song to the Israelites: "Remember the days of long ago; think about the generations past.

Ask your father and he will inform you. Inquire of your elders, and they will tell you" (Deuteronomy 32:7, NLT).

Moses continued to remind them of how God had watched over them in the wilderness. He reminded them of God's protection: "He guarded him as the pupil of his eye. Like and eagle that stirs up its nest, that hovers over its young, he spread his wings and caught them, he carried them on his pinions" (Deuteronomy 32:10b–11, NASB). Moses wanted the Israelites to remember God's never-ending protection and care.

Samson was a man of great strength as long as he stayed true to his Nazarite vow and did not cut his hair. When he married Delilah, she continually tried to get him to tell her the source of his strength. Samson became annoyed and revealed the secret to her: God had instructed him never to cut his hair. When Samson went to sleep, Delilah called for a man to come and shave his head.

> And she made him sleep on her knees, and called for a man and had him shave off the seven locks of his hair. Then she began to afflict him, and his strength left him. And she said, "The Philistines are upon you, Samson!" And he awoke from his sleep and said, "I will go out as at other times and shake myself free." But he did not know that the LORD had departed from him.
>
> Judges 16:19–20 (NASB)

Because of Samson's disobedience to the vow he made with the Lord, his strength was gone. He was captured by the Philistines and his eyes were gouged out. While in prison, his hair began to grow out. He called out to God for help: "Then Samson called to the Lord and said, 'O Lord God, please remember me and please strengthen me just this time, O God, that I may at once be avenged of the Philistines for my two eyes'" (Judges 16:28, NASB). He knew he would die in the process, but God empowered him to destroy more Philistines in one day than he had in the past. God remembered him.

Hannah was the favorite of Elkanah's two wives, but Hannah's womb was closed and she bore him no children. Hannah was distressed every year when they went to the temple to worship and make sacrifices to the Lord. She was so distraught that she cried out to God.

> And she made a vow and said, "O LORD of hosts, if thou wilt indeed look on the affliction of thy maidservant and remember me, and not forget thy maidservant, but wilt give thy maidservant a son, then I will give him to the LORD all the days of his life, and a razor shall never come on his head."
>
> 1 Samuel 1:11 (NASB)

No sound came from her mouth, but Eli the priest could see her lips moving and he thought she was drunk. She told him she was not drunk, but had poured out her heart to the Lord. "Then they arose early in the morning and worshiped before the Lord, and returned again to their house in Ramah. And Elkanah had relations with Hannah his wife, and the Lord remembered her" (1 Samuel 1:19, NASB). God remembered Hannah and she became pregnant with a son she named Samuel.

Simon Peter was a very dependable follower of Jesus and part of the inner-circle of disciples Jesus kept close to him. He had been in the inner part of the garden of Gethsemane with Jesus the night he prayed to the Father concerning his crucifixion. Jesus told the disciples many would fall away from him as the time came near. Peter said he would not fall away from him even though others might. "Jesus said to him, 'Truly I say to you that this very night, before a cock crows, you shall deny me three times'" (Matthew 26:34, NASB).

We know from the Scripture it happened just as Jesus said. After Peter denied knowing Jesus the third time, he heard a cock crow. "And Peter remembered the word which Jesus had said, 'Before a cock crows, you will deny me three times.' And he went out and wept bitterly" (Matthew 26:75, NASB). What a sad day this was for Peter when he remembered what the Lord had said to him earlier. Some memories bring sorrow to our hearts and some bring joy.

As we reflect on our past life, some memories are sad. What did you learn through these experiences in life? Did you learn more from the Lord during the times of trial than you did when things were going good?

The Exquisite Show of Lights

Doyal and I have just returned from a trip to Silver Dollar City in Branson, Missouri. We went to see the display of Christmas lights. The sign at the entrance of the park said there was a display of four million lights in the park. We arrived in the daylight so you did not realize the beauty of the decorations. It was about forty degrees and a light rain was falling, so we certainly moved about briskly, seeking refuge in the different shops. In fact, one could be a little disappointed arriving in the daylight thinking it was not going to be what they expected. We wondered why we were enduring the rain and cold for this experience. As darkness approached, we realized the atmosphere of the park was about to change. We had gone to see Dickens's *A Christmas Carol* at dusk, and when we came out, it was dark. It was a sight to behold as we walked out in the park and everything was covered with bright, colorful lights. Still, we did not realize the extent of the exquisite show of lights until we got to the entrance where they had a Christmas tree five stories high. At this time, there was a display of about five different colors. At 6:00 p.m., there was a display of colors far beyond one's imagination as the computerized tree showed its many different designs. It was an unbelievable sight. The tree had squares of different colors, stripes of different colors, the starting of one color at the top and the changing from one color to the other as it went down the tree. Of course, there was music setting the mood for the magnificent display of lights. The lights on trees and buildings all around were blinking on and off. Then to top it off, they had a parade of simple floats on Main Street. It was well worth enduring the cold and light rain to see the beauty of something created by man with the help of computers.

How do you think we would have felt if we had been present to experience the beginning of God's creation? I imagine we would have been overcome by the magnificent display of God's creative powers.

> In the beginning God created the heavens and the earth. Now the earth was formless and empty, darkness was over the surface of the deep, and the Spirit of God was hovering over the waters. And God said, "Let there be light," and there was light. God saw that the light was good, and he separated the light from the darkness. God called the light "day," and the darkness he called "night." And there was morning—the first day.
>
> Genesis 1:1–5 (NIV)

We can only imagine how it would have been when God created light. I am sure the display of lights at Silver Dollar City would not even compare with what it was like when God said, "Let there be light," and there was light. We would have been far more impressed by the presence of the light on the earth than the display of Christmas lights. The Bible tells us God added to his creation even more lights on the third day.

> God said, "Let there be lights in the expanse of the sky to separate the day from the night, and let them serve as signs to mark seasons and days and years, and let them be lights in the expanse of the sky to give light on the earth." And it was so. God made two great lights—the greater light to govern the day and the lesser light to govern the night. He also made the stars. God set them in the expanse of the sky to give light on the earth ...
>
> Genesis 1:14–17 (NIV)

God created the sun, moon, and stars to give light to the earth. It reminds me of walking outside at night in Malawi, Africa. If the moon and stars were not shining, it was pitch black. There was no light whatsoever. On the nights you could see the stars and the moon, it was much different. We have also experienced the difference here at home when the moon and stars are shining and when they are not. It makes all the difference in the world how one can see to get around at night, especially if they might be in wooded areas. God's creation of the lights is far beyond anything man might create with a computer.

God created you and me for a very special purpose. When we come to know Jesus as Savior, God wants to use us to accomplish his purpose. "You are the light of the world. A city set on a hill cannot be hidden. Let your light shine before men in such a way that they may see your good works, and glorify your Father who is in heaven" (Matthew 5:14, 16, NASB).

As a child of God, we are to be as lights to a lost and dying world. We are to show forth high moral standards in the way we live our life. We are to be people of integrity. We are to do good deeds in the name of the Lord to bring praise and glory to him. We know Jesus as Savior, so we are to be witnesses of how Jesus came as the light of the world. He offers to those who are lost in the darkness of sin the light of salvation.

Their judgment is based on this fact: The light from heaven came into the world, but they loved the darkness more than the light, for their actions were evil. They hate the light because they want to sin in the darkness. They stay away from the light for fear their sins will be exposed and they will be punished. But those who do what is right come to the light gladly, so everyone can see that they are doing what God wants.

John 3:19–21 (NLT)

Many people have no desire to know Jesus, the light of the world. They would rather continue in darkness because they do not want others to see their evil deeds. They think they can be free from the punishment of sin if they continue walking in darkness, the ways of the world. We as believers must allow the light of Jesus to shine through us to those who are in darkness.

The lights at Silver Dollar City were beautiful. It was an amazing display of lights, but I do not think it compares with the magnificent display of God's presence in the sun, moon, and stars as they give light to the earth. You and I can be light to a dark world as we share the message of salvation, Jesus Christ, with them.

What is the greatest display of lights you have ever seen?

What does it mean to you when God said that you are to be the light of the world?

How has your life changed since you came to know the true light of Jesus Christ?

The Dawning of Something We've Never Experienced

The year will end tonight when the clock strikes 12:00 midnight. At 12:01, the new year will begin. It will be a time of new beginning for all of us. Yesterday, our Sunday school teacher asked us to think about our life and consider how we had grown in the Lord this past year. This year has been an amazing year in my life. I am in awe of all God has done in one year. He has brought about events I never thought possible for me. I am simply amazed how he continues to use the devotional books the Lord and I have written together.

The apostle John was exiled on the island of Patmos for preaching the Word of God and speaking about Jesus. John had previously spoken about Jesus's return to earth and how his second coming would be visible to all. "And then they will see the Son of Man coming in clouds with great power and glory. And then he will send forth the angels, and will gather together his elect from the four winds, from the farthest end of the earth, to the farthest end of heaven" (Mark, 13:26–27, NASB).

John had an astonishing disclosure of future events, but also a revelation of how the children of God were to live in the present. Jesus made an amazing statement about himself: "'I am the Alpha and the Omega—the beginning and the end,' says the Lord God. 'I am the one who is, who always was, and who is still to come, the Almighty One'" (Revelation, 1:8 NLT). Jesus is the beginning and the end. All things began with him and all things will end with him. Then God gave John instructions as to what he was to do.

It was the LORD's Day, and I was worshiping in the Spirit. Suddenly, I heard a loud voice behind me, a voice that sounded like a trumpet blast. It said, "Write down what you see, and send it to the seven churches: Ephesus, Smyrna, Pergamum, Thyatira, Sardis, Philadelphia, and Laodicea."

Revelation 1:10–11 (NLT)

John heard the voice of the Lord and he wrote exactly what God told him to write to each of the seven churches. I am sure John was very humbled by God placing his confidence in him to write what he wanted to say to each of the seven churches.

I have been so humbled this past year and a half to hear God speaking and telling me what to write in these devotionals. It has been a task far beyond my ability, but with God at the helm, it has been accomplished. It has been a new beginning in my life. All I can say is "It is simply God!" I have no other explanation for what I have done. It is exciting to think about what God will do in my life in the new year if I will just be still and listen. "Let be and be still, and know (recognize and understand) that I am God" (Psalm 46:10a, AMP).

Think with me about what the Bible says about new beginnings. "In the beginning God created the heavens and the earth" (Genesis 1:1, NASB). This was a new beginning as God created the heavens and the earth. God then created everything in the heavens, the sun, moon, and stars. God continued creation by placing on the earth all the plants, trees, waters, fish, and every kind of creature. Finally, he created man and woman. It was a time of new beginnings.

Let's look at some other "new beginnings" in God's Word. "Fear of the Lord is the beginning of wisdom. Knowledge of the holy one results in understanding" (Proverbs 9:10, NLT). When we have deep respect for the Lord, this is the beginning of our possessing wisdom. We must come to the Lord in reverence and ask him for wisdom and understanding in life. "But if any of you lacks wisdom, let him ask of God, who gives to all men generously and without reproach, and it will be given to him. But let him ask in faith without any doubting, for the one who doubts is like the surf of the sea driven and tossed by the wind" (James 1:5–6, NASB).

For us to experience the beginning of wisdom, we must come seeking God, believing that he will give it to us. We must come in faith without doubting. This is a new beginning in our life as a believer as we learn to trust God.

In the Gospel of John, Jesus is introduced as the Word. "In the beginning was the Word, and the Word was with God, and the Word was God. He was with God in the beginning. Through him all things were made; without him nothing was made that has been made. In him was life, and that life was the light of men" (John 1:1–4, NIV).

God the Father, God the Son, and God the Holy Spirit were all present at the beginning of creation. Because of Jesus coming to earth, dying on the cross, and being raised from death, it is possible for us to have a new beginning. Salvation from sin is available to us. Jesus gave his life as payment for our sin. He arose from the grave, making it possible for us to have eternal life. "Truly, truly, I say to you, he who hears my word, and believes him who sent me, has eternal life, and does not come into judgment, but has passed out of death into life" (John 5:24, NASB). We have the opportunity for a new beginning in our life when we accept Jesus as Savior and Lord.

New beginnings make me think about planting a garden. We plow the ground, break up the clods, rake the ground smooth, and then make furrows in which to plant the seeds. We place the seed in a small hole, cover it with soil, and water it. We must wait patiently for the seed to die. When the seed dies, it swells up, breaks open, and roots begin to grow from the inside of the seed. "Truly, truly, I say to you, unless a grain of wheat falls into the earth and dies, it remains by itself alone; but if it dies, it bears much fruit" (John 12:24, NASB).

Within a short period of time—the time varies according to the type of seed—a small plant will begin to poke its head through a crack in the earth. It will grow into a large plant and begin bearing fruit. It is the same in our life as a Christian. For us to come to know Jesus, we must die to self, allowing Jesus Christ to be our Savior and Lord. When he becomes our Lord, we relinquish control of our life to him. The Holy Spirit comes to live in our heart and helps us know right from wrong. With God in control of our life, we will mature and be a witness for him. Others will come to know Jesus because of the seeds we plant through our witness and God's kingdom will grow.

This is just the tip of the iceberg about new beginnings in the Bible. Much could be written, but time or space does not allow this to be done. We are right on the verge of beginning a new year. Thank God for what he has done in this past year and look with anticipation towards the new year.

How do you evaluate your growth in the Lord this year? Do you feel that you have accomplished all God had for you to do?

Are you ready to take a bold step and tell God you will do whatever he purposes for you to do, even though it is far beyond your own human ability? Be still before the Lord and listen because he will speak to you. Something may come to mind God has already spoken to you about doing, what is it?

Filled to Overflowing

The second devotional book I wrote was entitled *My Cup Runneth Over*. When I concluded my first book, it seemed God had stirred in me an insatiable desire for his Word. I could not get enough of the Bible. Thoughts were continuing to flow from within me because of the Holy Spirit living in my heart. God led me to write a second book. When I completed the book, God continued to fill me to overflowing with a love for him and a desire to search deeper in his Word for more understanding. He led me to write my third book entitled, *Listen! What Do You Hear?* God had taught me so much about listening for his voice and doing what he said. I was not sure there was anything left in my life to write about, but I am now in the midst of the book you are reading. It seems impossible that God has opened so many doors of opportunity to me, a simple, Oklahoma country girl, this past year. I am just a sinner saved by the ever abundant grace of our Lord Jesus Christ. It is hard for me to fathom God counting me worthy to attempt and complete the task he has laid before me. God continually fills me with rivers of living water; the Holy Spirit empowers me to do what he says.

> That is what the Scriptures mean when they say, "No eye has seen, no ear has heard, and no mind has imagined what God has prepared for those who love him." But we know these things because God has revealed them to us by his Spirit, and his Spirit searches out everything and shows us even God's deep secrets. No one can know what anyone else is really thinking except that person alone, and no one can know God's thoughts except God's own Spirit. And God

has actually given us his Spirit (not the world's spirit) so we can know the wonderful things God has freely given us.

1 Corinthians 2:9–12 (NLT)

As Jesus taught in the synagogue, during the time of the Feast of Booths, he promised those who believed would be filled with rivers of living water: "If any man is thirsty, let him come to me and drink. He who believes in me, as the Scripture said, 'From his innermost being shall flow rivers of living water'" (John 7:37b–38, NASB).

Before Jesus ascended into heaven, he promised his disciples the Holy Spirit would come to empower them to do his work. They were to wait for the Holy Spirit to come upon them before they left Jerusalem. According to the Scriptures, they received the Holy Spirit on the day of Pentecost. "And they were all filled with the Holy Spirit and began to speak with other tongues, as the Spirit was giving them utterance" (Acts 2:4, NASB). He came to indwell their hearts and empower them to serve the Lord.

When we come to know Jesus as Savior, the Holy Spirit comes to live in our heart. "Peter replied, 'Repent and be baptized, every one of you, in the name of Jesus Christ for the forgiveness of your sins. And you will receive the gift of the Holy Spirit'" (Acts 2:38, NIV). He will strengthen, empower and give us direction in our life. "We can make our plans, but the Lord determines our steps" (Proverbs 16:9, NLT).

We are to continually ask God to fill us to overflowing with the Holy Spirit. We received the Holy Spirit at the time of our salvation, but we receive a fresh filling every day if our fellowship with the Lord is not broken by sin in our life.

Pay careful attention, then, to how you walk—not as unwise people but as wise—making the most of the time, because the days are evil. So don't be foolish, but understand what the Lord's will is. And don't get drunk with wine, which [leads] reckless actions, but be filled with the Spirit.

Ephesians 5:15–18 (HCSB)

As we spend quality time with the Lord in his Word and in intentional, fervent prayer, rivers of living water will flow from within us and we will have a witness to all around us.

I don't know about you, but as I begin the new year, I have a yearning for the fruits of the Spirit to grow so abundantly in my life that I will be filled to overflowing. "But the fruit of the Spirit is love, joy, peace, patience, kindness, goodness, faith, gentleness, self-control. Against such things there is no law. If we live by the Spirit, we must also follow the Spirit" (Galatians 5:22–23, 25, HCSB).

Can you imagine what would happen if each morning, when every believer got out of bed, they would ask God to fill them with the spirit of love, joy, peace, patience, kindness, goodness, faithfulness, gentleness, and self-control? There are enough Christians in this world to positively affect every business in the world. People would see a definite difference in the lives of believers and the Holy Spirit might stir within the lost the desire to be saved. Possibly, we might experience a great spiritual awakening. When God's people allow their lives to be under the control of the Holy Spirit, they become a living, vibrant, Spirit-filled example to the lost people of this world.

I never cease to be amazed at what God is doing in and through me, but I know I have only experienced a small part of what he has purposed for my life. There is still so much of my life I need to fully relinquish to the Lord and to the Holy Spirit's control.

"For I know the plans I have for you," declares the Lord, "plans to prosper you and not to harm you, plans to give you hope and a future. Then you will call upon me and come

and pray to me, and I will listen to you. You will seek me
and find me when you seek me with all your heart."

Jeremiah 29:11–13 (NIV)

What do you expect God to do in your life during the new year?
Are you anticipating a great adventure in the Lord? What will be
your response to what God calls you to do?

Am I a True Soldier of the Cross?

We have some young men in our community who will soon be going to Iraq. They will return to Fort Bliss today after spending Christmas with their families. They are soldiers of the United States Army who are putting their lives on the line for our country and the innocent people of Iraq. Because of their commitment, they will go and do whatever their job calls for in aiding the people of Iraq to have freedom, along with protecting the United States against terrorism. They are true soldiers of the United States Army because they are willing to give their lives, if necessary, for our country.

If your life as a believer were to be critiqued, would you be found to be a true, faithful, dependable, and willing soldier of the cross?

> In this you greatly rejoice, though now for a little while you may have had to suffer grief in all kinds of trials. These have come so that your faith—of greater worth than gold, which perishes even though refined by fire—may be proved genuine and may result in praise, glory and honor when Jesus Christ is revealed.
>
> 1 Peter 1:6–7 (NIV)

Are you ready to suffer grief and pain for the Lord? Is your foundation in the Lord strong enough to stand the test? People are faced with many trials and tests in life. When a believer is tested, he or she has someone to turn to for help, unlike an unbeliever who has no one with great power and strength. We go through trials so our faith can be proved genuine as we endure the fires of testing. Through these times of testing we learn to be more dependent on the Lord rather than on ourselves or others.

The testing of our faith will reveal whether or not we have built our life on the strong foundation of Jesus Christ. Paul was speaking to the Corinthian Christians about the foundation of their faith in the Lord: "For no one can lay any foundation other than the one already laid, which is Jesus Christ" (1 Corinthians 3:11, NIV).

For you and me to display great faith during times of testing, our faith must be built on the firm foundation of Jesus Christ. "Take particular care in picking out your building materials. Eventually there is going to be an inspection. If you use cheap or inferior materials, you'll be found out. The inspection will be thorough and rigorous. You won't get by with a thing" (1 Corinthians 3:12–13, MSG). This reminds me of people we have known who have used cheap materials to build a house, apartment building, or a place of business. As the years pass, the structure begins to fall apart because improper materials were used. The foundation may shift and the walls begin to crack because they did not put the right amount and size of steel in the foundation. They did not follow the list of materials given on the blueprint for the structure. They deceived the people they were working for. You can be sure their wrongdoing will catch up with them. Believers must build their lives on the firm foundation of God's Word.

> Therefore everyone who hears these words of mine, and acts upon them, may be compared to a wise man, who built his house upon the rock. And the rain descended, and the floods came, and the winds blew, and burst against that house; and yet it did not fall, for it had been founded upon the rock.
>
> Matthew 7:24–25 (NASB)

The house built on the firm foundation of the rock stood strong through the floods and wind. It is the same with us when we face trials and testing in life. If we have built our life on the strong foundation of God's Word, we will stand strong. As we pray, we build a strong relationship with God and he is attentive to us. In Psalm 40, David talks about waiting patiently for the Lord and how the Lord heard his cry. God lifted him out of the miry clay pit and set his feet upon a solid rock to give him sure footing. When we go through times of testing as a believer, God will hear us when we cry out to him and he will give us the strength we need. We must be like the tree Jeremiah talked about.

> Blessed is the man who trusts in the LORD and whose trust is the LORD. For he will be like a tree planted by the water, that extends its roots by a stream and will not fear when the heat comes; but its leaves will be green, and it will not be anxious in a year of drought nor cease to yield fruit.
>
> Jeremiah 17:7–8 (NASB)

The roots of the tree reached out for nourishment from the stream. As our roots go deep into God's Word, we receive nourishment from him.

Peter said we should feel blessed when we are counted worthy to suffer for doing right. He told those he was preaching to not to be afraid when this happens. Peter also gave us instruction as to what we are to do. "But in your hearts set apart Christ as Lord. Always be prepared to give an answer to everyone who asks you to give the reason for the hope that you have. But do this with gentleness and respect" (1 Peter 3:15, NIV). We must know what we believe and on what we base our belief. This will help a lost person know our foundation is strong in the Lord.

We as Christians have been chosen to go and fight in the battle for the Lord. What kind of soldier will you be? Have you been making preparation for battle or have you been ignoring the training required? The men going to Iraq from Wilburton have been in training at Fort Bliss. They are now ready to go and perform the work they need to do.

What happens when we are called into action as a Christian and we have not made the preparation needed? What preparation are you making for battle in our world today? Are your roots sinking deeper and deeper into the Word of God? If not, why not?

If God were to do an inspection of your training as a soldier, would he find you ready for battle? In who or what is your trust?

The Indescribable Power

When our two younger boys were growing up, we would go to the Oklahoma State Fair in Oklahoma City. We always went for the tractor pulls. Men and boys get excited about seeing the power of machinery in action. They love to see what extra additives to fuel can do to make the engine have more power so it can pull more weight. When the motors have great power, they make an almost deafening noise. For some reason, this brings joy to the hearts of men and boys. Doyal has great understanding of engines, so it was a good time for him to teach Anthony and Stevie how to make an engine have more power. It was good for them to be together and enjoy one another as they would talk on the way home about the different tractors. The power of man or machinery is important in the life of most men.

Let's consider the indescribable power of God portrayed in the lives of many biblical characters. David spoke of the great power of God on the day he sang a song of praise to the Lord when God delivered him from the hands of Saul and his enemies.

> The waves of death surrounded me; the floods of destruction swept over me. The grave wrapped its ropes around me; death itself stared me in the face. But in my distress I cried out to the Lord; yes, I called to my God for help. He heard me from his sanctuary; my cry reached his ears
>
> 2 Samuel 22:5–7 (NLT)

Not only did God hear him, but God showed his great power. The earth quaked, the foundations of heaven shook because of God's anger and smoke poured from his nostrils as flames came from his mouth from the burning coals. God opened the heavens and came down with dark clouds beneath his feet and he was on the mighty angel as he flew soaring on the wings of the wind. There was a great brightness around him. Lightning bolts blazed around him as the Most High thundered from heaven with a mighty shout. "He shot his arrows and scattered his enemies; his lightning flashed, and they were confused. Then at the command of the LORD, at the blast of his breath, the bottom of the sea could be seen, and the foundations of the earth were laid bare."

2 Samuel 22:15–16 (NLT)

God's great power was evident as he delivered David from his enemies.

God demonstrated his mighty power to Daniel and also to King Darius. The king had signed a document stating if any man prayed to any god or man other than to him in the next thirty days, he would be cast into the lions' den. Daniel knew this decree had been signed, but he stayed faithful to the Lord. "Now when Daniel knew that the document was signed, he entered his house (now in his roof chamber he had windows open toward Jerusalem); and he continued kneeling on his knees three times a day, praying and giving thanks before his God, as he had been doing previously" (Daniel 6:10, NASB).

The commissioners and satraps found Daniel praying to his God and reported him to King Darius. This distressed the king because Daniel had found favor with him. The king had to follow the decree he had signed. "Then the king gave orders, and Daniel was brought in and cast into the lions' den. The king spoke and said to Daniel, 'Your God whom you constantly serve will himself deliver you'" (Daniel 6:16, NASB).

The stone was placed over the mouth of the lions' den and the king sealed it with his signet ring so the orders could not be changed. The king rose early the next morning to go check on Daniel. He called out to Daniel as he neared the lions' den. "Then Daniel spoke to the king, 'O king, live forever! My God sent his angel and shut the lions' mouths, and they have not harmed me, inasmuch as I was found innocent before him; and also toward you, O king, I have committed no crime'" (Daniel 6:21–22, NASB). God's power was seen in the closing of the lions' mouths so they did not harm Daniel.

King Sennacherib of Assyria was taunting Hezekiah and the inhabitants of Jerusalem. He wanted the people to know Hezekiah was deceiving them. He made note of Hezekiah being the one who had torn down all of the shrines and altars. Sennacherib reminded them no god of any nation had been able to rescue his people from the Assyrians in the past, so why should they think their God would be able to rescue them. The Assyrian officials even went so far as to mock the Lord God and Hezekiah, his servant. They talked about the Lord as if he were one of the pagan gods.

> Then King Hezekiah and the prophet Isaiah son of Amoz cried out in prayer to God in heaven. And the LORD sent an angel who destroyed the Assyrian army with all its commanders and officers. So Sennacherib returned home in disgrace to his own land. And when he entered the temple of his god, some of his own sons killed him there with a sword. That is how the LORD rescued Hezekiah and the people of Jerusalem from King Sennacherib of Assyria and from all the others who threatened them. So there was peace at last throughout the land.
>
> 2 Chronicles 32:20–22 (NLT)

God proved his power to King Hezekiah and the prophet Isaiah by sending an angel to destroy the whole army and all its commanders and officers. Absolutely nothing is impossible for the Lord. He brought peace instead of oppression. Hezekiah and Isaiah knew who to cry out to in their time of need. God heard them and answered their prayer.

After King Ahab's death, the nation of Moab declared its independence and refused to pay taxes to Israel. Ahaziah, the new king of Israel, fell through the latticework of an upper room in his palace in Samaria. He was seriously injured and sent messengers to the temple of Baal-zebub to ask the god of Ekron if he would recover.

> But the angel of the LORD told Elijah, who was from Tishbe, "Go and meet the messengers of the king of Samaria and ask them, 'Why are you going to Baal-zebub, the god of Ekron, to ask whether the king will get well? Is there no God in Israel? Now, therefore, this is what the LORD says: You will never leave the bed on which you are lying, but you will surely die.'" So Elijah went to deliver the message.
>
> 2 Kings 1:3–4 (NLT)

When the messengers returned quickly to the king, he questioned why they had returned so soon. They told him about meeting a man who had given them this message. He asked for a description of the man and realized it was Elijah, the Tishbite. The men returned to Elijah with the request from the king to come to him. "But Elijah replied to the captain, 'If I am a man of God, let fire come down from heaven and destroy you and your fifty men!' Then fire fell from heaven and killed them all" (2 Kings 1:10, NLT).

The king once again sent fifty men to him with the message to come to him. Once again Elijah called on the power of God and the fifty men were destroyed by fire.

> Once more the king sent a captain with fifty men. But this time the captain fell to his knees before Elijah. He pleaded with him, "O man of God, please spare my life and the lives of these, your fifty servants. See how the fire from heaven has

destroyed the first two groups. But now please spare my life!" Then the angel of the LORD said to Elijah, "Don't be afraid. Go with him." So Elijah got up and went to the king.

1 Kings 1:13–15 (NLT)

Elijah depended on God to show him what to do. He sought the Lord to display his mighty power by sending fire from heaven to consume the captain and his fifty men two times. When the third group came in humility and bowed before him, fire from heaven did not consume them and Elijah went to the king. Because of the king's disobedience in calling on a foreign god instead of the God of Israel, he died in his bed.

God's great power is made evident throughout the Scriptures in many different ways. How has God's power been seen in your own personal life? Think back of things in the past, or maybe just recently you have experienced. How have you seen the power of God at work in your life?

If you have not seen God's power at work in your life, why do you think this is so?

Blessed, Happy: The Beatitudes

One of my greatest blessings has been to have the friendship of a very special older woman. Juanita has brought much joy into my life, as I have had the privilege to minister to her, pray with her, be a true friend, and simply enjoy her company. She has become a spiritual advisor to me over the past few years as she read and digested the devotionals I have written. She always gives me feedback as to whether they speak to the point I am trying to make. She has become a very dear friend and mentor to me. We have enjoyed many happy moments together, visiting and sharing our lives with one another. She is getting ready to move from Wilburton to Oklahoma City, and it will really leave a void in my life when she moves away. I must reflect on the abundant blessings God has brought into my life through her and be thankful God has allowed me to be close to her and enjoy her friendship. "A friend is always a friend" (Proverbs 17:17a, CEV).

I want us to consider the Beatitudes found in Matthew 5. In Matthew 5–7, we have Jesus's message called the Sermon on the Mount. Jesus was preaching this sermon on the hillside near Capernaum. It is thought this message was preached over several days. The opening sentences describe the quality of life Jesus desires for a born-again believer. These Beatitudes set forth the spiritual principles of the kingdom of God. They define the character of a child of God. These are blessings given for everyone who is a believer. Each one of the Beatitudes carries with it a strong promise of ultimate good for those who develop the blessed life.

"God blesses those people who depend only on him. They belong to the kingdom of heaven!" (Matthew 5:3, CEV). We are blessed when we realize our strength comes from God and we are dependent on him. Even though storms come into our life, we can look beyond those storms and still praise the Lord for his goodness, mercy, and grace. I have found this to be so with my sweet friend this past year when she lost her husband of sixty-three years. In spite of the void in her life, she has been able to praise the Lord for his loving care. God opened a place for her within twenty-four hours at the Baptist Village in Oklahoma City even though she was number twenty on the list of people needing an apartment. God sold her home in a short time, so she closed before she moved. God can do miraculous things in the lives of those who depend solely on him.

"God blesses those people who grieve. They will find comfort" (Matthew 5:4, CEV). A person is blessed when he is grieved over the sin in his life and comes repenting of his sin. He finds comfort for his soul. Jesus healed the people who were sick, but he also dealt with the condition of their souls. "The Spirit of the Lord is on me, because he has anointed me to preach good news to the poor. He has sent me to proclaim freedom for the prisoners and recovery of sight for the blind, to release the oppressed" (Luke 4:18, NIV). Jesus came for the special purpose of preaching the gospel to all people and to free them from the bondage of sin.

"God blesses those people who are humble. The earth will belong to them!" (Matthew 5:5, CEV). The word meek is used in place of humble in several translations, not referring to weakness, but it speaks about those who totally depend on God for strength. They have been brought to this point through coming to know Jesus as Savior. One writer said it was like a person breaking a horse so he could control him. Many times the horse becomes gentle and easy to handle. When we allow the Lord to take total control of our life, we should have a humble, gentle spirit.

"Blessed are those who hunger and thirst for righteousness, because they will be filled" (Matthew 5:6, HCSB) A person develops a strong desire to live a life of righteousness, being in right standing with God. When we come to this place in our relationship with the Lord, we will experience happiness beyond our greatest imagination. We desire to be more Christ-like. One paraphrase talks about us working up a good appetite for God. We are never satisfied with just a little, but we hunger for more of the Lord.

"Blessed are the merciful, for they will be shown mercy" (Matthew 5:7, NIV). I think of Jesus as he walked from city to city and encountered different people with infirmities. When Jesus was traveling to Jericho, Bartimaeus, a blind beggar, was sitting by the road. "And when he heard that it was Jesus the Nazarene, he began to cry out and say, 'Jesus, Son of David, have mercy on me!'" (Mark 10:47, NASB). Many people tried to make him be quiet, but he called out all the more for the mercy of the Lord. "'What do you want me to do for you?' Jesus asked him. The blind man said, 'Rabbi, I want to see.' 'Go,' said Jesus, 'your faith has healed you.' Immediately he received his sight and followed Jesus along the road" (Mark 10:51–52, NIV). Jesus showed great mercy to him.

"God blesses those whose hearts are pure. They will see him!" (Matthew 5:8, CEV). As believers, we are to strive daily to live a clean life for the Lord. Our desire should be to keep our hearts pure and filled with God's love. When we have our heart and mind in tune with the Lord, we will make a difference in our world by allowing God to use us as his witness. Paul, in writing to Timothy about his pastoral responsibilities, instructed him to warn those who were teaching strange doctrines, fables, or myths. Lead them to lean on God with absolute trust and confidence. "The purpose of my instruction is that all the Christians there would be filled with love that comes from a pure heart, a clear conscience, and sincere faith" (1 Timothy 1:5, NLT).

"God blesses those people who make peace. They will be called his children!" (Matthew 5:9, CEV). There are people who can exert a calming influence in our life even in the midst of a storm. They have the peace of God within them and, therefore, that peace flows from them into the lives of others. Jesus had a calming effect on the disciples when they were in a boat at sea. A great storm came and Jesus was asleep in the boat. They awoke him and cried out for him to save them. "And he said to them, 'Why are you timid, you men of little faith?' Then he arose, and rebuked the winds and the sea; and it became perfectly calm" (Matthew 8:26, NASB).

"God blesses those who are persecuted because they live for God, for the kingdom of heaven is theirs" (Matthew 5:10, NLT). This verse deals with faithfulness under stress. We will suffer when we live for the Lord. Many are persecuted because they believe in the Lord and follow his teachings. A young lady in Malawi denounced her Muslim beliefs and decided to follow Jesus. Her family disowned her, making her leave their home. They even threatened to have her killed. She was destitute, but determined to live her life for Jesus Christ. The world will ridicule us and speak out against us because the life we live is opposite to what the world lives. "In this world you will have trouble. But take heart! I have overcome the world" (John 16:33b, NIV). We will have strength in the power of the Lord to endure any persecution we face.

What does it mean to you to be blessed by the Lord?

What is the greatest blessing you have received?

Amazing Feats of God

One of our mission trips took us to the town of Aracaju in Brazil. To board the plane, we had to walk out on the tarmac. There were rain showers just before boarding and as we walked toward the plane there was a double rainbow in the sky. It was a beautiful sight to behold. Only God could accomplish this feat.

We went to Russia and Estonia on a mission trip, and as we were driving through the countryside of Estonia, we saw an amazing sight. Sitting atop a telephone pole was a nest, about eight feet across, made of small limbs from trees, grass, and straw. I was surprised to see storks in the nest. I really had not thought about storks being real birds because all I had seen were advertisements of a stork with a baby in a cloth hanging from its beak. I thought it was something a cartoonist or artist had drawn. In a five mile stretch, we saw several huge nests with storks resting in them. It was amazing how this huge nest could sit on top of the pole and not fall off. Only God could make this happen.

One of the main attractions of Malawi, Africa, is Lake Malawi. This lake is about 363 miles long and it measures fifty-five miles across at its widest point. The country of Malawi is about 454 miles long. The lake covers one fifth of the area of Malawi. Its maximum depth is 2,310 feet and it has 1350 species of fish, of which 350 are endemic to Lake Malawi. The lake has more species of fish than any lake in the world. In many areas, the lake is absolutely beautiful. A man from Europe came to live in Malawi and established a business exporting these unusual species of small fish around the world. The winds will blow in southern Malawi, causing the water of the lake, even in the far north, to be extremely rough and dangerous. The waves come against the shore just as they do along the ocean. We serve an amazing God who can place a beautiful lake such as this in a very small African country and cause it to behave much like the ocean.

Our God continually did amazing things throughout the Bible. The children of Israel had once again strayed from the Lord and were living sinful lives. They were worshiping foreign gods. The Philistines were always causing them problems. Samuel instructed them as to what they were to do: "Then Samuel spoke to all the house of Israel, saying, 'If you return to the Lord with all your heart, remove the foreign gods and the Ashtaroth from among you and direct your hearts to the Lord and serve him alone; and he will deliver you from the hand of the Philistines" (1 Samuel 7:3, NASB).

The children of Israel did as Samuel instructed. Samuel then spoke a very important word to them. It would be to our benefit if we would pay strict attention to his words. "Then Samuel said, 'Gather all Israel to Mizpah, and I will pray to the Lord for you'" (1 Samuel 7:5, NASB). They gathered at Mizpah and poured water on the ground before the Lord as a sign of repentance of their sin. They removed their foreign gods and vowed to worship God only. The Philistines heard what was happening at Mizpah and they came against the Israelites. The children of Israel were very fearful of the Philistines. They asked Samuel not to cease calling out to God for them, praying God would rescue them from the hands of the Philistines. Samuel offered a burnt offering of a lamb to the Lord. God heard Samuel's cry and answered his prayer. "Now Samuel was offering up the burnt offering, and the Philistines drew near to battle against Israel. But the Lord thundered with a great thunder on that day against the Philistines and confused them, so that they were routed before Israel" (1 Samuel 7:10, NASB). This was another amazing feat our God performed.

The time came for God to take Elijah to heaven. Elijah told Elisha, who was to replace him, to stay where he was because he must go to Bethel. Elisha refused, saying he would not leave him.

When they got to Bethel, Elijah told Elisha to stay there because he must go to Jericho, but once again Elisha refused. They came to the Jordan River and God did an amazing thing with the cloak of Elijah. "And Elijah took his mantle and folded it together and struck the waters, and they were divided here and there, so that the two of them crossed over on dry ground" (2 Kings 2:8, NASB).

Man could not do this alone. Elisha then made a tough request of Elijah. He asked Elijah to give him a double portion of his spirit.

> And he said, "You have asked a hard thing. Nevertheless, if you see me when I am taken from you, it shall be so for you; but if not, it shall not be so." Then it came about as they were going along and talking, that behold, there appeared a chariot of fire and horses of fire which separated the two of them. And Elijah went up by a whirlwind to heaven. And Elisha saw it and cried out, "My father, my father, the chariots of Israel and its horsemen!" And he saw him no more. Then he took hold of his own clothes and tore them in two pieces.
>
> 2 Kings 2:10–12, (NASB)

Elisha received the double portion of Elijah's spirit because he actually saw Elijah taken. There suddenly appeared a chariot of fire and horses of fire that came between them, and Elijah was taken away in the midst of a whirlwind. Another amazing feat performed by God our Father.

Korah, Dathan, Abiram and On incited a rebellion against Moses. They accused Moses and Aaron of considering themselves better than the other Israelites. The men were of the tribe of Levi that had been chosen to serve in the tabernacle. Moses accused them of wanting to be priests. He instructed them to come to the entrance of the tabernacle the next day with their incense burners with incense on them. The next morning all 250 of their followers appeared.

> Meanwhile, Korah had stirred up the entire community against Moses and Aaron, and they all assembled at the tabernacle entrance. Then the glorious presence of the LORD appeared to the whole community, and the LORD said to Moses and Aaron, "Get away from these people so that I may instantly destroy them."
>
> Numbers 16:19–21 (NLT)

Moses and Aaron pleaded with the Lord not to destroy all these men because of Korah. God instructed them to tell the people to get away from the tents of Korah, Dathan, and Abiram. The people moved away from their tents.

> And Moses said, "By this you will know that the LORD has sent me to do all these things that I have done—for I have not done them on my own. If these men die a natural death, then the LORD has not sent me. But if the LORD performs a miracle and the ground opens up and swallows them and all their belongings, and they go down alive into the grave, then you will know that these men have despised the LORD."
>
> Numbers 16:28–30 (NLT)

The Bible tells us that the earth suddenly split open and the men and their families were swallowed up. They went down alive into the hole and the earth closed over them. The people of Israel fled from that place, afraid of what would happen to them. The other 250 men who came to offer incense with them also died. "Then fire blazed forth from the Lord and burned up the 250 men who were offering incense" (Numbers 16:35, NLT). God performed unbelievable feats to rid the earth of those who had rebelled against him.

What are some other amazing feats God performed in the Bible and why did he use these to demonstrate his power?

What has happened in our world today that should wake America up as to the condition of our country?

Come, Listen, Seek, Call

The title of this devotion contains commands we have continually given our children as they were growing up. I can remember many times saying to my boys, "Come here!" Whether they came or not depended on their selective hearing. They learned very quickly if they did not come, they would be in trouble. How many times have we taken the face of a child in our hands, turning their face to us and said, "Listen to me!" We wanted our child to realize they were to pay strict attention to us. Many times my boys would come to me and say, "Mom, I can't find my coat." I, in turn, would say to them, "Go search (seek) for your coat. It is there if you will just look for it." As our children became teenagers and began driving, how many times did we say, "Call us if you are going to be late" or "Call if you have any trouble." We were saying, "Stay in touch with us." We wanted to know what our children were doing.

Our God uses the same words to give commands to us. He desires to have fellowship with us. God offers free nourishment to believers if we will simply obey his commands. "Is anyone thirsty? Come and drink—even if you have no money! Come, take your choice of wine or milk—it's all free!" (Isaiah 55:1, NLT).

Everyone is welcome to come to God; Jew and Gentile alike. Isaiah makes this very clear throughout his book. God's salvation is for all people. He offers to all of us a drink that satisfies so we will never thirst again. The story of the woman of Samaria is an excellent example. Jesus was traveling to Galilee and he had to go through Samaria. He stopped by the well to rest because the walk had been very long. As he was sitting there, a woman of Samaria came to draw water. Jesus asked her for a drink of water. She questioned him as to why he would ask her, a Samaritan, for a drink since he was a Jew. The Jewish people had nothing to do with the Samaritans.

> Jesus replied, "If you only knew the gift God has for you and who I am, you would ask me, and I would give you living water." "But sir, you don't have a rope or a bucket," she said, "and this is a very deep well. Where would you get this living water?" Jesus replied, "People soon become thirsty again after drinking this water. But the water I give them takes away thirst altogether. It becomes a perpetual spring within them, giving them eternal life."
>
> John 4:10–11, 13–14 (NLT)

The water spoken of here is a picture of the Holy Spirit. Jesus was offering her salvation where the Holy Spirit would come to dwell in her heart. "Now on the last day, the great day of the feast, Jesus stood and cried out, saying, 'If any man is thirsty, let him come to me and drink. He who believes in me, as the Scripture said, 'From his innermost being shall flow rivers of living water'" (John 7:37–38, NASB).

To everyone who comes and believes in him, Jesus offers rivers of living water (Holy Spirit) that will flow from within. Every believer will receive a continual filling of the Holy Spirit if we surrender ourselves to him and accept his blessing.

God's second command was for us to listen to him. "Come to me with your ears wide open. Listen, for the life of your soul is at stake. I am ready to make an everlasting covenant with you. I will give you all the mercies and unfailing love that I promised to David" (Isaiah 55:3, NLT).

God told them to come to him and listen to his Word. The Word of God has the power to draw all men to him. "I assure you, those who listen to my message and believe in God who sent me have eternal life. They will never be condemned for their sins, but they have already passed from death into life" (John 5:24, NLT).

Even though we are believers, Jesus is continually knocking at our heart's door desiring to enter. "Behold, I stand at the door and knock; if anyone hears my voice and opens the door, I will come in to him, and will dine with him, and he with me" (Revelation 3:20, NASB).

We forget to give attention to the Lord because we get so tied up with earning money, having material possessions, or other things in life. When we do this, many times we close the door of our heart to the Lord and his work. We must continually keep the door open to him as we study his Word and pray. He is there to speak to us if we will just listen. He will not enter unless we ask him to come in. He wants to have fellowship with us.

The third command given by God is for us to seek him. "Seek the Lord while he may be found" (Isaiah 55:6a, NASB). It reminds me of the parable of the lost coin in the Book of Luke. The woman had ten silver coins and she lost one. Commentators say the Palestinian women are given ten silver coins when they marry. They had the same sentimental value to them as a wedding ring does to us. She was distressed over losing the one coin and she lit a lamp and began searching for the coin. The Bible says she swept her house carefully, every little nook and cranny, trying to find the coin. She was determined to search for it until she found it. She called her friends together to rejoice with her when she found the coin. When one lost soul repents of their sin and turns to God, the angels in heaven rejoice and so should we. As a Christian, I must continually seek the very presence of the Lord. I am not to allow other things to interfere with my fellowship with the Lord. If I sin, I must come to the Lord and confess my sin so nothing will hinder the working of the Holy Spirit in my life. If I want to know more about the Lord, I will continually seek to find out about him in his Word. The Bible gives me all the information I need about God the Father, God the

Son, and God the Holy Spirit. But, I must have a desire to know more about him and seek him with all my heart. "And you will seek me and find me, when you search for me with all your heart" (Jeremiah 29:13, NASB).

The fourth command God gave to us was for us to call on him: "Call upon him while he is near" (Isaiah 55:6b, NASB). A lost person needs to respond (come) immediately to the Lord when Holy Spirit convicts his heart of the need of forgiveness of sin. There is a time when the invitation will cease, if we do not respond to the stirring of Holy Spirit in our heart. In the first chapter of Proverbs, it talks about wisdom calling out to the people in the streets. Wisdom is pictured as a person who reveals to us the mind of God. He questions those who are called simpletons about how long will they continue being simpleminded. How long will they mock the Lord and fight against the information he is giving them about the Lord?

> Come here and listen to me! I'll pour out the spirit of wisdom upon you and make you wise. I called to you so often, but you didn't come. I reached out to you, but you paid no attention. You ignored my advice and rejected the correction I offered. So I will laugh when you are in trouble! I will mock you when disaster overtakes you—when calamity overcomes you like a storm, when you are engulfed by trouble, and when anguish and distress overwhelm you. I will not answer when they cry for help. Even though they anxiously search for me, they will not find me.
>
> Proverbs 1:23–28 (NLT)

A lost person needs to immediately repent of his sin and turn to God for salvation. The longer you wait to accept Jesus as Savior, the harder it gets. As you become older, it becomes more difficult to completely submit to someone's leadership and control. In the instance of a child of God, the Lord does not go away from us, but sometimes we allow things in our life to take us away from God. Sin entangles the life of a believer and his fellowship with the Lord is broken. Don't hesitate to return to the Lord as soon as you realize this is happening. The longer you wait, the harder it gets.

When you think of your relationship with the Lord, what do the terms come, listen, seek, and call mean?

Questions, Questions, Questions

What is a question? Webster's Dictionary says a question is an interrogative expression often used to test knowledge; an act or instance of asking for information; an inquiry; a request. Many of us look back on our teenage years with great fondness. It was an exciting time in our life as we began to spread our wings and make some decisions on our own. Our parents gradually released this privilege to us as they felt we were mature enough to handle it. Many times when we came home from being with friends, we would be met with what seemed to be a thousand questions. Who were you with? Where have you been? What have you been doing? Why are you late? How much money did you spend? What did you see? How many young people were with you? Whose car were you in? Did you obey the rules? Were you a good example to others? Did you remember who you are and act accordingly? On and on the questions would go. They were concerned about what we did and wanted to know all that happened. All of us who have children, I am sure, have treated our children the same way. We asked every question we could think of to try to determine the thoughts and intents of the hearts of our children.

Jesus got into a boat and went to the other side of the lake to his hometown. "Just then some men brought to him a paralytic lying on a stretcher. Seeing their faith, Jesus told the paralytic, 'Have courage, son, your sins are forgiven'" (Matthew 9:2, HCSB).

Jesus had forgiven the sins of this man. The scribes and Pharisees were always questioning Jesus. They sought to trap him by his answers. The scribes were discussing among themselves Jesus claiming to be God. This would make him guilty of blasphemy. Jesus answered a question with a question of his own.

But perceiving their thoughts, Jesus said, "Why are you thinking evil things in your hearts? For which is easier: to say, 'Your sins are forgiven,' or to say, 'Get up and walk'? But so you may know that the Son of Man has authority on earth to forgive sins"—then he told the paralytic, "Get up, pick up your stretcher, and go home."

(Matthew 9:4–6, HCSB).

By answering with a question, Jesus caused the scribes to consider what he had done and to realize he had power beyond their thinking and understanding. Jesus knew the thoughts and intents of their hearts, so he questioned them as to whether it was easier to forgive a person's sin or to enable a man who had been a paralytic for a long time to get up and walk. Jesus not only forgave the man's sin, but he healed the paralytic right before their eyes. The man got up from his mat and walked home.

Jesus called Matthew to be one of his apostles. "As Jesus went on from there, he saw a man named Matthew sitting at the tax office, and he said to him, 'Follow me!' So he got up and followed him" (Matthew 9:9, HCSB).

Jesus went to his house to eat and many tax collectors and sinners were also guests there. "When the Pharisees saw this, they asked his disciples, 'Why does your teacher eat with tax collectors and sinners?'" (Matthew 9:11, HCSB).

The Pharisees believed you were not to associate with these people. Jesus overheard what they were saying and gave them a direct answer. We need to remember what Jesus said. "But when he heard this, he said, 'Those who are well don't need a doctor, but the sick do. Go and learn what this means: I desire mercy and not sacrifice. For I didn't come to call the righteous, but sinners'" (Matthew 9:12–13, HCSB).

The people who already believed in Jesus did not need him as desperately as the person who was still living a life of sin without the Lord. Jesus's main mission was to lead lost people to believe in him, seek his forgiveness, and follow him. This should also be our mission as children of God.

The children of Israel were continually questioning Moses during their wilderness journey. "So the people grumbled at Moses, saying, 'What shall we drink?'" (Exodus 15:24, NASB). They came to water at Marah, but it was bitter. The Lord showed Moses a tree to put in the water and when he did the water became sweet. Then the people began to grumble again. "And the rabble who were among them had greedy desires; and also the sons of Israel wept again and said, Who will give us meat to eat?" (Numbers 11:4, NASB).

They not only questioned Moses, but when Moses heard them weeping in front of their tents, he became aggravated with them. God also became angry with the people. This time, Moses was the one who asked questions.

> And Moses said to the LORD, "Why are you treating me, your servant, so miserably? What did I do to deserve the burden of a people like this? Are they my children? Am I their father? Is that why you have told me to carry them in my arms—like a nurse carries a baby—to the land you swore to give their ancestors? Where am I supposed to get meat for all these people? They keep complaining and saying, 'Give us meat!'"
>
> (Numbers 11:11–13, NLT).

The Israelites were an obstinate people as they traveled through the wilderness, always complaining and questioning Moses.

Some of the last words of Jesus were in the form of a question. As Jesus hung on the cross, he experienced the terrible pain of the crucifixion. He also sorrowed over the separation from his Father because he had taken upon himself our sin. Sin separates all people from God. Jesus cried out to God from the cross. "And about the ninth hour Jesus cried out with a loud voice, saying '*Eli, Eli, lama sabachthani?*' that is, "My God, my God, why hast thou forsaken me?" (Matthew 27:46, NASB). Jesus's greatest pain was being separated from his Father.

Jesus had told the disciples to stay in Jerusalem until they received the Holy Spirit and then they were to go into all parts of the earth to be his witnesses. As he finished speaking, he was lifted up and a cloud received him.

> And as they were gazing intently into the sky while he was departing, behold, two men in white clothing stood beside them; and they also said, "Men of Galilee, why do you stand looking into the sky? This Jesus, who has been taken up from you into heaven, will come in just the same way as you have watched him go into heaven."
>
> Acts 1:10–11 (NASB)

The angels questioned Jesus's followers why they were gazing into the sky. They explained to the disciples that Jesus would return to earth in the same way he went into heaven. I am sure this raised questions in the minds of the disciples.

Questions seem to be a part of every conversation. People are always asking questions. Why did this happen? Where did it happen? Who was responsible for what happened? What made it happen? When did it happen? They want answers to their questions.

If you were to come face to face with the Lord right now, what question would you ask him?

If the Lord should ask you, "Why should I let you into my heaven?" what would be your answer?

Satan's Enticement

When the boys and I were fishing one day, an interesting thing happened. We had caught several fish and they were on a stringer in the pond. There was a water moccasin swimming around them. All of a sudden I looked down and the water moccasin had one of the fish in its mouth. The snake tried to swallow a catfish and when he got to the two bone-like fins right below the head, they kept the snake from swallowing the fish. The snake could not spit the fish out, so it was really in a predicament. The boys and I contemplated what to do since the water moccasin, cottonmouth common to Oklahoma, is poisonous. We finally got a gun and shot the snake after getting a picture of this amazing sight.

Many times in the Bible the word serpent refers to Satan. Satan likes nothing better than enticing a believer with worldly things and causing them to stumble in their walk with the Lord. We are acquainted with Genesis 3 when the serpent convinced Eve it was okay to eat the fruit forbidden by God. This was the tree of the knowledge of good and evil.

In Genesis 12–14, God told Abram to move from Haran to the land he would show him. He settled in southern Canaan. Lot, Abram's nephew, was with him and there was not enough grazing land to support the livestock of both of them. Their herdsmen began to quarrel amongst themselves. Abram was a fair man, so he gave Lot first choice of the land he wanted.

> And Lot lifted up his eyes and saw all the valley of the Jordan, that it was well watered everywhere—this was before the Lord destroyed Sodom and Gomorrah—like the garden of the Lord, like the land of Egypt as you go to

Zoar. So Lot chose for himself all the valley of the Jordan; and Lot journeyed eastward. Thus they separated from each other. Abram settled in the land of Canaan, while Lot settled in the cities of the valley, and moved his tents as far as Sodom.

Genesis 13:10–12 (NASB)

Lot's choice of Sodom would change his life radically. Apparently, Lot struggled to make right choices in life and did not look beyond the enticement of the rich fertile land of the valley of the Jordan. He did not have the forethought to look ahead to the consequences of his actions. "Now the men of Sodom were wicked exceedingly and sinners against the Lord" (Genesis 13:13, NASB).

The lure of the fertile valley placed Lot in the midst of a sinful people. He was surrounded by every sin imaginable. Lot selfishly chose the most fertile land and did not consider what God desired. When we make decisions without consulting the Lord, we leave an opening for Satan to get a foothold in our life. Making right choices in life is very important.

In a simple situation, such as hunger, Satan can entice us to do wrong. Jacob and Esau were twin brothers. Esau was the older of the two. Esau was a burly looking man with much hair on his body and he was an outdoorsman with a love for hunting. Jacob was a peaceful man who lived in tents. Isaac loved Esau more because of his love for wild game. Rebekah loved Jacob more. While Esau was out hunting, Jacob had cooked a pot of stew. When Esau came home from hunting, he was starving for something to eat.

He said to Jacob, "Quick, let me have some of that red stew! I'm famished!" (That is why he was also called Edom.) Jacob replied, "First sell me your birthright." "Look, I am about to die," Esau said. "What good is the birthright to

278

me?" But Jacob said, "Swear to me first." So he swore an oath to him, selling his birthright to Jacob.

Genesis 25:30–33 (NIV)

Esau's second name or nickname was Edom meaning "red stuff." The name Jacob means "he grasps the heel" or "he deceives." Jacob deceived Esau into giving up his birthright during his time of great hunger. Thinking only of his immediate hunger, Esau did not consider the consequences of his actions. Satan has a way of deceiving us, enticing us to make wrong decisions. Isaac, their father, was old and almost blind. Continuing his deception, Jacob covered his arm with the skin of a goat, took a bowl of his father's favorite food, and went to Isaac to receive the blessing belonging to Esau. Esau became very angry and threatened to kill Jacob when he found out Jacob had received his blessing. Jacob fled for his life. In the Book of Hebrews, Christians are given a warning to beware of allowing immediate satisfaction to lure us into sin. "Make sure that no one is immoral or godless like Esau. He traded his birthright as the oldest for a single meal. And afterward, when he wanted his father's blessing, he was rejected. It was too late for repentance, even though he wept bitter tears" (Hebrews 12:16–17, NLT). Even though we may come in repentance and seeking forgiveness from the Lord, we still must suffer the consequences for the sin we committed.

Solomon was a very wise king and God had blessed him in abundance. "So King Solomon became greater than all the kings of the earth in riches and in wisdom. And all the earth was seeking the presence of Solomon, to hear his wisdom which God had put in his heart" (1 Kings 10:23–24, NASB). Solomon gathered many material possessions for himself. People coming to seek his wisdom brought many gifts of silver, gold, garments, spices, horses, mules, and many other things to him. He had many chariots and horses. Solomon went against what God desired for a king to possess.

Now King Solomon loved many foreign women along with the daughter of Pharaoh: Moabite, Ammonite, Edomite, Sidonian, and Hittite women, from the nations concerning which the LORD had said to the sons of Israel, "You shall not associate with them, neither shall they associate with you, for they will surely turn your heart away after their gods." Solomon held fast to these in love.

1 Kings 11:1–2 (NASB)

Solomon was enticed by Satan and was lured away from God. He allowed his foreign wives to lead him to worship their foreign gods. Even though Solomon was considered the wisest man who ever lived, he still had his weaknesses. He could still be enticed by Satan to sin against God.

The water moccasin was enticed by the catfish hanging on the stringer in the pond. He proceeded to take what he thought was a delicacy. It ultimately brought about his death. Lot, Jacob, Esau, and Solomon were enticed by the things of the world, and it caused them to sin. They did not think beyond their immediate satisfaction as to what would be the consequences of their actions.

When you are tempted to sin, do you look beyond immediate gratification to what the consequences of your actions will be? What is the first thing we should do when this happens?

Read Luke 4:1–13. Jesus had just been baptized by John the Baptist in the wilderness. He was led away by the Spirit of God to be tempted for forty days by the devil. What was the weapon Jesus used against the temptations of Satan? What should you use when you are tempted by Satan to sin?

Jesus knew the Scriptures, so he could use them against the temptations of Satan. Do you know what the Scriptures say? If not, delve deep into the Word of God, so you can be prepared to stand against the temptations of Satan in your life.

Hunger and Thirst

Doyal and I served as International Service Corp missionaries three different times in Malawi, Africa. While there, we worked on the Jacob's Well Project for the Oklahoma Baptist Convention. We would leave home early in the morning and arrive home late in the afternoon. We took enough drinking water with us for the day. We had snacks to eat, but had to be careful not to eat in front of the people. We spent the time teaching and working on the wells. We did not have lunch until we returned to our home late in the afternoon. We would be tired, hungry, and ready for a hot cup of coffee or tea. It reminds me of the following scripture when Jesus spoke to his disciples about the food they had brought him. "Jesus said to them, 'My food is to do the will of him who sent me, and to accomplish his work. Do you not say, 'There are yet four months, and then comes the harvest?' Behold, I say to you, lift up your eyes, and look on the fields, that they are white for harvest'" (John 4:34–35, NASB).

We went to Malawi to do the work God called us to do. Whatever it took, we were willing to do it. Most days, we were physically hungry and thirsty after being gone for long periods of time. We did not have access to food we have at home. However, God sustained us physically by feeding us spiritually.

Throughout the Bible, we are given examples about hungering and thirsting for the Lord. One example is in the Beatitudes. "Blessed are those who hunger and thirst for righteousness, for they shall be satisfied"(Matthew 5:6, NASB).

How do you approach the Word of God? Do you dread getting your Bible out each day to try to read and understand the Scriptures? Before you open his Word, ask God to open your mind and give you understanding. Ask God to open your eyes so you can see those pebbles of wisdom hidden within the Scriptures. You must ask God to open your ears so you can hear as he speaks to you through his Word. Ask God to open your heart and give you a heart of flesh in place of a heart of stone, so you can receive the word he has for you and apply it in your life. The scripture above told us we are blessed when we have a hunger and a thirst to know more about the Lord. Through the writing of my devotional books, God has given me an insatiable desire for his Word. He has stirred in me a hunger and a thirst to know and understand the Bible from Genesis to Revelation. Jeremiah expressed it well when he said, "Thy words were found and I ate them, and thy words became for me a joy and the delight of my heart; for I have been called by thy name, O Lord God of hosts" (Jeremiah 15:16, NASB).

Don't allow anyone or anything to rob you of the joy you gain in life by spending time with the Lord in his Word. Our earthly father and mother want to be with us because we are their children. Don't you think God the Father desires to meet with his children? The main way he spends time with us is when we read his Word. "For he has satisfied the thirsty soul, and the hungry soul he has filled with what is good" (Psalm 107:9, NASB).

We must approach the Word of God with a hunger and a thirst to know him better. We need to seek him with all our heart. God will prepare us to meet the challenges of the workday if we will ask him. The sweet morsels hidden in God's Word are from his heart to all people in the world. "So I opened my mouth, and he fed me the scroll. 'Eat it all,' he said. And when I ate it, it tasted as sweet as honey" (Ezekiel 3:2–3, NLT).

David wanted to experience all God had for him in his daily life. The Book of Psalms offers much encouragement to us as children of God. "O God, you are my God; I earnestly search for you. My soul thirsts for you; my whole body longs for you in this parched and weary land where there is no water" (Psalm 63:1, NLT).

David was in the wilderness of Judah and the land was parched because of lack of water. He also had a longing, a yearning, and a thirst for the Lord to be prevalent in his life. He intentionally searched for the Lord with earnestness. More than anything in the world, he wanted to meet with the Lord. He had seen the Lord's power and he wanted to experience all God had for him. "Your unfailing love is better to me than life itself; how I praise you! I will honor you as long as I live, lifting up my hands to you in prayer. You satisfy me more than the richest of foods. I will praise you with songs of joy" (Psalm 63:3–5, NLT).

David acknowledged God's love for him. He promised to honor the Lord as long as he lived and praised him for all he had done. God brought great satisfaction to him even more than the richest of foods. David went on to say, "I lie awake thinking of you, meditating on you through the night" (Psalm 63:6, NLT). David knew what it was to keep company with the Lord and desired to fellowship with the Lord once again.

What is the greatest desire of your heart concerning the Lord?

What changes do you need to make to be able to meet with the Lord daily?

Learning to Depend On God

At birth, we are totally dependent on our parents to feed, bathe, clothe, and take care of us. When we are young and we begin to learn to do things for ourselves, each day is a time of growth. Through our teenage years there is a certain amount of care we need. We are still dependent on the care of our parents for many things.

As adults, the roles reverse and our parents become dependent on us as they get up in their later years. We then have to care for them in the same way they cared and provided for us from the time of our birth. They are dependent on us for their needs.

God, our Father, desires for us to live our life in total dependence on him. Sometimes people forget where their provision comes from. The Lord had told the Israelites they would be blessed if they were obedient to him. "If you walk in my statutes and keep my commandments so as to carry them out, then I shall give you rains in their season, so that the land will yield its produce and the trees of the field will bear their fruit. I will also walk among you and be your God, and you shall be my people" (Leviticus 26:3–4, 12, NASB).

The Lord went on to tell them what would happen if they were disobedient to his commandments.

> However, if you do not listen to me or obey my commands, and if you break my covenant by rejecting my laws and treating my regulations with contempt, I will punish you. You will suffer from sudden terrors, with wasting diseases, and with burning fevers, causing your eyes to fail and your life to ebb away. You will plant your crops in vain because your enemies will eat them. I will turn against you, and you

will be defeated by all your enemies. They will rule over you, and you will run even when no one is chasing you!

Leviticus 26:14–17 (NLT)

If they did not learn to depend on God, he would turn against them and they would be defeated by their enemies. God constantly had to speak to the children of Israel about their disobedience. Do you think God is speaking to us today about our disobedience? Are we turning a deaf ear to him? What do you think God will do if we continue to be disobedient and fail to depend on his promises?

The army of Israel and Philistia were waging battle across the Ellah Valley. During the time of the Exodus, the Israelites had been afraid to enter the promised land because it was inhabited by giants who were living there. Once again they were faced with a giant as they encountered the nine foot tall giant named Goliath. They ran in fear because they were cowards. They forgot to depend on the Lord who promised to strengthen and uphold them in battle if they would do what he said. Goliath was huge and David was a young boy. The Israelites had looked at Goliath from a human standpoint, but David looked at the giant from God's perspective, knowing God would be with him in battle.

> Then David said to the Philistine, "You come to me with a sword, a spear, and a javelin, but I come to you in the name of the LORD of hosts, the God of the armies of Israel, whom you have taunted. This day the LORD will deliver you up into my hands, and I will strike you down and remove your head from you. And I will give the dead bodies of the army of the Philistines this day to the birds of the sky and the wild beasts of the earth, that all the earth may know that there is a God in Israel, and that all this assembly may know that the LORD does not deliver by sword or by spear; for the battle is the LORD's and he will give you into our hands."

1 Samuel 17:45–47 (NASB)

David was victorious over the giant because he placed his faith and trust in the Lord. David showed his dependence on the Lord.

To depend on God means we will trust in him, rely on him to show us what we are to do. David prayed for victory over his enemies. In his prayer, he emphasized his dependence on the Lord. "Now I know that the Lord saves his anointed; he answers him from his holy heaven with the saving power of his right hand. Some trust in chariots and some in horses, but we trust in the name of the Lord our God" (Psalm 20:6–7, NIV).

This prayer may have been prompted by what took place when David defeated the Syrians. The Ammonite king died and his son Hanun replaced him. Because Hanun's father, Nahash, had been loyal and kind to David, he decided to show his respect to him. He sent ambassadors to him to express his regrets concerning his father's death. Hanun took wrong advice and felt they had come to spy out the city. He treated David's men badly. When David saw what happened and heard Hanun was bringing a host of men against them, David sent Joab with his army to fight. One statement Joab made needs our undivided attention: "Be strong and let us fight bravely for our people and the cities of our God. The Lord will do what is good in his sight" (2 Samuel 10:12, NIV). Joab knew they must fight with all their strength, but the Lord was in control. He knew, as did David, that they were dependent on God for victory. When we learn to depend on God, all things are possible.

Who do you depend on when you encounter challenging situations?

If you are dependent on God, what will be the first thing you will do when trials come?

Repentance

The Bible dictionary defines repentance as a feeling of regret, a changing of the mind, or a turning from sin to God. When our children between the ages of three to five years were told not to pick an item up, they would do it anyway. All of a sudden, when it slipped from their hand, fell to the floor, and broke in many pieces, we would slap their hands or swat them for disobeying. We probably became angry with them. After disobeying us, they would seek our forgiveness. They would come to us and say, "Momma, I am sorry. Please don't be mad at me." They were admitting to us that they had done wrong and did not want us to continue to be upset with them. They were sorry and wanted us to take them in our arms and love on them. When our children came seeking our forgiveness, our anger would leave and our hearts would become soft and receptive to them. Speaking for myself, I would usually take them in my arms and hold them tight. I would tell them I loved them, but they needed to obey me and do as I instructed. I still loved them, but did not love the wrong they had done. I would always forgive them and we would continue the teaching and learning processes of life.

Repentance in the Scripture is turning away from sin and turning to God. "In the twelfth year of Judah's King Ahaz, Hoshea son of Elah became king over Israel in Samaria; [he reigned] nine years. He did what was evil in the Lord's sight, but not like the kings of Israel who preceded him" (2 Kings 17:1–2, HCSB).

After King Shalmaneser attacked and defeated King Hoshea, Israel had to pay heavy taxes to Assyria. King Hoshea decided to conspire with King So of Egypt to try to defeat the Assyrians. This was very foolish and King Hoshea was not doing what God had commanded. The king of Assyria became aware of the conspiracy and that King Hoshea had not paid the taxes due to Assyria for several years. He attacked and invaded the whole land of Samaria, arrested King Hoshea, and put him in prison. Samaria was forced to pay heavy taxes to Assyria. Why did God allow Israel to be defeated by the king of Assyria?

> All this took place because the Israelites had sinned against the LORD their God, who had brought them up out of Egypt from under the power of Pharaoh king of Egypt. They worshiped other gods and followed the practices of the nations the LORD had driven out before them as well as the practices that the kings of Israel had introduced. The Israelites secretly did things against the LORD their God that were not right.
>
> 2 Kings 17:7–9a (NIV)

They did everything imaginable to go against the teaching of the Lord. The Lord sent prophets and seers to tell them to turn from their evil ways and keep God's commandments, but they were a very obstinate people.

> "But they would not listen and were as stiff-necked as their fathers, who did not trust in the Lord their God. They imitated the nations around them although the Lord had ordered them, 'Do not do as they do,' and they did the things the Lord had forbidden them to do."
>
> (2 Kings 17:14, 15b, NIV)

The Lord became very angry with their disobedience and their refusal to repent. He removed them from his presence. At that time, they had no remorse or regret for the wrongs they had committed. The way of sin was more enticing to them.

Some of the children of Israel believed they were being punished for the sins of their ancestors. God spoke to Ezekiel and gave him the message he wanted delivered to the people. The person who commits the sin is the one who will be punished by death. The Lord gave several explanations for Ezekiel to deliver to the Israelites. "But if a wicked man turns away from the wickedness he has committed and does what is just and right, he will save his life" (Ezekiel 18:27, NIV).

If a wicked man turns from the sins he has committed and makes a change in his life, he is repenting of his sins.

> "Therefore, O house of Israel, I will judge you, each one according to his ways, declares the sovereign Lord. Repent! Turn away from all your offenses; then sin will not be your downfall. Rid yourselves of all the offenses you have committed, and get a new heart and a new spirit."
>
> (Ezekiel 18:30–31a, NIV)

I believe the same message is being delivered to our nation today. It is time for us to repent and return to God. "The one who conceals his sins will not prosper, but whoever confesses and renounces them will find mercy" (Proverbs 28:13, HCSB).

David committed adultery with Bathsheba while Uriah, her husband, was on the battlefield. After she returned home, she sent a message to David to inform him she was pregnant. David sent a message to Joab, his commanding officer, to send Uriah to him. David told him to go home and sleep with Bathsheba. Uriah did not feel it was right for him to go home while the other men were on the battlefield, sleeping in tents. After a few days, Uriah still had not slept with Bathsheba. David sent a message to Joab to put Uriah on the front line so he would die. David committed another sin to cover up the first sin. When he knew Uriah was dead, David had Bathsheba brought to him to become his wife.

> So the LORD sent Nathan to David. When he arrived, he said to him: There were two men in a certain city, one rich and the other poor. The rich man had a large number of

sheep and cattle, but the poor man had nothing except one small ewe lamb that he had bought. It lived and grew up with him and his children. It shared his meager food and drank from his cup; it slept in his arms, and it was like a daughter to him. Now a traveler came to the rich man, but the rich man could not bring himself to take one of his own sheep or cattle to prepare for the traveler who had come to him. Instead, he took the poor man's lamb and prepared it for his guest.

2 Samuel 12:1–4 (HCSB)

The story Nathan, the prophet, told David made him very angry with the rich man. He told Nathan this man must die and the rich man must repay the one lamb with four lambs from his flock. Nathan informed David he was the man. God had given him much, but he was not satisfied. He had committed sin by disobeying the command of the Lord. He had Uriah murdered with the Ammonite's sword. Nathan told him the sword would never leave his house. The Lord went on to say he would bring disaster on David and his family. The Lord would not put up with David's disobedience.

"David responded to Nathan, 'I have sinned against the Lord.' Then Nathan replied to David, 'The Lord has taken away your sin; you will not die. However, because you treated the Lord with such contempt in this matter, the son born to you will die.'"

(2 Samuel 12:13–14, HCSB)

David repented of his sin and the Lord forgave him, but he still suffered the consequences of his sin.

How often must we confess our sins to the Lord?

What does 1 John 1:9 say will happen when we confess our sins to the Lord?

Faith that Moves Mountains

Mary Slessor was from a very poor family in Scotland. Her father was a drunkard, but her mother was a godly woman. Mary worked in factories for twelve hours a day, six days a week from the time she was eleven years old. Even though her circumstances were hard, she served the Lord faithfully. The life she lived growing up prepared her for the hardships she would experience when she went as a missionary to Africa at the age of twenty-nine. Mary had a burning desire to take the gospel and civilization to the "dark continent" of Africa. In September of 1876, Mary boarded a steamer and headed down the Calabar River on the slave coast of Africa. This was an area known as White Man's Grave and only fools entered this area without great fear. Much of the area was unexplored and inhabited by killer elephants and lions, swarms of insects, witch doctors, and cannibals. To enter this land meant death for most people. Mary arrived at the mission station in Duke Town. The missionaries at the station had been successful in helping to stop some of the worst heathen practices through their school, hospital, orphanage, and chapel. Mary Slessor began working at the mission station and she would go out to the coastal and river villages. As soon as she learned the language, she began to travel alone without a translator. She was warned by others that this was very dangerous, but she found she could get to know the people in a more personal way if she went alone. She could identify with Paul when he said, "I have been on frequent journeys, in dangers from rivers, dangers from robbers, dangers from my countrymen, dangers from the Gentiles, dangers in the city, dangers in the wilderness, dangers on the sea, dangers among false brethren" (2 Corinthians 11:26, NASB).

The further Mary went from the mission station, the greater

needs she found. She shared with the natives the good news of Jesus Christ. Mary taught them not to worship the skulls of dead men, not to be afraid of evil spirits, and not to kill the wives of men who died. She taught the women how to cook healthy food and how to keep their children clean. One night as Mary slept on the dirt floor of a hut in a coastal village, she prayed, "Oh Lord, I thank thee that I can bring these people thy Word. But Lord, there are other villages back in the jungle where no white man has gone. They need Jesus, too. Help me reach them!" She went home to Scotland for a short furlough, and when she returned she was thrilled to find she was on her own at an outstation. She had a real burden for the Okoyong tribe who had never heard the gospel. She wondered how she could bring the love of Christ to these people who valued only three things: guns for power, chains to keep slaves, and liquor to dull their minds. Mary was willing to place complete faith in the Lord to show her how to win these savage people to him.

> The Spirit of the LORD is upon me, because he anointed me to preach the gospel to the poor. He has sent me to proclaim release to the captives, and recovery of sight to the blind, to set free those who are downtrodden, to proclaim the favorable year of the LORD.
>
> Luke 4:18–19 (NASB)

This Scripture could have been Mary Slessor's motto as she shared the Gospel with people. In June of 1888, Mary quietly announced she would go up river alone and find a place to settle. Others warned her she might be killed. The further she went up river, the more fearful the natives became who were paddling her canoe. They wanted to turn back, but the Lord was with the group and they arrived safely. The Lord went ahead of her and prepared the heart of the chief to receive her. She was the first outsider to ever be allowed to live in their village. The only things these people respected were vengeance and cruelty. To a people who did not know love, Mary brought the love of Christ. They referred to her as "White Ma." Many of the Okoyong people came to know Jesus, and civilization was brought more quickly to this village than to other villages.

I believe Mary's slogan must have been, "I can do all things through him who strengthens me" (Philippians 4:13, NASB). God began to stir within Mary's heart the need to go even deeper into the jungle. The converts among the Okoyong protested her going for they felt those people would kill her. But her call was, "Onward! I dare not turn back."

> "I will lift up my eyes to the mountains; from whence shall my help come? My help comes from the Lord, who made heaven and earth. The Lord will protect you from all evil; he will keep your soul. The Lord will guard your going out and your coming in from this time forth and forever."
>
> (Psalm 121:1–2, 7–8, NASB)

She went to the area of the Azo people, a dreaded cannibal tribe. At first they did not pay much attention to what Mary was teaching, but within time, many of the Azo people came to know Jesus. In just one town there were two hundred converts. She did all she could do in the time she had left. She walked the paths until she was old and feeble. Some in Scotland even sent a cart so she could travel from village to village. They urged her to return to Scotland. She had wanted to do so, but the desire of her heart was to continue sharing Jesus with the many who did not know him. She prayed God would give her strength and as the strength came, she worked faster and harder.

> "So everywhere we go, we tell everyone about Christ. We warn them and teach them with all the wisdom God has given us, for we want to present them to God, perfect in

their relationship to Christ. I work very hard at this, as I depend on Christ's mighty power that works within me."

(Colossians 1:28–29, NLT)

Two years later, in January 1915, the Lord took Mary home to be with him. Her body was taken back to Duke Town and she was buried on the hillside by the mission station. She literally gave her life to share with many unreached people groups the message of salvation. I think the words of Paul could have been engraved on the headstone of Mary Slessor: "I have fought a good fight, I have finished the race, and I have remained faithful" (2 Timothy 4:7, NLT).

Mary Slessor gave her all to the cause of Christ. God, the Creator of the universe, has called every believer to be on mission with him. "You did not choose me, but I chose you, and appointed you, that you should go and bear fruit, and that your fruit should remain, that whatever you ask of the Father in my name, he may give to you" (John 15:16, NASB).

We may not go to the "dark continent" of Africa, as it was referred to years ago, but we are chosen by God to go wherever he leads. It may simply be to our next door neighbor. We have a responsibility as a believer and are held accountable by God to share the good news of Jesus with people in all parts of the world. God will empower us to do the work he calls us to do.

What is God calling you to do? Are you willing to go wherever he wants to send you? Do you have a real burden about people of all nations hearing the Gospel?

Doubt: No Faith

All of us have prayed for someone's needs, but as we prayed, doubt was prevalent in our heart and mind. We lacked confidence in the Lord to answer our prayer. I know I have certainly been guilty of this in the past, particularly as I was struggling to grow spiritually. God has proven over and over in my life how he hears and answers my prayers. I had to get past the doubting stage and place my complete faith and trust in the Lord. When our youngest son was struggling, having become entangled in the ways of the world, I prayed fervently for the Lord to bring him back to him. I prayed God would do whatever it took to get his attention. God answered my prayer. Today he serves the Lord in his church. I remember when Mother was struggling to stay alive, her system was shutting down, and I prayed God would relieve her suffering. I released her to God to do whatever was needed. Very soon my mom entered the gates of heaven where there was no more suffering. I think of times we have been preparing to go on a mission trip overseas, and we were not sure where the money would come from to pay for our travel. We prayed fervently about this, and God provided through the sale of a piece of our land or a church bond reaching maturity. I prayed God would open doors of opportunity for me to share him with others through speaking, leading seminars, and different ministry projects. It is amazing what God has done. God is not just concerned about the big things in our life, but also the many tasks we perform throughout the day. The past couple of weeks, I have been printing many copies of a Bible study in a bag God led me to create. This is done on cardstock and each sheet contains four copies. I was wasting so much cardstock because the machine would not pull it through as it should. It finally dawned on me that I needed to pray with faith about what I was doing, asking God to help the machine to work correctly. It was amazing how the machine began performing as it should and the mistakes were fewer. We must pray with confidence without any doubting. "Therefore I say to you, all things for which you pray and ask, believe that you have received them, and they shall be granted you" (Mark 11:24, NASB).

Jesus had spent the day teaching and healing the crippled and sick. As evening came, he told the disciples they were going to go to the other side of the Sea of Galilee. They got in the boat together and as they were making their way across the sea there was a great storm. "And behold, there arose a great storm in the sea, so that the boat was covered with the waves; but he himself was asleep. And they came to him, and awoke him, saying, 'Save us, Lord; we are perishing!'" (Matthew 8:24–25, NASB).

I don't know about you, but when I am abruptly awakened from deep sleep, I am not in a very pleasant mood. I wonder how Jesus felt when they woke him up. Do you think he was a little upset with the disciples for waking him and for the doubt he heard in their voices? And he said to them, "'Why are you timid, you men of little faith?' Then he arose, and rebuked the winds and the sea; and it became perfectly calm" (Matthew 8:26, NASB).

I can imagine the disciples' bewilderment as they observed what happened. Right before their eyes, the waves quieted and the water became calm. I am sure what Jesus said cut to the inner core of their hearts when he emphasized they had doubted, showing they possessed little faith. How do you think Jesus feels when we doubt that he can bring peace to our lives in the midst of a storm?

Many people live a life of doubt, never thinking positively about how God desires to bless them. What would have happened to blind Bartimaeus if he had doubted Jesus's ability to heal him?

Then they came to Jericho. As Jesus and his disciples, together with a large crowd, were leaving the city, a blind man, Bartimaeus (that is, the Son of Timaeus), was sitting by the roadside begging. When he heard that it was Jesus of Nazareth, he began to shout, "Jesus, Son of David, have mercy on me!" Jesus stopped and said, "Call him." So they called to the blind man, "Cheer up! On your feet! He's calling you."

Mark 10:46–49 (NIV)

Possibly, Bartimaeus recognized Jesus as the Messiah. He had faith in Jesus's power to heal him. Even though the people around him tried to quiet him, he was persistent because he wanted to be able to see. Jesus had the disciples bring Bartimaeus to him. "'What do you want me to do for you?' Jesus asked him. The blind man said, 'Rabbi, I want to see.' 'Go,' said Jesus, 'Your faith has healed you.' Immediately he received his sight and followed Jesus along the road" (Mark 10:51–52, NIV). Bartimaeus believed in Jesus's healing power. Because he had faith and did not doubt, Jesus healed him.

Many times we doubt because we do not see things from God's perspective. We have failed to ask the Lord to give us wisdom to understand what is happening around us. James spoke to this thought: "If any of you lacks wisdom, he should ask God, who gives generously to all without finding fault, and it will be given to him. But when he asks, he must believe and not doubt, because he who doubts is like a wave of the sea, blown and tossed by the wind" (James 1:5–6, NIV).

James compared doubting to one who is being tossed hither and thither by the strong winds. We have been on a lake when strong winds came causing the waves to become large and toss us to and fro. It was a frightening experience. We had to trust, not doubt, the Lord's capability to get us to safety. God will provide whatever we need if we ask in faith without doubting.

Jesus fed the 5,000 men, plus women and children, with five loaves of bread and two fish. He was weary after a day of teaching and performing this great miracle. He went up on the mountain to be alone and pray to his Father. Evening was approaching and the disciples were in their boat as Jesus had instructed them and were headed to the other side of the lake. The wind was strong and the waves came with great force. All of a sudden, they looked up and saw someone coming toward them walking on the water. They were very afraid and thought it was a ghost. Jesus spoke to them, telling them not to be afraid, it was him.

> And Peter answered Him and said, "LORD, if it is you, command me to come to you on the water." And he said, "Come!" And Peter got out of the boat, and walked on the water and came toward Jesus. But seeing the wind, he became afraid, and beginning to sink, he cried out, saying, "LORD save me!" And immediately Jesus stretched out his hand and took hold of him, and said to him, "O you of little faith, why did you doubt?"
>
> Matthew 14:28–31 (NASB)

Do you think the Lord feels the same way about us when we waver in unbelief concerning whether he will do as he has promised? The Scripture very clearly tells us that God does not break a promise. "Praise the Lord who has given rest to his people Israel, just as he promised. Not one word has failed of all the wonderful promises he gave through his servant Moses" (1 Kings 8:56, NLT).

The Scripture tells us what we must do in order to live our life trusting God to fulfill His promises.

> But you, dear friends, must continue to build your lives on the foundation of your holy faith. And continue to pray as you are directed by the Holy Spirit. Live in such a way that God's love can bless you as you wait for the eternal life that our LORD Jesus Christ in his mercy is going to give you.
>
> Jude 20–21 (NLT)

NEVER THE SAME AGAIN

When Jesus Christ comes again, our salvation will be completed. In the meantime, we are to continually build a stronger foundation on the Lord Jesus Christ. May our motto be, "On Christ the solid rock I stand."

Blessed by God

Many thoughts run through my mind when I think about God's abundant blessings. I was blessed by being born to Christian parents who taught me about the Lord. The blessing was mine when I came to know the Lord at eight years of age. God blessed me as a teenager by opening doors of opportunity to serve him. One of those blessings was interpreting for deaf people in our churches. He blessed me when he sent me to Camp Nunny Cha Ha; our Girls in Action camp for Oklahoma Baptist. There I met a missionary to the deaf from California and decided to go to California Baptist College in Riverside, California. I had the opportunity to work with and teach children from the school for the deaf and deaf adults at one of our churches there. I married my first husband when I had one semester of college left, but continued in school and graduated at the end of the semester. God blessed me with two healthy boys. Even though my first husband died when they were young, God's blessing continued to be on my life. God blessed me with my present husband, Doyal. God's abundant blessings have been mine through experiencing the ups and downs of life. Even through those tough times, God's blessings have continued to flow into my life as I have learned to be more dependent on him. Blessings beyond number have been ours as we have served the Lord in missions in Brazil, Russia, Estonia, and Malawi. God amazingly blessed me through a special friend, Cecilia, who suggested I consider writing about my life experiences in the form of devotional books. She encouraged me to pray concerning this matter and offered to assist me by editing what I wrote. God's abundant blessings have been mine as he has led me through his Word, leading me to dig deeper and deeper to come to know him better. He has blessed me by opening many doors of opportunity for me to share Jesus with people in many different places. I am blessed by God's very presence in my life, his everlasting, never-ending and unconditional love for me. He promises he will equip me to do all he purposes for my life. I look with expectation to the future and what God has in store for me. The prayer of my heart is found in the following scripture:

> I pray that from his glorious, unlimited resources he will give you mighty inner strength through his Holy Spirit. And I pray that Christ will be more and more at home in your hearts as you trust in him. May your roots go down deep into the soil of God's marvelous love. And may you have the power to understand, as all God's people should, how wide, how long, how high, and how deep his love really is. May you experience the love of Christ, though it is so great you will never fully understand it. Then you will be filled with the fullness of life and power that comes from God.
>
> Ephesians 3:16–19 (NLT)

Jabez is a man in the Bible who was mentioned only in 1 Chronicles. He is known for his prayer to the Lord seeking his blessing.

> Jabez was more honorable than his brothers. His mother had named him Jabez, saying, "I gave birth to him in pain." Jabez cried out to the God of Israel, "Oh, that you would bless me and enlarge my territory! Let your hand be with me, and keep me from harm so that I will be free from pain." And God granted his request.
>
> 1 Chronicles 4:9–10 (NIV)

His mother remembered the time of his birth because of the pain she had to endure. A mother can reflect on these times, yet she can rejoice because of the joy the child has brought into her life. The name Jabez would remind him to love and honor his mother who experienced great pain to bring him into the world. The son who caused her the most pain brought the most joy into her life. Apparently, Jabez spent time alone with the Lord. He prayed, not to the gods of the Gentiles, but to the God of Israel, the living and true God. He knew God alone could answer his prayer. Jabez asked God for his blessing. Jabez wanted God's blessing and was willing to do whatever was needed to receive his blessing.

Jabez asked the Lord to increase his territory, his boundaries or his coastline. He entreated God to take whatever he received by work or war and to increase it so he might prosper. As children of God, we need to pray, asking God to enlarge our hearts and increase our desire to have more of him, less of ourselves. We need to have a love for others based on his great love for us.

> And may the LORD make your love grow and overflow to each other and to everyone else, just as our love overflows toward you. As a result, Christ will make your hearts strong, blameless, and holy when you stand before God our Father on that day when our LORD Jesus comes with all those who belong to him.
>
> 1 Thessalonians 3:12–13 (NLT)

As children of God, we need to ask God to increase our boundaries and give us a larger area of witness for him.

Jabez prayed for God's hand to be on him in all he did. The children of Israel were a stubborn people and Moses prayed God would go with them because he knew he needed God's help. "And he said, 'My presence shall go with you, and I will give you rest.' Then he said to him, 'If thy presence does not go with us, do not lead us from here'" (Exodus 33:14–15, NASB). Jabez desired the presence of the Lord in what he did, as did Moses as he led the children of Israel to the promised land.

Jabez prayed God would protect him from trouble and pain.

David continually cried out to God for help. "Oh, the joys of those who are kind to the poor. The Lord rescues them in times of trouble. The Lord protects them and keeps them alive. He gives them prosperity and rescues them from their enemies" (Psalm 41:1–2, NLT).

God heard the prayer of Jabez and God granted him his requests. Jabez was specific about what he asked God to do for him. God truly blessed Jabez because of his seeking him through prayer.

Nehemiah heard about the walls of Jerusalem being destroyed all around the city and the gates burned. "Now it came about when I heard these words, I sat down and wept and mourned for days; and I was fasting and praying before the God of heaven" (Nehemiah 1:4, NASB). Nehemiah came to the Lord in confession for himself and all the sons of Israel. He reminded the Lord of what he had said to Moses about scattering the people to many lands if they continued to be unfaithful to him. Nehemiah quoted to God the promise he had made to Moses. "But if you return to me and keep my commandments and do them, though those of you who have been scattered were in the most remote part of the heavens, I will gather them from there and will bring them to the place where I have chosen to cause my name to dwell" (Nehemiah 1:9, NASB).

Nehemiah was the cupbearer to the king. He asked the Lord to go with him as he went to the king asking him to grant his return to Jerusalem to rebuild the wall. When Nehemiah approached the king, he allowed him to return to Jerusalem. Nehemiah had prayed and fasted before the Lord and the Lord had been attentive to his cry. God blessed Nehemiah because of his faithfulness to him.

Not only did Nehemiah ask the king's permission to go to Jerusalem, but he presented the king with other requests.

I also said to the king, "If it please Your Majesty, give me letters to the governors of the province west of the Euphrates

River, instructing them to let me travel safely through their territories on my way to Judah. And please send a letter to Asaph, the manager of the king's forest, instructing him to give me timber. I will need it to make beams for the gates of the temple fortress, for the city walls, and for a house for myself." And the king granted these requests, because the gracious hand of God was on me.

Nehemiah 2:7–8 (NLT)

Nehemiah was asking the king to increase his territory, to give him freedom to move about, and to obtain materials for the job. God blessed him by granting his requests.

Jabez, David, Moses, and Nehemiah were specific in their prayers to the Lord. God blessed them by hearing their prayers and meeting their needs.

Why do we need to be specific when we pray to God?

What are some ways God has blessed you because you came to him in prayer seeking his blessing?

The Amazing Creative Plan of Almighty God

Last spring, while working in my flower bed there were two beautiful butterflies flying around the shrubs and flowers. The prettiest butterfly was blue and black with a delicate touch of white and orange. It was interesting to watch them go from one plant to the other. I understand when they drink the nectar from a flower some grains of pollen cling to their body, but then, some of that pollen will drop onto the next flower it visits.

Think about how this amazingly, beautiful butterfly developed. In my research concerning the process of the egg becoming a butterfly, I found the following facts. First, the egg turns into a caterpillar. A caterpillar has many legs and is a strange-looking creature. It continually eats all kinds of leaves and other foods until it is full grown. When it gets to this point, it turns into a pupa. It gradually weaves, from the liquid in its body, a hard shell around itself. Inside the hard shell an amazing process takes place. Many different kinds of butterflies will spend all winter in this stage and some only six to eight months. After it reaches complete maturity, it begins to separate itself from this hard shell and emerges, feet first. The butterfly hangs from the shell with its wings down for about thirty minutes. During this time, it is pumping air and blood through its body and wings. It is then ready to fly. Doyal and I visited the Butterfly Palace in Branson, Missouri and it was amazing to see the many different kinds of butterflies God created.

God begins an amazing creation in the womb of a woman when the egg produced by the woman comes in contact with and is fertilized by the sperm from a man. Within the womb a baby begins to develop. The first births recorded in the Bible were those of Cain and Abel.

> "Now the man had relations with his wife Eve, and she conceived and gave birth to Cain, and she said, 'I have gotten a manchild with the help of the Lord. 'And again, she gave birth to his brother Abel. And Abel was a keeper of flocks, but Cain was a tiller of the ground"
>
> (Genesis 4:1–2, NASB).

This was in God's plan for husband and wife to have union with one another, so they would populate the earth.

Consider what took place here as Cain and Abel were formed in the womb of Eve.

> For you created my inmost being; you knit me together in my mother's womb. I praise you because I am fearfully and wonderfully made; your works are wonderful, I know that full well. My frame was not hidden from you when I was made in the secret place. When I was woven together in the depths of the earth, your eyes saw my unformed body. All the days ordained for me were written in your book before one of them came to be.
>
> Psalm 139:13–16 (NIV)

God knew from the conception of Cain and Abel in Eve's womb what would take place in their lives. He knew Abel would be a shepherd and Cain a farmer. At harvest time when they brought their offering to the Lord, Cain brought the produce of his land, but Abel brought several of the choicest lambs from his flock. God accepted Abel's offering, but rejected Cain and his offering. Cain became very angry. God knew what would happen next. "Later Cain suggested to his brother, Abel, 'Let's go out into the fields.' And while they were there, Cain attacked and killed his brother"

(Genesis 4:8, NLT). God knows all about us and what will happen in our entire life.

God had a special plan for Jochebed and Amram when they united with one another and a baby was conceived in her womb. Jochebed gave birth to a baby whose name was Moses. "During this time, a man and woman from the tribe of Levi got married. The woman became pregnant and gave birth to a son. She saw what a beautiful baby he was and kept him hidden for three months" (Exodus 2:1–2, NLT).

The reason Jochebed had to hide their son was because Pharaoh had given the Hebrew midwives the order to kill every male Hebrew baby. They were to allow only the girl babies to live. Pharaoh was afraid the Israelites were too many and would be a threat to the Egyptians. Jochebed hid him as long as she could, but as he grew she could no longer hide him. "But when she could no longer hide him, she got a little basket made of papyrus reeds and waterproofed it with tar and pitch. She put the baby in the basket and laid it among the reeds along the edge of the Nile River" (Exodus 2:3, NLT).

Miriam, his sister, watched at a distance to see what would happen to Moses. One of Pharaoh's daughters came down to bathe in the Nile. She saw the little basket floating in the water. When she opened the basket and saw the baby, she realized it must be one of the Hebrew children. Miriam approached the princess and asked her if she wanted her to find a Hebrew woman to nurse the baby for her. God's provision in life is all we need, if we will wait for God to work. This is proven by what happened next in the story. "'Yes, go,' she answered. And the girl went and got the baby's mother. Pharaoh's daughter said to her, 'Take this baby and nurse him for me, and I will pay you.' So the woman took the baby and nursed him" (Exodus 2:8–9, NIV).

From the time of Moses' conception in his mother's womb, God knew all of this would take place. God had a special plan for Moses.

After he was older and weaned from his mother, she took him to the palace. It was then the princess named him Moses and said, "Because I drew him out of the water." In later years, Moses had to flee the palace because he had killed an Egyptian who was beating an Israelite slave. When Pharaoh heard about it, he gave orders to find Moses and kill him. This was all in God's plan. Moses then encountered the Lord at the burning bush and he revealed his plan for Moses' life.

> There the angel of the LORD appeared to him in flames of fire from within a bush. Moses saw that though the bush was on fire it did not burn up. So Moses thought, "I will go over and see this strange sight—why the bush does not burn up." When the LORD saw that he had gone over to look, God called to him from within the bush, "Moses! Moses!" And Moses said, "Here I am."
>
> Exodus 3:2–4 (NIV)

Moses had to come aside, be still before the Lord and then God spoke to him. God selected Moses to lead the children of Israel out of slavery in Egypt to the promised land.

God knew from the time the egg was laid, that the egg would become a caterpillar, the caterpillar would become a pupa, and the pupa would become a beautiful butterfly. God knew Cain would be the firstborn of Eve and that Cain would kill Abel. God knew Moses would not be killed at birth and would be put in a position to lead the children of Israel out of Egypt towards the promised land. What God planned was always accomplished.

Looking back, can you see where God's hand was on your life, preparing you for what you are doing today? What is the special purpose God has for your life?

What does Jeremiah 29:11–12 say about God's plan for your life?

Listen to Me!

I can remember my parents telling me many times to listen to them as they spoke to me. I did the same thing with my boys in their preschool, elementary, junior high, and high school years. Sometimes I have felt like saying the same thing to them in their adult years, but it is not my place to do so. I can remember when Anthony was two or three years old and if his dad or I were not listening to him, he would come and take our face in his little hands and say, "Mama, listen to me," or "Daddy, listen to me." He wanted our utmost attention. I recall as a school teacher asking my class when they were chattering instead of listening, "Class, are you listening to me?" I wanted them to pay attention to what I had to say.

How many times in your life do you think God has wanted to take your face in his hands and say, "Are you listening to what I am saying to you?" I imagine each of us could count numerous times in our life when we have attempted to do something in our own strength, not listening to what God was telling us to do. More than likely, we have fallen flat on our faces in our attempts and have had to turn to God and say, "Lord, please help me. I cannot do this alone."

In the story of Elijah at Mount Carmel, he prayed to God.

At the customary time for offering the evening sacrifice, Elijah the prophet walked up to the altar and prayed, "O LORD, God of Abraham, Isaac, and Jacob, prove today that you are God in Israel and that I am your servant. Prove that I have done all this at your command. O LORD, answer me! Answer me so these people will know that you, O LORD, are God and that you have brought them back to yourself." Immediately the fire of the LORD flashed down from heaven and burned up the young bull, the wood, the stones, and the dust. It even licked up all the water in the ditch! And when the people saw it, they fell on their faces and cried out, "The LORD is God! The LORD is God!"

1 Kings 18:36–39 (NLT)

Afterwards, Elijah had all the prophets of Baal taken to the Kishon brook and killed. Elijah again prayed to God on Mount Carmel asking for God to send rain. After this took place, Jezebel, the wife of King Ahab, threatened to kill Elijah.

In fear for his life, Elijah fled to Beersheba. "Then he went on alone into the desert, traveling all day. He sat down under a solitary broom tree and prayed that he might die. 'I have had enough, Lord,' he said. 'Take my life, for I am no better than my ancestors'" (1 Kings 19:4, NLT).

Elijah had two great spiritual experiences with the Lord's help when he defeated the prophets of Baal and God had sent rain from heaven. He was now very tired and going through a time of depression. He cried out to God. I can imagine how God felt after he had shown himself so faithful to Elijah and now Elijah was running in fear. I just know God wanted to say to Elijah, "Have you been listening to me and recognized my power in the things I have done? You are not alone, I, the Lord God, am standing with you." God sent an angel to speak to Elijah and tell him to get up and eat for he had a long journey ahead of him. He traveled forty days and forty nights to Mount Horeb. He stayed in a cave on the mountain overnight. God came to Elijah and called out to him.

There he came to a cave, where he spent the night. But the LORD said to him, "What are you doing here, Elijah?" Elijah replied, "I have zealously served the LORD God Almighty. But the people of Israel have broken their covenant with you, torn down your altars, and killed every one of your prophets. I alone am left, and now they are trying to kill me, too."

1 Kings 19:9–10 (NLT)

The Lord told him to go out on the mountain and stand before him. God sent a terrible, mighty windstorm that tore the rocks apart. The Lord then caused an earthquake, and then he brought fire, but God was not in any of these. The Bible then specifically tells us how Elijah heard the voice of God. "And after the fire there was the sound of a gentle whisper. When Elijah heard it he wrapped his face in his cloak and went out and stood at the entrance of the cave" (1 Kings 19:12b–13a, NLT).

So often, we think God only speaks through the miraculous deeds he performs, through loud thunder or a mighty bolt of lightning. We expect him to do something exciting to get our attention. Elijah knew the gentle whisper was the voice of God. We may miss hearing the voice of God if we fail to sit quietly and humbly before the Lord. God speaks in many different ways, but we must be listening to him.

I love the book by Jim Cymbala, *Fresh Wind, Fresh Fire*. Jim Cymbala came to pastor a small black church in New Jersey when he was in his late twenties. He worked another job in the business world as he tried to pastor this church in a very difficult part of Newark. His father-in-law who was a preacher called him one night and asked him for a favor. He wanted Jim to go to the multiracial Brooklyn Tabernacle and preach four Sunday nights in a row. This was a church his father-in-law supervised. The church had hit an all time low and had major problems. The worship style was almost chaotic with no sense of direction. After Jim's second Sunday there, the pastor told him he planned to resign and asked Jim to please tell his father-in-law. There was a question as to whether the church should even stay open. His father-in-law was not ready to give up.

He asked Jim if he would consider serving as pastor of both churches for the time being and see if he could help to turn the church around. Jim went along with the plan, racing back and forth across New York each Sunday. The church usually did not collect enough money to pay its mortgage payment, so there were many anxious moments. The church paid him no salary, making it difficult to live. The schedule going back and forth between the two churches was very tiring and life was discouraging. They were ministering to an array of people: homosexuals, druggies, alcoholics, street people, prostitutes, and many others. It was extremely difficult. One night he stood behind the pulpit so depressed he could not preach. He told them he could not preach in that atmosphere, so he asked his wife to come play music on the piano and he called the people to come to the altar and pray. "Hear my prayer, O Lord; listen to my cry for mercy" (Psalm 86:6, NIV).

Carol played the song, "I Need Thee, Oh, I Need Thee," and all of a sudden a young usher came running down the aisle and threw himself on the altar and began to pray. As Jim went to him, he admitted he had been taking money from the offering plate and sought forgiveness for what he had done. This was one reason the church had trouble meeting their mortgage payments. At one of Jim Cymbala's greatest times of weakness, there had been a spiritual breakthrough, but there were many struggles still ahead.

Jim became sick with a lingering cough. He was becoming very weak and his in-laws suggested he come to Florida for some rest and warm sunshine. He went, but had to leave his wife and little girl behind. One day he went out on a fishing boat. The other tourists were talking about the fish they hoped to catch, but Jim moved to the other end of the boat. He knew they needed a great outpouring of the Holy Spirit on their church. He began to pray and he said,

"Lord, I have no idea how to be a successful pastor," I prayed softly out there on the water. "I haven't been trained. All I know is that Carol

and I are working in the middle of New York City, with people dying on every side, overdosing from heroin, consumed by materialism, and all the rest. If the gospel is so powerful…" He said he could not ever finish his prayer and he began to shed tears. Jim said that very quietly, but yet forcefully, in words heard not with his ears but deep within his spirit, he sensed God speaking: "If you and your wife will lead my people to pray and call upon my name, you will never lack for something fresh to preach. I will supply all the money that's needed, both for the church and for your family, and you will never have a building large enough to contain the crowds I will send in response."

God restored his confidence in him. "I sought the Lord, and he answered me; he delivered me from all my fears" (Psalm 34:4, NIV). He heard God speak through the avenue of prayer. Through the years, great revival has come when God's people have fervently prayed. Jim returned to his church with fresh wind and fresh fire for the Lord.

When do you sit quietly before the Lord and listen for him to speak to you through his Word, through prayer, through a stirring of your spirit and soul, through someone else or through a circumstance in your life?

Have you responded when God spoke to you about a specific matter? What does it mean to you to totally surrender yourself to the will of God? Are you willing to surrender to him without reservation?

From Dusk to Dawn

I drove to Oklahoma City to attend the Evangelism Conference. I left early in the morning so I could arrive in time to gather my senses after the long drive. I wanted be ready to listen for what God had for me in the messages I would hear. The first couple of hours I drove, it was dark and a light mist was falling, which made it rather difficult to see at times. It seems my night vision is not very good anymore, but with God's help, I made it fine. It was such a relief, though, when the sun began to rise on the horizon. It brought to my mind what happens in those hours between dusk and dawn.

One day, we were traveling to an animal park with a missionary couple that had been in Malawi for many years. As we passed a pond, the missionaries said that it was very important to be careful traveling late in the evening. The crocodiles would come out of the water and lay across the road during the night. Of course, if you did not see them, it could cause great damage to your vehicle if you hit one because they are quite large. In the animal parks, they warn people to stay in their cabins after dark because hippos come out of the water to graze on the grass around the huts. They are very dangerous. In certain areas, poisonous snakes begin to move at night. Here at home if you go into the woods at night you hear all kinds of sounds. If you are alone in the woods in the dark of night, it is quite frightening. Many animals prowl in the dark.

This reminds me of the story of Jesus in the garden of Gethsemane. After eating the Last Supper with his disciples, Jesus said there would be one who would betray him. He leaned over to Judas Iscariot and told him to do quickly what it was he was going to do. Jesus and the disciples then went to the garden of Gethsemane. Jesus took Peter, James, and John with him farther into the garden and told them to keep watch for him. Jesus knew what was going to happen to him and his soul was very grieved.

> And he withdrew from them about a stone's throw, and he knelt down and began to pray, saying "Father, if thou art willing, remove this cup from me; yet not my will, but thine be done." Now an angel from heaven appeared to him, strengthening him. And being in agony he was praying very fervently; and his sweat became like drops of blood, falling down upon the ground.
>
> Luke 22:41–44 (NASB)

When Jesus returned to the three disciples, he found them asleep because they were weary and in great sorrow. While Jesus was speaking to them, Judas came with a multitude of people following him. He came and placed a kiss on Jesus's face identifying him as the one they were to arrest.

> And Jesus said to the chief priests and officers of the temple and elders who had come against him, "Have you come out with swords and clubs as against a robber? While I was with you daily in the temple, you did not lay hands on me; but this hour and the power of darkness are yours."
>
> Luke 22:52–53 (NASB)

Why do you think they did not approach Jesus during the day when he was in the temple? Do you think they were afraid the crowd of people might come against them if they did? It seems people who do much of the evil in the world prowl around at night.

The Bible tells us about the ten plagues God sent on the land of Egypt. The ninth plague was darkness over the land.

> Then the LORD said to Moses, "Stretch out your hand toward the sky so that darkness will spread over Egypt—

darkness that can be felt." So Moses stretched out his hand toward the sky, and total darkness covered all Egypt for three days. No one could see anyone else or leave his place for three days. Yet all the Israelites had light in the places where they lived.

Exodus 10:21–23 (NIV)

It was so dark around the Egyptians that they could not move or see one another. The darkness was not pierced by the light around them. We have been in several different caverns in Arkansas and Missouri. When they turned off the lights, we could not see our hand in front of our face. It was pitch black in the caves. Darkness can be very frightening in certain situations.

The Lord spoke to Abram promising to give him a son to inherit all he had given him. The Lord showed him all the stars in the sky and told him his descendants would be as numerous as the stars. "And Abram believed the Lord, and the Lord declared him righteous because of his faith" (Genesis 15:6, NLT).

The Lord then reminded Abram that he had brought him from Ur of the Chaldees to give him the land where he was as an inheritance. Abram wanted God's assurance this would be so. A great darkness surrounded Abram and he had a vision of intense fear and horror while in a deep sleep.

Now when the sun was going down, a deep sleep fell upon Abram; and behold, terror and great darkness fell upon him. And God said to Abram, "Know for certain that your descendants will be strangers in a land that is not theirs, where they will be enslaved and oppressed four hundred years. But I will also judge the nation whom they will serve; and afterward they will come out with many possessions."

Genesis 15:12–14 (NASB)

The Israelites would be taken into captivity by the Babylonians and be their slaves for four hundred years. It would be a time of great darkness in their lives. They would see the light in the midst of darkness when God rescued them from Babylon.

Jesus told the disciples he would be with them only for a short time.

> Then Jesus told them, "You are going to have the light just a little while longer. Walk while you have the light, before darkness overtakes you. The man who walks in the dark does not know where he is going. Put your trust in the light while you have it, so that you may become sons of light." When he had finished speaking, Jesus left and hid himself from them.
>
> John 12:35–36 (NIV)

The light referred to Jesus who would leave them in the near future. He instructed his disciples to walk in the light, take advantage of his presence while he was with them so they would be a light to others. He wanted their lives to shine in places of darkness where the gospel message had not been preached. They were to go and preach the gospel so others could hear the truth and come to know Jesus. When people are saved, they come out of darkness, a life of sin, to walk in the light of Jesus Christ.

When I was driving to the city in the early morning darkness, as the dawn began to break, it was as if a curtain was lifted and things looked much brighter. Even though I could not yet see the sun rising in the east, I knew it was there because of the light around me. Very soon, I looked in my rear view mirror and saw the sun coming up over the mountains.

Different creatures, some very dangerous, choose to roam in the darkness of night. People who live a life of sin often choose to commit their bad deeds in the darkness. Judas Iscariot was a supreme example. The children of Israel continued to live a life of disobedience to the Lord so God allowed them to be taken into captivity to the Babylonians for four hundred years. It was a dark time of slavery and oppression. People who walk in sin are in darkness, but Jesus Christ, the light of the world, offers to free them from the bondage of sin. Jesus Christ will bring joy into the hearts of those who believe in him as Savior and Lord.

Think about a time when you experienced darkness in your life, a time when it seemed there was no hope, but God rescued you from that darkness. Thank God for his display of grace in the midst of darkness.

What does your life show to others today, light or dark? Do they see the light of Jesus Christ in you?

The Sweet Morsels of the Word of God

A Bible study I taught by T.W. Hunt, *The Mind of Christ*, made a great impact on my life. T. W. Hunt had a master of music and doctor of philosophy degree from North Texas State University. He was a professor of church music at Southwestern Baptist Theological Seminary. He authored many different books on prayer, music, and discipleship. He realized he was in bondage to sin as he strived to obtain the virtues of Christ taught in James and Galatians. He thought he could obtain these virtues by study and hard work, but discovered this was not so. He had allowed humanism to control his thinking. He said he struggled to "let go and let God have his way." In order to overcome this deep-seated humanism present in his life, he vowed to the Lord not to read anything but the Bible until God signaled him that he had begun to think in biblical terms. He read nothing but the Bible for four years. He memorized Scripture passages, chapters, and books of the Bible. He studied continually, praying constantly, and found there was a change taking place in the deepest parts of his mind. He literally saturated his mind with God's Word. He began to understand the deeper meaning of the virtues of Jesus he was to demonstrate in his life. Through his study, he realized a real cleansing was taking place in his heart and mind. He said the Word of God reaches into the deepest recesses of our mind and impacts all areas of our mind, including our subconscious, when it is stored there.

Do you truly know the Word of God? Would you know enough Scripture to sustain you and help you to stand strong in your faith if your Bible was taken from you? T. W. Hunt had God's Word stored in his heart and he had come to understand it because of many hours of reading and meditating on the Scripture. What about you?

The Bible was divinely inspired by God. Every word written in the Bible was given to men so they could write it down. "The words of the Lord are pure words; as silver tried in a furnace on the earth, refined seven times" (Psalm 12:6, NASB).

God's Word is without error and was given for us to have a standard to live by. "All Scripture is inspired by God and profitable for teaching, for reproof, for correction, for training in righteousness; that the man of God may be adequate, equipped for every good work" (2 Timothy, 3:16–17, NASB).

It is God's word to us, even though it was put on paper by ordinary men called by God for this purpose. "But know this first of all, that no prophecy of Scripture is a matter of one's own interpretation, for no prophecy was ever made by an act of human will, but men moved by the Holy Spirit spoke from God" (2 Peter 1:20–21, NASB).

Men such as Moses, Ezekiel, Jeremiah, Amos, Matthew, Mark, Luke, John, and Paul did not write their own words and thoughts, but those of God. The writers I have mentioned and others were directed by Holy Spirit what to write. Here is an example. Many of the disciples were in Jerusalem in the upper room where they were staying. The disciples and some women were devoting themselves to earnest prayer. Peter stood and spoke to the group: "Brethren, the Scripture had to be fulfilled, which the Holy Spirit foretold by the mouth of David concerning Judas, who became a guide to those who arrested Jesus" (Acts 1:16, NASB).

We can go back in the Old Testament to the Book of Psalm and find where David spoke these words. "Even my close friend, in whom I trusted, who ate my bread, has lifted up his heel against me" (Psalm 41:9, NASB).

In the Gospel of John, we find these words: "I do not speak of all of you. I know the ones I have chosen; but it is that the Scripture may be fulfilled, 'He who eats my bread has lifted up his heel against me'" (John 13:18, NASB).

Jesus knew Judas Iscariot would be the one to betray him. It was the fulfillment of what had been written by David in the Old Testament. The Bible was divinely inspired by God and the Holy Spirit moved in the hearts and minds of men to write down what God spoke.

The Bible is food for the soul of man. Great satisfaction is found in partaking of God's Word. Moses was giving instruction to the children of Israel before they went in to possess the promised land. "And he humbled you and let you be hungry, and fed you with manna which you did not know, nor did your fathers know, that he might make you understand that man does not live by bread alone, but man lives by everything that proceeds out of the mouth of the Lord" (Deuteronomy 8:3, NASB).

Job answered the questions and thoughts of Eliphaz the Timanite, who told him to receive the instruction from the mouth of the Lord and to hide his words in his heart. "Your word I have laid up in my heart, that I might not sin against you" (Psalm 119:11, AMP). In Job's answer, he said these words, "I have not gone back from the commandment of his lips; I have esteemed and treasured the words of his mouth more than my necessary food" (Job 23:12, AMP).

Could this be said of you and me? Do we have such a hunger, for the Word of God that it satisfies our hunger more than the actual food we eat to sustain our physical bodies? While writing these devotional books, a verse in the Book of Jeremiah has become the cry of my heart: "Your words were found, and I ate them; and your words were to me a joy and the rejoicing of my heart, for I am called by your name, O Lord God of hosts" (Jeremiah 15:16, AMP). God's Word has become my most precious possession and I want to hide it deeply in my mind and heart so I can have it to use when I need it.

The Word of God is to be written in our hearts. "And these words, which I am commanding you today, shall be on your heart; and you shall teach them diligently to your sons and shall talk of them when you sit in your house and when you walk by the way and when you lie down and when you rise up" (Deuteronomy 6:6–7, NASB).

To me, this is telling us to always keep God's Word before us, in our view, in our hearts, and in our minds. It is to be of uppermost importance to us. "Let the word of Christ richly dwell within you, with all wisdom teaching and admonishing one another with psalms and hymns and spiritual songs, singing with thankfulness in your hearts to God" (Colossians 3:16, NASB).

May God's Word permeate every part of our being and may we use it as we pray and sing praises to the Lord. I believe God loves to hear his Word spoken back to him because it means we are claiming what his Word says.

How much time do you spend reading and meditating on the Word of God? How much Scripture have you taken to memory so you have it on the tip of your tongue to use in witnessing to other people?

What is a verse you have memorized from the Word of God and have claimed it as your life verse? Why did you choose this verse?

Encountering the Unrelenting
Trials of Life

Many times we encounter unrelenting trials in life because of the wrong decisions we make. We do not think through the things we do, and in the future they come back to haunt us. This is very true concerning financial decisions we make in life. I don't think our children are any different than other people's children in the way they overextend themselves financially with unneeded purchases. When the bills begin to come in, they feel like they are in the midst of a blazing fire with no way to get out. I know, as adults, we have been in the same predicament because of wrong decisions. Either we, or possibly our husband or wife, have made wrong decisions, but we must stand good for the financial agreements made. It seems we have more money going out than we have coming in. As a child of God, we must strive to do what we have said we will do. "Give to everyone what you owe them: Pay your taxes and import duties, and give respect and honor to all to whom it is due" (Romans 13:7, NLT).

In all honesty, we must pay to others what we have agreed to pay. When we find ourselves in the midst of these unrelenting trials, as a last resort, we turn to God. What do you think would have happened if we had turned to God before we made the decision to buy a new car, a new boat, or a new house? Do you think God would have advised us to wait until we were financially stable? Do you think God might have questioned whether our faith was in the material possessions we desired or if we were willing to faithfully wait for him to provide the things we actually needed? Even though we make wrong decisions in life and we have to endure the trials, he promises to be with us. "When you pass through the waters, I will be with you; and through the rivers, they will not overflow you. When you walk through the fire, you will not be scorched, nor will the flame burn you" (Isaiah 43:2, NASB). God will help us walk through the trials. We have to endure the consequences for wrong decisions, but he will protect us as we walk through the fire or the overflowing streams.

The story of the widow's oil is a good illustration of this point.

> One day the widow of one of Elisha's fellow prophets came to Elisha and cried out to him, "My husband who served you is dead, and you know how he feared the LORD. But now a creditor has come, threatening to take my two sons as slaves." "What can I do to help you?" Elisha asked. "Tell me, what do you have in the house?" "Nothing at all, except a flask of olive oil," she replied.
>
> 2 Kings 4:1–2 (NLT)

This woman was concerned for the safety of her children and all she had to offer the creditors or anyone was one flask of oil. One could see why she would be so disturbed at this moment. God gave Elisha great wisdom in what he did next.

> And Elisha said, "Borrow as many empty jars as you can from your friends and neighbors. Then go into your house with your sons and shut the door behind you. Pour olive oil from your flask into the jars, setting the jars aside as they are filled." So she did as she was told. Her sons brought many jars to her, and she filled one after another. Soon every container was full to the brim! "Bring me another jar," she said to one of her sons. "There aren't any more!" he told her. And then the olive oil stopped flowing.
>
> 2 Kings 4:3–6 (NLT)

I can just imagine what this widow thought when Elisha told her to fill all these jars from this one little flask of oil. I can see the bewildered look on her face. Our response probably would have been, "You have got to be kidding me!" But in obedience to what Elisha told her to do, she began to fill the jars. She ran out of jars before her flask was empty. The situation appeared absolutely hopeless, but God proved his provision. Elisha instructed her as to what she was to do. "When she told the man of God what had happened, he said to her, 'Now sell the olive oil and pay your debts, and there will be enough money left over to support you and your sons'" (2 Kings 4:7, NLT). What would happen if we trusted God, as this widow did, to help us find solutions to our problems?

Susanna Wesley was the mother of John and Charles Wesley, whose ministries impacted the world with the Gospel of Jesus Christ. She was the youngest of twenty-five children born into the family of Dr. Samuel Annesley, a well-known, powerful minister. When Susanna was nineteen years old, she married Samuel Wesley. She did not anticipate the hard life she would have in the future. He was a newly ordained minister in the Church of England and had to wait for appointments to preach where they would pay him sufficient salary. By the time he was made rector at Epworth, they were deep in debt. To make matters worse, Samuel was a very poor money manager. His investments seemed to sink them deeper in debt. He even left the family for a year, and Susanna had to care for the children alone. If it had not been for generous friends willing to help, it would have proven disastrous. Susanna stayed faithful to the Lord and cared for her family in the best way possible. Because of limited resources, she started a school for her children. She was more concerned with the saving of their souls, so academics did not take priority over her instruction in the Bible. She taught her children well, disciplined them when needed, and set aside a time for an appointment with each child each week. The bond of faith and love she established with each child helped all to endure the hardships they faced. Her faith sustained her through tough times. God promises the same for you and me. "Look at the proud! They trust in themselves, and their lives are crooked; but the righteous will live by their faith" (Habakkuk 2:4, NLT). Susanna Wesley endured trying circumstances, but through her faith she was at peace with the Lord.

Paul experienced different visions and revelations from the Lord. He told about things that had happened in his life, but then said he was not boasting in these things. Paul said the only thing for him to boast about were his weaknesses.

> And because of the surpassing greatness of the revelations, for this reason, to keep me from exalting myself, there was given me a thorn in the flesh, a messenger of Satan to buffet me—to keep me from exalting myself! Concerning this I entreated the LORD three times that it might depart from me. And he has said to me, "My grace is sufficient for you, for power is perfected in weakness." Most gladly, therefore, I will rather boast about my weaknesses, that the power of Christ may dwell in me.
>
> 2 Corinthians 12:7–9 (NASB)

Paul knew the source of his power. He realized there was nothing he could do on his own. We do not know exactly what the thorn in the flesh was, but we do know it kept Paul humble about the things God accomplished through him. What he accomplished in life was by the mercy, grace, and power of Almighty God.

When we sink ourselves deep in debt and see no way out, our only hope is for God to have mercy on us and give us wisdom to know how to overcome our financial problem. The widow listened to Elisha and did what he said in spite of the fact it appeared impossible. Susanna Wesley placed her faith in the Lord when her husband did not manage their money well and left her and the children destitute for one year. Paul could have boasted about the things God had allowed him to see, but God gave him a thorn in the flesh to prevent his boasting. He knew what he accomplished was only because of God's power working through him.

When you encounter the unrelenting trials of life, do you turn to the Lord or to other things?

Think about a trial you have come through in your life. What was the outcome and did it change you in any way?

Who was faithful to you and provided what you needed during this time?

Wanted Dead or Alive

All of us have watched old western movies and have seen the posters on the board outside the jail or the stack on the marshal's desk. When a suspicious character rides into town, the marshal goes quickly to his office to see if he is wanted. We have watched *Gunsmoke* and seen Marshal Dillon riding off into the areas surrounding Dodge City in search of a man wanted for murder or robbery. It is always exciting to watch how Festus helps him to track this wanted man. He is wanted for a crime and he can be brought in dead or alive. They just want to be sure he is found and justice is served. Most of the time, Marshal Dillon tries to bring him in alive so he can stand trial.

In thinking about this illustration in relation to the Lord, we could turn this title around to read; "Wanted: Those Who Are Dead in Sin. Reward: Everlasting Life." When a person comes to accept Jesus as Savior and Lord, his sin is forgiven. He passes from being dead in sin into the assurance of life everlasting. "I tell you the truth, whoever hears my word and believes him who sent me has eternal life and will not be condemned; he has crossed over from death to life" (John 5:24, NIV).

One night Paul had a vision of a man who asked him to come to Macedonia and help them. He believed the vision was from God and proceeded to Macedonia. He took Timothy along with him to Philippi, the chief city of the district of Macedonia. The Sabbath day came, and they sought the place of worship.

> On the Sabbath we went outside the city gate to the river, where we expected to find a place of prayer. We sat down and began to speak to the women who had gathered there. One

of those listening was a woman named Lydia, a dealer in purple cloth from the city of Thyatira, who was a worshiper of God. The LORD opened her heart to respond to Paul's message. When she and the members of her household were baptized, she invited us to her home. "If you consider me a believer in the LORD," she said, "come and stay at my house." And she persuaded us.

Acts 16:13–15 (NIV)

Lydia had accepted Jesus as Savior and desired to learn more from Paul and Timothy. I believe God immediately put a hunger in Lydia's heart to know more about him. She wanted Paul and Timothy there to teach her what she wanted to know about the Lord. Lydia was a good business woman and was well thought of in the community where she lived. She was known for weaving beautiful purple cloth. The dye she used to produce this beautiful cloth came from a shellfish found along the seashore. The juice of the shell fish is white while in the veins, but when extracted and exposed to the sun, it is transformed into the most brilliant purples and crimsons. According to different writers, the first church in Philippi met within the walls of Lydia's home. Lydia was dead in her trespasses and sins, but when she met Jesus she received life everlasting.

Think with me about the parable of the marriage feast.

The kingdom of heaven can be illustrated by the story of a king who prepared a great wedding feast for his son. Many guests were invited, and when the banquet was ready, he sent his servants to notify everyone that it was time to come. But they all refused! So he sent other servants to tell them, 'The feast has been prepared, and choice meats have been cooked. Everything is ready. Hurry!' But the guests he had invited ignored them and went about their business, one to his farm, another to his store. Others seized his messengers and treated them shamefully, even killing some of them.

Matthew 22:2–6 (NLT)

Like the guests, some have experienced the nudging of the Holy Spirit on their hearts to make a decision, but they have ignored it and refused to come to Jesus. The Lord's abundance of rich blessings and food for a hungry soul has been made available to them. Yet, they have refused to listen and continue to be dead in sin. There is no hope for them unless they turn to the Lord.

The king became so angry with those who refused to come that he sent his servants out to the street corners to invite everyone they saw.

So the servants brought in everyone they could find, good and bad alike, and the banquet hall was filled with guests. But when the king came in to meet the guests, he noticed a man who wasn't wearing the proper clothes for a wedding. "Friend," he asked, "how is it that you are here without wedding clothes?" And the man had no reply. Then the king said to his aides, "Bind him hand and foot and throw him out into the outer darkness, where there is weeping and gnashing of teeth." For many are called, but few are chosen.

Matthew 22:10–14 (NLT)

According to one commentator, this man really did not want to be at the feast, so he had refused to put on the proper clothing. When the Holy Spirit stirs within a person the need for salvation, he offers to clothe him in righteousness. One must be in right standing with God to enter the kingdom of heaven. This man was thrown into outer darkness because he was not a child of God. He was still dead in his trespasses and sins. He had not read the sign: Wanted: Those Who Are Dead in Sin. Reward: Everlasting Life

It is a choice each person must make to accept Jesus as Savior and be assured of everlasting life or continue to walk the path of sin. There is hope for the one who follows Jesus as Lord and Savior. "In the same way, count yourselves dead to sin but alive to God in Christ Jesus" (Romans 6:11, NIV).

Praise God! When we die to our old way of life and accept Jesus as Savior, we can live in unbroken fellowship with him. All our sins were nailed to the cross when Jesus was crucified. He paid the price for all our sin. Our reward for accepting Jesus as Savior is eternal life.

When you see the poster "Wanted Dead or Alive," what do you think?

What is the condition of your life? Are you dead in your sin or are you alive in Christ Jesus?

Angels of Mercy

Doyal and I traveled to Fort Smith, Arkansas, for me to have a medical procedure done. It is so reassuring to a person facing this sort of thing to be surrounded by compassionate people who want to do all they can to make you comfortable. The lab technicians, the nurses, the anesthesiologist, and the doctor did their very best to make me feel at ease. The people at Cooper Clinic have a love and compassion for people that you do not find in some medical offices and hospitals today. They wanted me to know and understand everything they were planning to do and even those things they might need to do if something out of the ordinary was found. There was no doubt they were very concerned about my physical condition and my mental well-being. I had prayed for God's guidance and protection in all I did yesterday and firmly believe he worked through these medical personnel to make me feel at ease. I had entrusted the whole situation to the Lord and he was faithful. "For you have made the Lord, my refuge, even the Most High, your dwelling place. For he will give his angels charge concerning you, to guard you in all your ways" (Psalm 91:9, 11, NASB). We are to seek the Lord's guidance and protection in all we do. When we make God our refuge, he will send his angels to protect us.

Jesus showed compassion towards all people.

> And Jesus was going about all the cities and the villages, teaching in their synagogues, and proclaiming the gospel of the kingdom, and healing every kind of disease and every kind of sickness. And seeing the multitudes, he felt compassion for them because they were distressed and downcast like sheep without a shepherd.
>
> Matthew 9:35–36 (NASB)

As Jesus healed all those brought to him, he was giving evidence of the truth of his teaching. Jesus compared these people to sheep who wander around like they are lost without a shepherd. We must share with others how God has helped us through different situations in life, whether the healing of an illness, our salvation, or delivering us from some type of danger. People must go share love and compassion to those who are lost and help lead them to the Lord. Jesus showed compassion in every aspect of a person's life.

Ezekiel compared Israel to lost sheep:

And they were scattered for lack of a shepherd, and they became food for every beast of the field and were scattered. My flock wandered through all the mountains and on every high hill, and my flock was scattered over all the surface of the earth; and there was no one to search or seek for them.

Ezekiel 34:5–6 (NASB)

The children of Israel were scattered all over the earth. God spoke through Ezekiel concerning those who claimed to be shepherds of his people, but they were not ministering to them. They were more concerned about themselves than they were the people. The sheep Ezekiel was talking about were the children of Israel who had been taken into captivity by the Babylonians. Because these leaders had failed in shepherding the flock, Ezekiel spoke of the one God the Father would send. God promised to send the true Shepherd, the Messiah, to come and care for his people. When Jesus came to earth, he showed compassion and mercy to all people. He was concerned about the needs of the people and he ministered to them. " …That the Lord is full of compassion and is merciful" (James 5:11b, NASB).

Jesus traveled throughout Galilee preaching in the synagogues, driving out demons, and healing the sick. "A man with leprosy came to him and begged him on his knees, 'If you are willing, you can make me clean.' Filled with compassion, Jesus reached out his hand

and touched the man. 'I am willing,' he said. 'Be clean!' Immediately the leprosy left him and he was cured" (Mark 1:40–42, NIV).

Whenever Jesus saw a person in need, he stopped to help. He showed them mercy and healed them because of their faith in him. Jesus healed blind Bartimaeus, the woman with the blood hemorrhage, the man possessed by demons that the disciples could not heal, the Syrophoenician woman's demon-possessed daughter, the Centurion's paralyzed servant that was at his home many miles away, and many more.

The story of the Good Samaritan is a great example of one who showed compassion to another. There was a man traveling from Jerusalem to Jericho, and on the way he was attacked and beaten severely by robbers. A priest saw the injured man, but passed by on the opposite side of the road. A Levite came by, but he also passed by. "But a certain Samaritan, who was on a journey, came upon him; and when he saw him, he felt compassion, and came to him, and bandaged up his wounds, pouring oil and wine on them; and he put him on his own beast, and brought him to an inn and took care of him" (Luke 10: 33–34, NASB). The Samaritan man, who was not well thought of by the Jews, went out of his way to help the injured man. He imitated Jesus Christ in his actions.

When Paul and other prisoners were being sent to Rome for trial, they were on a large ship with other people. A strong wind came, and the waters became very rough. It hindered the ship's progress. The wind had blown strongly for over fourteen days. The captain of the ship tried to make it to shore, but struck a reef where two seas met. They ran the vessel aground and the ship stuck fast. The stern of the ship was repeatedly smashed by the strong waves and began to break apart. When daylight came, they could see where they were. "Once safely on shore, we found out that the island was called Malta. The islanders showed us unusual kindness. They built a fire and welcomed us all because it was raining and cold" (Acts 28:1–2, NIV).

Not only did the natives show kindness toward all on board the ship, but the main official of the island, Publius, fed them for three days. Paul, even though a prisoner on the ship, showed compassion toward the father of Publius. "His father was sick in bed, suffering from fever and dysentery. Paul went in to see him and after prayer, placed his hands on him and healed him" (Acts 28:8, NIV). God's compassion for all people is shown by the things we do in his name.

All of those I came in contact with at Cooper Clinic showed compassion and mercy towards me in preparation and performance of the medical procedure. Jesus showed love and compassion for all who were ill, crippled, and possessed of demons. Ezekiel cared about the Israelites. He listened to God and delivered the messages God gave him. He spoke of how the coming Messiah would meet the needs of the people. The man from Samaria showed mercy to the man beaten by robbers. The people of Malta showed compassion on Paul, the other prisoners, and people on the ship. Paul, in turn, showed mercy on the chief official's father by healing him. God desires for us to show love and compassion to all people.

Think of a time in your life when you needed help in some way and God sent an angel of mercy to show compassion toward you. Thank God for his provision.

How did you feel when you were the recipient of mercy and compassion?

Technology Versus God's Purpose

For years, many of us existed without computers, cell phones, answering machines, and satellite TV. There are times these things can bring considerable anxiety in the life of a person sixty years of age or above. Yesterday morning, I wrote a devotional using my computer. I went to copy it and it disappeared. I searched for it with my limited knowledge of computers. It was to no avail. I sat in front of my computer very frustrated with technology. This was not the first time this happened. Webster's Dictionary gives this definition of technology: "A manner of accomplishing a task using technical methods or knowledge." If this was so, why could I not find my devotion that suddenly disappeared? As I write, I type what God shows me at that time. It is difficult for me to recall all I have written when suddenly it is gone. By God's grace, I remembered I had copied what I had finished before breakfast to read to my husband. I was so relieved that I had at least two-thirds of my devotional. All I needed to do was to complete the last one-third of the writing. I don't think I suffer anxiety in any way like I do when something malfunctions on the new technical equipment of today. I know it is due to my limited ability because all our children and grandchildren have no problem with new technology. Think about the ministry of Jesus and how burdened down he would have been to carry all this "technological stuff" with him. We get so entangled in modern technology that our attention is taken away from the real purpose God has for us.

Joshua was reviewing with the children of Israel how their ancestors had chosen to serve gods other than the one true God. He reminded them about God calling Abraham to go to the land of Canaan and sending Moses and Aaron to lead them out of slavery in Egypt. He recalled many other things for them and then talked to them about their purpose in life.

> Now, therefore, fear the LORD and serve him in sincerity and truth; and put away the gods which your fathers served beyond the River and in Egypt, and serve the LORD. And if it is disagreeable in your sight to serve the LORD, choose for yourselves today whom you will serve: whether the gods which your fathers served which were beyond the river, or the gods of the Amorites in whose land you are living; but as for me and my house, we will serve the LORD.
>
> Joshua 24:14–15 (NASB)

Joshua let his allegiance be known. He stood secure in his belief in the only true God and had a reverential fear of him. Everyone who lived in his house would worship God.

We are to continually seek the Lord and strive to learn more about him. "Do not be anxious then, saying, 'What shall we eat?' or 'With what shall we clothe ourselves?' But seek first his kingdom and his righteousness; and all these things shall be added to you" (Matthew 6:31, 33, NASB).

Why do we question God's ability to care for us when he cares for everything else he created? We get so caught up in the things of this world and having material possessions that we forget God's instruction to put him first in our life. He will take care of all we need. We are to turn to God first when we need help and not to some person or method. He knows our every need and abides with us to meet our need. We need to saturate our hearts and minds with what God desires for our life, not our own selfish desires. We are to imitate God in the way we live. "Therefore be imitators of God, as beloved children; and walk in love, just as Christ also loved you, and gave himself up for us, an offering and a sacrifice to God as a fragrant aroma" (Ephesians 5:1–2, NASB).

How does your life imitate the life of Jesus Christ? Do others see him in you in the things you say and do? When we have an intimate relationship with the Lord, he takes care of every need we have. Sometimes we allow all this technological stuff to get in the way of sitting quietly, listening intently for the still small voice of the Lord to speak to us.

We are to seek to do the will of God. "Jesus said to them, 'My food is to do the will of him who sent me, and to accomplish his work" (John 4:34, NASB). This should be the intent of a believer. Jesus often forgot about physical hunger because he was so intent on doing the will of God, accomplishing his purpose. Do you have the same type of desire to accomplish God's will for your life?

Right before Jesus was betrayed and arrested, he prayed to his Father.

> Father, the time has come. Glorify your Son so he can give glory back to you. For you have given him authority over everyone in all the earth. He gives eternal life to each one you have given him. And this is the way to have eternal life—to know you, the only true God, and Jesus Christ, the one you sent to earth. I brought glory to you here on earth by doing everything you told me to do. And now, Father bring me into the glory we shared before the world began.
>
> John 17:1b–5 (NLT)

Jesus knew he was getting ready to fulfill the purpose God sent him to earth to accomplish. He knew he had shared the good news of Jesus Christ with all people. He had glorified the Father here on earth and he was asking the Father to return him to the glory they had shared before his coming to earth.

Paul did not know what would happen in his life from one day to the next. He did his best to do the will of God.

And now I am going to Jerusalem, drawn there irresistibly by the Holy Spirit, not knowing what awaits me, except that the Holy Spirit has told me in city after city that jail and suffering lie ahead. But my life is worth nothing unless I use it for doing the work assigned me by the LORD Jesus—the work of telling others the good news about God's wonderful kindness and love.

Acts 20:22–24 (NLT)

Paul realized by himself he was nothing, but with God he could accomplish great things. God sent him to share Jesus Christ with all people. He was determined, even though it might mean being beaten or thrown into prison, to accomplish the purpose God had for him.

No, dear brothers and sisters, I am still not all I should be, but I am focusing all my energies on this one thing: Forgetting the past and looking forward to what lies ahead, I strain to reach the end of the race and receive the prize for which God, through Christ Jesus, is calling us up to heaven.

Philippians 3:13–14 (NLT)

Technology is great as long as we do not allow it to interfere with our serving the LORD and accomplishing his purpose for our life. Sometimes it helps us acquire information and do our work more quickly. We should never allow technology to replace sitting down with the Bible in hand, reading and meditating on God's Word and asking him to show us his will.

Where do you find God's purpose for your life?

In what ways do you attempt to achieve God's purpose? Do you believe God is pleased with your efforts?

Learning to Lean

Our pastor has been preaching about the relationship between a husband and wife. Doyal and I both had been married before our marriage in 1979. Each of our mates had died quite suddenly. I had been a widow for one and a half years and Doyal a widower for six months when we married after a courtship of six weeks. Our first few years together were really a time of getting to know one another, plus we had children at home. Since our children left home, God has led us to serve him in overseas missions. We have stayed four and five months three different times in Malawi, Africa. Malawi is about four hundred fifty miles in length and we traveled up and down the country. We would move every few weeks to a different area to help them learn how to dig water wells by hand. Being in a foreign country and traveling together continually caused us to be more dependent on one another. Our love and respect for one another grew. Many times, we were the only Caucasian people in the midst of a sea of Malawians. We learned to watch out for one another and to be aware of all that was going on around us. I had my driver's license in Malawi, but only drove a few times. The laws were different, the steering wheel was on the opposite side of the car, and we drove on the opposite side of the road. Also, I did not know where everything was, so I did not go places by myself. I learned to be more submissive and depend on Doyal. Now, this was quite an adjustment for a woman who had been a schoolteacher, a widow alone with two young boys, and also the manager of our rental hardware store where I made most of the decisions. Truly, I was very independent. "Wives be subject to your own husbands, as to the Lord" (Ephesians 5:22, NASB).

During these times abroad, God worked in each of our lives to show us he had brought us together for a very special purpose. We were to complement one another and help the other to grow in the Lord and learn his purpose for our life together. First of all, we were to depend on him, and secondly, we were to depend on one another. There were times we had some frightening experiences, but knowing God was there for us gave us the assurance of his protection. I also knew my husband was there to protect me and he would not allow anything bad to happen to me if he could prevent it. We definitely grew in our love and respect for one another as we were learning to lean on each other. Doyal would have gone very hungry if I had not been there to cook for him because there were very few places, if any, where a person could go to get food. He would have really struggled to cook for himself and to care for his personal needs in these situations. We did not have the comforts we possess here in the United States. Through these experiences, we learned to use our God-given talents. We learned the special skills God had for each of us and how he intended for man and woman to meet the needs of their mate. "Husbands, love your wives, just as Christ also loved the church and gave himself up for her" (Ephesians 5:25, NASB). Doyal loves the Lord, but I firmly believe God helped him to have the type of love for me Christ had for the church. I know, beyond the shadow of a doubt, Doyal would have given his life for me, if necessary.

Before Doyal leaves for work, we have a time of prayer together. We believe this has strengthened our relationship and love for one another. The work I do for our concrete construction company is performed from our home, so I no longer have to go out to work. After we eat our breakfast, we usually read the devotional I have written for the day or one from my previous books. We read the list of our missionaries serving at home and abroad from Open Windows. When we pray together, each of us prays for one another. It has become a sweet time together as we join our hearts in prayer. I believe each of us can see how the other has grown over the years as we have prayed together. Praying for one another has made our marriage much stronger.

> Don't worry about anything; instead, pray about everything. Tell God what you need, and thank him for all he has done. If you do this, you will experience God's peace which is far more wonderful than the human mind can understand. His peace will guard your hearts and minds as you live in Christ Jesus.
>
> Philippians 4:6–7 (NLT)

As we pray together, we share with one another the concerns of our heart. When you hear a person voice a concern, you pray along with them about this matter. We pray concerning Doyal's work for the day. Many things affect his work, particularly the weather, so this is always a matter of concern. We pray for God's protection of him as he is out working around equipment. We pray God will give him wisdom in dealing with the men who work for us and also in dealing with the people he works for. We have learned in our life to turn things over to the Lord and he has given us a peace about his provision in every situation.

The Pharisees were questioning Jesus concerning whether it was lawful for a man to divorce his wife. I think the answer Jesus gave to their question is a truth we all need to take to heart.

> And he answered and said, "Have you not read, that he who created them from the beginning made them male and female, and said, 'For this cause a man shall leave his father and mother, and shall cleave to his wife; and the two shall become one flesh'? Consequently they are no longer two, but one flesh. What therefore God has joined together, let no man separate."
>
> Matthew 19:4–6 (NASB)

I know there are things each of us does that irritate the other, but God has enabled us to pray and ask for help. We take very seriously the vows we spoke when we married. We were each raised by parents who believed marriage was to last a lifetime. We strive to stay faithful to one another. As we pray each day, the prayer of our hearts is for God to keep our hearts and minds on one another. We strive to not allow Satan to lead us astray. We pray for God to help us flee from any temptation Satan throws in our paths. We know each of us can easily be subject to temptation if we allow Satan to get a foothold in our lives. We believe as we pray together it helps us to have a better understanding of each other. Our relationship becomes more closely knitted together. We have learned not only to lean on Jesus, but he has enabled us to lean on one another for love and support.

How have you learned to lean on Jesus for all that you need? What does the Bible teach us about supporting our husband or wife with love?

The Divine Guidance of Our Lord

The heart of a parent grieves when they see their children struggling with the trials of life. When our children were growing up, we were always able to help them as problems arose. Many times we could find the solution to the situations they got themselves into. Our children grew up, got married, and established themselves in life. We sit back and watch as they make some of the same mistakes we did in our younger adult life. We want so much to advise them and guide them in the right direction, but they are now adults so this is hard to do. It grieves our hearts as we watch them struggle with finances and raising their children. We want to fix the situation, but many times we must allow them to go through the struggles of life so they will learn a lesson from the decision they made. If they ask us for guidance and direction, we will try to help them. We pray what we have taught them will guide them to do what is right. "Teach your children to choose the right path, and when they are older, they will remain upon it" (Proverbs 22:6, NLT).

As our shepherd, the Lord offers divine guidance in his Word. He brings comfort to us as he leads us. "Because the Lord is my shepherd, I have everything I need! He lets me rest in the meadow grass and leads me beside the quiet streams. He gives me new strength. He helps me do what honors him the most" (Psalm 23:1–3, Living Bible).

The Lord will provide all we need when we walk in obedience to him in all our ways. I can see in my mind a flock of sheep on the hillside, in grass up to their bellies, eating all they desire. The provision of our Lord is sufficient to meet their every need. By eating what God has provided, their strength will be renewed. God offers the same to you and me if we daily partake of the exquisite banquet he has prepared for us in his Word. We must come and sit quietly before him savoring every word. It will be like sitting down to a juicy, marinated steak dinner with someone we love.

He promises to guide us through every situation we face. "He leads the humble in what is right, teaching them his way" (Psalm 25:9, NLT).

The guidance our Heavenly Father gives to His children is for eternity. "For that is what God is like. He is our God forever and ever, and he will be our guide until we die" (Psalm 48:14, NLT).

It seems God would get discouraged with us when we continue to make the same mistake over and over, but we have the assurance in his Word of his continual guidance. He will allow us to suffer the consequences of our decisions, but he promises to always be there for us. "Yet I still belong to you; you are holding my right hand. You will keep on guiding me with your counsel, leading me to a glorious destiny. Whom have I in heaven but you? I desire you more than anything on earth" (Psalm 73:23–25, NLT).

Remember, we are God's children and he will support us with his strong right hand. He will give us guidance and wise counsel in life if we will seek him. The desire of our heart should be for his comforting presence in our life each day.

When we come with a humble spirit, seeking his direction, he will show us the path we are to take. "The Lord says, 'I will guide you along the best pathway for your life. I will advise you and watch over you'" (Psalm 32:8, NLT).

God's Word gives direction for every aspect of our life. As our children grow into adulthood, we pray they will live by the Word of God. Our Father promises to lead each person along "the best pathway for your life." He promises to give us the advice we will need, if we will ask. He assures us he will watch over and protect us in our struggles.

When we came to accept Jesus as our Savior and Lord, the Holy Spirit came to abide in our heart. He will direct us when we are living our life in obedience to him. "Whether you turn to the right or to the left, your ears will hear a voice behind you, saying, 'This is the way; walk in it'" (Isaiah 30:21, NIV). Be quiet before the Lord and listen for his voice. You will hear him as he speaks to you and tells you which way to turn.

He promises to be there to guide us through the uncertainties of life. "I will lead the blind by the ways they have not known, along unfamiliar paths I will guide them; I will turn the darkness into light before them and make the rough places smooth. These are the things I will do; I will not forsake them" (Isaiah 42:16, NIV).

When it seems our world is crashing in around us and the pressures of life are more than we can bear, God our loving Father promises to be there for us. He is there to guide us along those unfamiliar paths of life. He will go ahead of us, making those rough places smooth if we will trust him.

He promises to give us rest and comfort for our weary souls and bodies. "Come to me, all you who are weary and burdened, and I will give you rest. Take my yoke upon you and learn from me, for I am gentle and humble in heart, and you will find rest for your souls. For my yoke is easy and my burden is light" (Matthew 11:28–30, NIV). My! What a sweet invitation from our Lord! He tells us to come to him because he is there for us to help us bear our heavy, wearisome burdens. The yoke Jesus is speaking of is our being united or joined with God. If we will come and lay our burdens of life at Jesus's feet, he will carry those burdens for us. He knows what is best for us and he will give us strength for living. The burden he will give to us is much lighter than the burdens of life we carry. The burden referred to here is living our life in the will of God. When we determine to live in his will, his hand will be upon us and he will lead us in the right way.

We can't carry all the burdens our children have in their lives, but God can and he promises he will. If you are carrying a burden in your life and it is so heavy you can hardly move, come, lay it at the feet of Jesus and ask him for help. He is ready and willing to help you through the trials of life.

State of Contentment

Our blue heeler puppy does everything in her power to entertain herself. She has chewed the wire to our TV antenna, part of our rubber tire doormat, and numerous other things. She rolls the bottom half of a five gallon plastic bucket around and throws a tennis ball with her mouth and chases after them. She is energy in motion. She thinks she needs to be doing something all the time. The other day I looked out and she had two tennis balls in the yard. She had one in her mouth and was trying to get the other one in her mouth. The second one would roll around and she would pounce on it. In the process of trying to get the second one, she would drop the ball she had in her mouth. After several tries, she finally managed to get both of the balls in her mouth at one time. The next day I gave her a large milk bone. A tennis ball was lying on the driveway, so I threw it, and she chased after it with the milk bone in her mouth. She did not let go of the milk bone, but she managed to get the tennis ball in her mouth also. It was a sight to behold. In the end, she decided she wanted the milk bone more than she wanted to fool with the tennis ball.

Watching this reminded me of how we are not content with what we have in life. We continually want more. There is a story in the Bible about a landowner who hired men to work in his vineyard. "For the kingdom of heaven is like a landowner who went out early in the morning to hire laborers for his vineyard. And when he had agreed with the laborers for a denarius for the day, he sent them into his vineyard" (Matthew 20:1–2, NASB).

A denarius was equal to a penny, which was a day's wage at that time. There was an agreement made about pay with the first laborers hired. The landowner went out again at the third hour, the sixth hour, the ninth hour, and the eleventh hour and found men standing around and sent them into the vineyard to work with the agreement he would pay them a fair wage at the end of the day.

> And when evening had come, the owner of the vineyard said to his foreman, "Call the laborers and pay them their wages, beginning with the last group to the first." And when those hired about the eleventh hour came, each one received a denarius. And when those hired first came, they thought that they would receive more; and they also received each one a denarius.
>
> Matthew 20:8–10 (NASB)

The men who began work early in the morning started to grumble because those who were hired last received the same pay as they did. The first laborers hired had insisted on an agreement with the landowner, but the rest of the men hired agreed to take whatever the owner paid them. This was the landowner's way of showing the men how generous he was. The first ones were paid according to their agreement and all the rest were paid the same showing his generosity. This parable is dealing with having the right attitude in our service.

Jesus was teaching the disciples principles about living and working for the Lord. Our purpose in working for the Lord should not simply be the rewards we will receive. We must trust the Lord to give us what he sees fit. Our God is gracious and generous and we must serve him because we love him.

> Obey them not only to win their favor when their eye is on you, but like slaves of Christ, doing the will of God from your heart. Serve wholeheartedly, as if you were serving the LORD, not men, because you know that the LORD will reward everyone for whatever good he does, whether he is slave or free.
>
> Ephesians 6:6–8 (NIV)

When we serve others, we are to do good work as if we were doing it for the Lord. The blessing and contentment come from knowing we are giving the Lord our very best. We are demonstrating to others the love of Jesus and the working of the Holy Spirit in our heart and life.

> Follow God's example in everything you do, because you are his dear children. Live a life filled with love for others, following the example of Christ, who loved you and gave himself as a sacrifice to take away your sins. And God was pleased, because that sacrifice was like sweet perfume to him.
>
> Ephesians 5:1–2 (NLT)

The way in which we serve is an example of what the Lord is doing in our heart. We are imitating him when we serve with a willing and loving heart, not worrying about the pay or reward we might receive.

> Do not lay up for yourselves treasures upon earth, where moth and rust destroy, and where thieves break in and steal. But lay up for yourselves treasures in heaven, where neither moth nor rust destroys, and where thieves do not break in or steal; for where your treasure is, there will your heart be also.
>
> Matthew 6:19–21 (NASB)

What we have here on earth is of no importance to the Lord. In the sight of the Lord, we lay up treasures in heaven as we serve him with a gracious heart. When others see Jesus in us, it may stir in their hearts a desire to know him. What about you and me? Have we come to the place in life where we are content with what God supplies or do we always want more? Our dog wanted so much to have both tennis balls in her mouth and one time she managed to do so. She was not content with just one.

When the men who came to work later in the day received

one denarius, the men hired early in the morning expected more pay even though they received what they agreed to work for. We must determine in our hearts why we are serving the Lord. God is pleased when we serve him because we love him. "Whoever serves me must follow me; and where I am, my servant also will be. My Father will honor the one who serves me" (John 12:26, NIV).

What is your definition of contentment in the Lord? Pray and ask God to help you be content in Him.

Does your life exemplify the contentment found in the Lord?

Hated by the World

When we live for Jesus, it makes many people feel uncomfortable around us. Sometimes they make fun of those who take a stand for the Lord. I remember when I was in high school I would experience this at times. Sometimes as I would approach a small group laughing and talking, one would say, "Shh, here comes Nancy, change the subject." I knew they were talking about something they did not want me to hear they had done or it was not good for them to be discussing. They knew what I stood for and the beliefs I had. I tried to live for the Lord in spite of any ridicule I received for my beliefs. I was raised in a very traditional Baptist preacher's family and one of the things we were taught was we should not dance. This was embedded firmly in my mind and it really did not bother me not to dance. One night the people, who were supposedly my friends, invited me to a birthday party for a close friend. I quizzed them as to what was going to happen at this party, and they assured me we were simply going to play games and celebrate the friend's birthday. I asked them specifically if there was going to be dancing and they said no. My parents gave me permission to go when they learned the type of party it was going to be. Now, you may think it is silly what I am going to say next, but this is the way I was taught and the way I believed. When I got to the party, I knew within a short time I should not have gone. Very soon, they began dancing, and I cannot tell you how it hurt me to know my friends had deceived me. I knew I must leave the party. I telephoned my parents and my dad came to pick me up. I went home in tears because my friends had lied to me about what they were going to do at the party. They knew what I believed and it did not bother me not to be included in activities. I was not in trouble with my parents because they knew the standard I tried to live by. What does it do to us when others ridicule, make fun, or despise us for what we believe? In my particular situation, I began to question whether or not these young people were really my friends. If they were my friends, why would they put me in a position such as this? It certainly caused me to have a lack of trust in them. More importantly, even though this may seem very minor to some of you, I knew I must stand up for what I believed.

Jesus gave the disciples the authority to cast out evil spirits and to heal men of disease and illness. They were to go preaching and teaching to the lost sheep of Israel, the Jews. They were not to go to the Gentiles or the Samaritans at this time. "Go and announce to them that the kingdom of heaven is near. Heal the sick, raise the dead, cure those with leprosy, and cast out demons. Give as freely as you have received!" (Matthew 10:7–8, NLT).

They had been blessed by God, and they were to be a blessing to others. They were to show love and concern for all people. Jesus told them not to take anything with them, but to depend on the hospitality of the people they were going to minister to. He then instructed them as to how they could expect to be treated.

> Look, I am sending you out as sheep among wolves. Be as wary as snakes and harmless as doves. But beware! For you will be handed over to the courts and beaten in the synagogues. And you must stand trial before governors and kings because you are my followers. This will be your opportunity to tell them about me—yes, to witness to the world.
>
> Matthew 10:16–18 (NLT)

As the disciples traveled, teaching about the Lord, life was not easy. Jesus had warned them what might happen when they stood up for their beliefs. "And everyone will hate you because of your allegiance to me. But those who endure to the end will be saved" (Matthew 10:22, NLT). A believer must be willing to endure persecution from others. We are to stand strong for the Lord, committed to him, no matter what comes about. How we respond when others despise and reject us is evidence of our commitment to the Lord. "Therefore, my beloved brethren, be steadfast, immovable, always abounding in the work of the Lord, knowing that your toil is not in vain in the Lord" (1 Corinthians 15:58, NASB).

How do you respond when others speak out against you because of your beliefs? When you are passed over for a promotion at work because you will not bow to their dishonest requests, how do you react? "In this world you will have trouble. But take heart! I have overcome the world" (John 16:33b, NIV). We must stand strong knowing the Lord is with us and will protect us in every circumstance.

In the Book of Daniel, Shadrach, Meshach, and Abed-nego refused to bow down and worship foreign gods. They were reported to Nebuchadnezzar, the king. He ordered these men to be brought to him. "Nebuchadnezzar responded and said to them, 'Is it true, Shadrach, Meshach, and Abed-nego, that you do not serve my gods or worship the golden image that I have set up?'" (Daniel 3:14, NASB). They worshiped the only true God so they stood strong in their beliefs.

Shadrach, Meshach and Abed-nego answered and said to the king, "O Nebuchadnezzar, we do not need to give you an answer concerning this matter. If it be so, our God whom we serve is able to deliver us from the furnace of blazing fire; and he will deliver us out of your hand, O king. But even if he does not, let it be known to you, O king, that we are not going to serve your gods or worship the golden image that you have set up.

Daniel 3:16–18 (NASB)

They trusted God to deliver them from the blazing fire if they were thrown in the furnace for worshiping him. How do you think you would respond in this situation? I have often wondered if I were put to a test such as this how I would react. I pray I would be steadfast in my faith even in the midst of persecution.

The Scripture very clearly tells us we will suffer hatred, ridicule, and persecution if we live a life of obedience to the Lord. Jesus was teaching the disciples concerning his return to earth to claim those who had placed their faith and trust in him. The disciples questioned Jesus as to how they were going to know when this was going to happen.

> Jesus answered: "Watch out that no one deceives you. For many will come in my name, claiming, 'I am the Christ,' and will deceive many. You will hear of wars and rumors of wars, but see to it that you are not alarmed. Such things must happen, but the end is still to come. Nation will rise against nation, and kingdom against kingdom. There will be famines and earthquakes in various places. All these are the beginning of birth pains."
>
> Matthew 24:4–8 (NIV)

Jesus tried to help the disciples understand the terrible things that would be evidence of the time of his return being near. When the time is near, not only will these things happen, but many of those who claim to know Jesus will begin to fall away from him. Many people in foreign lands are persecuted when they denounce the beliefs of their family and decide to follow Jesus. Some are put to death for their beliefs or ostracized from their family. Jesus warned the disciples about what would happen and the same warning stands for us today.

> Then you will be arrested, persecuted, and killed. You will be hated all over the world because of your allegiance to me. And many will turn away from me and betray and hate each other. And many false prophets will appear and will lead many people astray. Sin will be rampant everywhere,

and the love of many will grow cold. But those who endure to the end will be saved.

Matthew 24:9–13 (NLT)

Much of this is happening today, but we do not know when Jesus will return. Through the years, preachers have preached about the end of times being near. We have no idea when this will be, but one thing we do know: we must be ready spiritually for his return. We must consistently live our life in obedience to him. "But thanks be to God that though you were slaves of sin, you became obedient from the heart to that form of teaching to which you were committed, and having been freed from sin, you became slaves of righteousness" (Romans 6:17–18, NASB).

Has there been an instance in your life when you had to take a stand for what you believed?

How did others around you respond to the allegiance you showed to the Lord and for what you believed?

What do you think you would do if you were told you would be shot if you did not denounce the Lord?

Saturated Beyond Measure

We recall things of the past when something happens in the present to trigger our memory. Saturday it rained most of the day and into the night. It rained so hard, at times it sounded like a herd of buffaloes running across our metal roof. Late in the evening, I looked outside and water was standing on top of the ground. Our yard drains very well, but it had become saturated beyond measure. It reminded me of the early 1980s when it rained for two weeks straight. Our property borders the Robbers Cave State Park. Lake Wayne Wallace, one of the lakes in the park, is between our property and Highway 2. The lake became so full within this two-week period that the waters overflowed the banks. The property between us and the lake was covered with water. The water came up in our lower pasture about 150 yards. It was as if we had our own lake right in our pasture. The ground and every growing plant were literally saturated with water. It took some time for the water to go down even after the rains subsided.

Our pastor preached a message about faith using the scripture about the mustard seed. Jesus was speaking to the disciples. "'You didn't have enough faith,' Jesus told them. 'I assure you, even if you had faith as small as a mustard seed you could say to this mountain, 'Move from here to there,' and it would move. Nothing would be impossible'" (Matthew 17:20, NLT). Jesus was discussing faith with the disciples because of what happened. "When they came to the crowd, a man approached Jesus and knelt before him. 'Lord, have mercy on my son,' he said. 'He has seizures and is suffering greatly. He often falls into the fire or into the water. I brought him to your disciples, but they could not heal him'" (Matthew 17:14–16, NIV).

How do you think Jesus felt when he heard the man tell him

the disciples could not cast out the demon? He had given authority to the disciples to cast out demons and to heal. They had been able to do this earlier. Why were they not able to do it at this time? "Jesus replied, 'You stubborn, faithless people! How long must I be with you until you believe? How long must I put up with you? Bring the boy to me'" (Matthew 17:17, NLT).

I can imagine how the disciples felt when the Lord rebuked them for their lack of faith. He told them even if they had faith the size of the mustard seed great things would happen. We all know a mustard seed is extremely small. When planted in the right type of climate and soil, a mustard seed will produce a tree-like plant six to eight feet tall. It is strong enough for the birds to perch on the limbs of the tree. Our pastor used this illustration to speak to us about our faith. He mentioned that our faith is as small as a grain of mustard seed when we become a Christian, but this is not how it should remain. As we mature in the Lord, our faith should begin to blossom and grow like the mustard tree.

How does this happen? As our pastor preached last night, it was an affirmation to my heart of what God had done in my life the past two years. I believe the only way our faith can grow is by saturating our heart and mind with God's holy Word.

Ezekiel was a prophet and God had a special job for him to do.

Then he said to me, "Son of man, eat what you find; eat this scroll, and go, speak to the house of Israel." So I opened my mouth, and he fed me this scroll. And he said to me, "Son of man, feed your stomach, and fill your body with this scroll which I am giving you." Then I ate it, and it was sweet as honey in my mouth. Then he said to me, "Son of man, go to the house of Israel and speak with my words to them."

Ezekiel 3:1–4 (NASB)

I love what Ezekiel said about the Word of God being as sweet as honey. David said the same thing in the Book of Psalms. "How sweet are thy words to my taste! Yes, sweeter than honey to my mouth!" (Psalm 119:103, NASB).

Not only are we to sit down to a royal feast and partake of the sweet morsels that are sweet as honey, but we are to put God's Word in action in our lives. We can saturate our heart and mind with the Bible, but unless we put it into action, it is of no value to us or to God. Head knowledge is not all we need. What needs to take place is described well by the psalmist: "But his delight is in the law of the Lord, and in his law he meditates day and night. And he will be like a tree firmly planted by streams of water, which yields its fruit in its season, and its leaf does not wither; and in whatever he does, he prospers" (Psalm 1:2–3, NASB).

A person who delights in God's Word will ponder and study the Word of God day and night. He has a continuous hunger that causes him to saturate his heart and mind with the Scriptures. Did you notice what the scripture said? It not only said a person found delight in the teachings of the Lord, but he would be like a tree planted by streams of water. What happens when a tree receives all the nutrients it needs from the soil and the moisture in the soil?

> Blessed is the man who trusts in the LORD and whose trust is the LORD, for he will be like a tree planted by the water, that extends its roots by a stream and will not fear when the heat comes; but its leaves will be green, and it will not be anxious in a year of drought nor cease to yield fruit.
>
> Jeremiah 17:7–8 (NASB)

The roots of a tree somehow senses water is near and begins to reach outward to the water. It receives the nourishment it needs, and even when drought comes, its leaves are still green and it does not cease yielding fruit. Do you simply have head knowledge of the

Word of God or is your life a testimony of what God has done in your life through the study of his Word?

Our faith should not remain as small as a grain of mustard seed. I am now sixty-three years old, and as I look back at my life, I can see the progression of God's purpose for my life. But, I must say, the past two years God has done such an amazing thing in my life that I stand in awe in his presence. If someone had told me three years ago I would be doing what I am today, I would have told him he was crazy. Never in my wildest dreams did I think I would ever write something people would read! When I think about it today, it humbles me far beyond what I can express to you in this writing. I know it is simply a work of God in my life. " ... For it is God who works in you to will and to act according to his good purpose" (Philippians 2:13, NIV).

Because of what God has done in my life through the study of his Word, I must live out the faith he has instilled in me. I have come to know him much better and to understand more about what he desires for my life. It is my responsibility to put into action what he has taught me. This is why I share it with you through these devotions. I am not in any way a Bible scholar. I am just a common, ordinary person willing to be used by God. Was it easy to take this bold step of faith and allow God to use me in this way? No, it was not. It was the most unnerving thing I have ever attempted in my life. I am glad I took this bold step of faith. Yes, it has been the most thrilling trip I have ever taken. Doyal and I have taken many trips for the Lord overseas. We have been involved in missions in several different countries, but nothing compares to the journey God has led me on the past two years as I have written these books.

My faith is no longer the size of a grain of mustard seed, because I have spent so much time in God's Word. It is more like a tree used by God to produce fruit for his kingdom. I have become steadfast in my faith in the Lord. "I have set the Lord continually before me; because he is at my right hand, I shall not be moved" (Psalm 16:8, AMP).

God is my strength. He is my fortress. The Lord is my deliverer. He is my stronghold. The Lord God Almighty is the rock on which I stand. He is the rock to which I flee for refuge in those times of weakness. The rains saturate the earth with abundant water. Why not saturate your heart and mind with the Word of God, so you are prepared to go out into the world and produce fruit for the Lord?

How do you define your faith?

What must you do to help your faith to grow and flourish for the Lord?

All to Jesus I Surrender

As I was praying this morning, the song "I Surrender All" was playing in the background. Sitting in front of my computer, the thought came to my mind, do I really surrender all I am or ever hope to be to the Lord? I think of Corrie ten Boom, her sister Betsy, and their father who gave their all for the Jewish people in Holland. They determined in their hearts to hide the Jews from the soldiers of Nazi Germany. They even had to endure the terrible conditions of Ravenbruck concentration camp for protecting the Jews. Betsy and their father both died in the confines of the prison camp. Corrie was released through a clerical error one week before all the women her age were put to death. These courageous people literally gave their all for what they felt God was leading them to do. Corrie and Betsy took many chances with their own lives while in the camp when they did things to share with others the message of Jesus Christ. Corrie ten Boom promised the Lord, if she were ever released, to spend her life sharing with people the love and forgiveness of Jesus Christ. She also did this while in prison, and miraculously, she was given a New Testament to use while there. These three people were totally surrendered to the Lord to do whatever he led them to do.

What about you and me? Do we give every little nook and cranny of our life to the Lord or are there certain areas we never surrender to him? "Delight yourself in the Lord; and he will give you the desires of your heart. Commit your way to the Lord, trust also in him, and he will do it" (Psalm 37:4–5, NASB).

When we commit our ways to the Lord and trust in him, we are surrendering our life to his control. We are saying to the Lord, "Here I am Lord. Use me!" David was faced with this decision when God told him to go and deliver Keilah from the hands of the Philistines.

> So David inquired of the LORD, saying, "Shall I go and attack these Philistines?" and the LORD said to David, "Go and attack the Philistines, and deliver Keilah." Then David inquired of the LORD once more. And the LORD answered him and said, "Arise, go down to Keilah, for I will give the Philistines into your hand."
>
> 1 Samuel 23:2, 4 (NASB)

When God told David to do this, the men who were in the army with David were frightened about fighting the Philistines. God still told David to go and he would deliver them into his hands. David and his men did as God said, and the people who lived in Keilah were delivered. Saul said God had delivered David into his hands because he was within the walls of the city of Keilah. David then sought the Lord and questioned the Lord as to whether the people of Keilah would be destroyed because of his being there.

> "Will the men of Keilah surrender me into his hand? Will Saul come down just as thy servant has heard? O LORD God of Israel, I pray, tell thy servant." And the LORD said, "He will come down." Then David said, "Will the men of Keilah surrender me and my men into the hand of Saul?" And the LORD said, "They will surrender you."
>
> 1 Samuel 23:11–12 (NASB)

David was faithful to the Lord and did what he commanded him to do, delivering Keilah from the hands of the Philistines. Because David was surrendered to the Lord, he enabled him to leave the city and live in the wilderness of the hill country of Ziph. Saul hunted him day after day, but God did not deliver David into his hands. God honored David's commitment to him.

Jesus gave us a great example of being totally surrendered to God the Father. This is clearly portrayed in the time of prayer Jesus had in the garden of Gethsemane. Jesus knew what the future held for him. He retreated deeper into the garden to pray after leaving Peter, James, and John. "And he went a little beyond them, and fell on his face and prayed, saying, 'My Father, if it is possible, let this cup pass from me; yet not as I will, but as thou wilt'" (Matthew 26:39, NASB). In speaking of the cup, Jesus was referring to his dying on the cross. He had no desire to do this, but if it was God's plan, he was willing to do it.

The story is told about Amy Carmichael's selfless dedication to Jesus, her Savior. She lived a life of discipleship and complete abandonment to the Lord. She was determined to make God's love known to as many people as possible that were trapped in the utter darkness of sin. She lived in Southern Ireland, and when she was eighteen years old, her father died. This caused Amy to begin thinking about what God had for her to do in the future. Even before she became a missionary, God gave her a glimpse of what she would do in life. One Sunday morning she and her brothers came across a ragged, older woman carrying a huge bundle. They really felt an urgency to help her, but also there was the thought of the embarrassment caused by others seeing them. They met many they knew as they helped the old woman and felt like their faces were crimson red with embarrassment. It is said as Amy passed a Victorian fountain, she heard these words:

Now if any man builds upon the foundation with gold, silver, precious stones, wood, hay, straw, each man's work will become evident; for the day will show it, because it is to be revealed with fire; and the fire itself will test the quality of each man's work. If any man's work which he has built upon it remains, he shall receive a reward.

1 Corinthians 3:12–14 (NASB)

Amy turned around to see who had said those words and no one was there. All she heard was the sound of the fountain's water and the laughter of those passing by. Amy had been enthralled by the social life around her, but now it seemed God had some things she must settle with him. She attended a conference in England with her family, and it was there God singled her out for service to him. The conference dealt with taking one's life to a higher plane, living it for the Lord. Amy Carmichael thought about how Jesus had lived his life with no worldly possessions and she knew God was calling her to do the same thing for him. In 1895, she was commissioned by the Church of England to go as a missionary to Dohnavur, India. She served the Lord for fifty-six years as his devoted servant, never taking a furlough. She spent a great deal of her time rescuing children who had been dedicated by their families to serve as temple prostitutes. Amy often recalled the situation with the little old lady who was in rags carrying the heavy bundle. She realized in her heart God was calling her to reach out to those of the world who were considered unlovely. It is said that "Obedience, total commitment, and selflessness were the marks of Amy Carmichael's life." [3] She surrendered her life totally to the Lord. Her sole existence was devoted to her Lord and Savior.

Pray and meditate on the words of the song "I Surrender All."
All to Jesus I surrender, All to him I freely give;
I will ever love and trust him, In his presence daily live.
All to Jesus I surrender, Make me, Savior, wholly thine;
Let me feel the Holy Spirit, Truly know that thou art mine.
All to Jesus I surrender, Lord, I give myself to thee;
Fill me with thy love and power, Let thy blessing fall on me.

What area of your life you have not surrendered to the Lord? Will you commit it to him today and follow God wherever he leads?

The Terrible Odor of a Rotten Egg

I was visiting with my sister, Ann, by phone the other night. We were discussing our older sister, Glenda, and how we wished she could find a better place to live. Glenda has always been the one to entertain us at family gatherings. She is always unpredictable in her actions. Ann spoke about the man Glenda rents a room from being gone, and he asked Glenda to gather the eggs from his laying hens. Glenda did as she was asked and gave some to one of her friends. When she cracked them they were rotten, and some had a baby chick in them. Glenda had not only gathered the fresh eggs, but she had gathered the eggs of a setting hen that had been there a long time. They definitely had an odor about them. This reminded me of the first year I taught mentally handicapped children in the California public school system. It was the week of Easter, and I had each child bring three colored, boiled eggs for the Easter egg hunt. One little boy was from an extremely poor family. The father was slow and the mother was mentally handicapped, but they kept their home and their children spotless. She sent the three eggs to school with James. We had our egg hunt that afternoon and a girl found one of James's eggs. When she cracked it to eat, the egg was rotten and had the beginning of a baby chick inside. Also it had not been boiled long enough to be firm. Oh, what an odor filled our classroom.

We all know what it would be like to bite into a rotten apple. We have seen how one rotten apple can affect a bushel of apples if it is not removed. How does the fruit of sinfulness in one person's life affect those around him? Moses reminded the Israelites of their past sins and how rebellious they had been even though they had seen God do mighty works in their lives. They continually deserved the punishment of the Lord, but God often showed mercy towards them when they would come in repentance to him. Moses recited an entire song to the children of Israel reminding them of the mistakes they had made and how they were to avoid committing those same sins again. He told them about the hope available to them if they would trust in the Lord. "But Israel soon became fat and unruly; the people grew heavy, plump, and stuffed! Then they abandoned the God who had made them; they made light of the rock of their salvation. They stirred up his jealousy by worshiping foreign gods; they provoked his fury with detestable acts" (Deuteronomy 32:15–16, NLT).

When the Israelites became prosperous, many times they turned away from the Lord. They would go astray by worshiping foreign gods and living a life of sin. "You neglected the rock who had fathered you; you forgot the God who had given you birth" (Deuteronomy 32:18, NLT).

The Lord became very angry with them and abandoned them to the ways of the world. God went so far as to say he would heap disasters upon them because of their sinful ways and their distaste for him. Moses reminded the Israelites that they were a nation lacking good sense. They were a foolish people without understanding. He wanted them to realize that their life of sin would affect all around them.

Israel became very prosperous during the reign of Jeroboam II. Israel took their eyes off the Lord and became very selfish. They used the money to build bigger altars and more beautiful idols. Their armies became very strong and they were doing well economically.

Israel is a luxuriant vine; he produces fruit for himself. The more his fruit, the more altars he made; the richer his land, the better he made the sacred pillars. Their heart is faithless; now they must bear their guilt. The LORD will break down their altars and destroy their sacred pillars.

Hosea 10:1–2 (NASB)

The more God gave them, the more they strayed from him. Does this sound familiar to you concerning our country? It seems the more affluent we become, the farther we stray from God. I do not believe God will continue to bless us when we are not good stewards of what he has given us. It is a sin unto the Lord for us to use the finances he has blessed us with simply for ourselves. This was what Israel was doing and God was very angry with them. The fruit produced here was the fruit of selfishness.

The Israelites produced the fruit of deceitfulness.

I said, "Plant the good seeds of righteousness, and you will harvest a crop of my love. Plow up the hard ground of your hearts, for now is the time to seek the LORD, that he may come and shower righteousness upon you." But, you have cultivated wickedness and raised a thriving crop of sins. You have eaten the fruit of lies—trusting in your military might, believing that great armies could make your nation safe!

Hosea 10:12–13 (NLT)

God had instructed the Israelites how they were to plant. If they planted righteousness, being in right standing with God, they would harvest a crop of love. The Israelites were not producing a crop of love because they had turned from the one true God to gods. Instead of planting seeds of righteousness, they were planting seeds of wickedness. These seeds had produced a thriving crop of sins. They trusted in themselves and their own military strength rather than trusting in our God who is all powerful and capable of destroying all the armies at once. They did not pay attention to the message being preached to them, but were deceitful in all their ways.

Paul wrote a letter to the church at Galatia describing their condition, but it also describes the condition of our world today.

The acts of the sinful nature are obvious: sexual immorality, impurity and debauchery; idolatry and witchcraft; hatred, discord, jealousy, fits of rage, selfish ambition, dissensions, factions and envy; drunkenness, orgies, and the like. I warn you, as I did before, that those who live like this will not inherit the kingdom of God.

Galatians 5:19–21 (NIV)

Many people today have taken their eyes off the Lord and strive only to satisfy their human, fleshly desires. Everywhere you look today, you see a multitude of sins being cultivated. We see this in TV, movies, the clothing people wear that leave nothing to the imagination, particularly the girls and women; we see the rampant growth of sexual misconduct, children born out of wedlock, demonic activities, the worshiping of false gods, and terrible crimes committed each day. Our world today produces many different fruits of the fleshly desires of humankind.

In my way of thinking, the sins of this world have the same horrible, distasteful, awful smell of a rotten egg. Those eggs the little boy brought to school that the children cracked, thinking they would be good to eat, almost made us throw up. How do you think God feels when he looks at us and sees how far we have strayed from him and how engrossed we are in the terrible sins of our flesh? I believe our involvement in the gross sins of this world puts off a horrible stench unto the Lord. One of these days, if we do not repent of our sin, he will turn from us like he did the children of Israel who refused to listen to him.

If God evaluated your heart and mind, what would he find?

Are you putting off a sweet aroma or a horrible stench unto the Lord?

Encourage One Another in Love

One of the greatest gifts God gives us is encouragement. As a believer, I am to allow the love of God to flow from within me to others. Expressing God's love to others is encouragement. I want to share with you when God impressed this so strongly upon my heart. When I was thirty-two years old, my first husband died after back surgery when a massive blood clot moved from his leg to his lungs. My two boys were two and five years of age. I arrived home from the hospital, ready to face my two boys who were there with their aunt and try to explain to them what had happened. Standing on my doorstep was the former dean of women of California Baptist College where I graduated. She was a widow who had been left with a young son when her husband died, though now she was much older. We also went to church together. It was such an encouragement to me for her to share advice concerning different situations. She offered strength to me when I really needed it. Later in the morning, the wife of our Sunday school teacher came by to encourage me. She brought a book dealing with death by Chuck Swindoll entitled *For Those Who Hurt*. The most important thing she did was to bring a book for Anthony to help him understand what happened to his daddy. She sat down on the couch with him and spent time reading the book and explaining it to him. This was not an expected death, and I was somewhat in shock by what had happened because he seemed to be progressing well. Stevie was not old enough to really understand what had happened. I realized from this experience how important it was to encourage people in the name of Jesus. Through this experience, God developed in me the gift of encouragement. To be able to encourage others in times of need is kind of the "icing on the cake" for me. God is truly my friend and it brings great joy to my life to be able to help others understand God wants to be their friend also. "A friend loves at all times, and is born, as is a brother, for adversity" (Proverbs 17:17, AMP).

David had the opportunity to encourage the people after the death of his son Absalom. A short time before his death, Absalom had led the children of Israel to follow him as king and not David, his father. David sent his troops out to fight against Absalom's army with the instructions to go easy on Absalom. He had come upon some of David's men and as he fled on his donkey, his hair caught in a tree and he was left dangling. Joab had actually plunged three daggers into his heart and ten young men surrounded him and killed him. David did not know the details, but he was in his chambers mourning the death of his son. "The king covered his face with his hands and kept on weeping, 'O my son Absalom! O Absalom, my son, my son!'" (2 Samuel 19:4, NLT).

Joab, David's military leader, came to David and made an important statement to him.

> Then Joab went into the house to the king and said, "Today you have humiliated all your men, who have just saved your life and the lives of yours sons and daughters and the lives of your wives and concubines. You love those who hate you and hate those who love you. You have made it clear today that the commanders and their men mean nothing to you. I see that you would be pleased if Absalom were alive today and all of us were dead. Now go out and encourage your men."
>
> 2 Samuel 19:5–7a (NIV)

David needed to encourage them if he wanted to have a following of any kind. They now wanted to restore David as king. In some ways this was an encouragement to the people so he could be restored to his place of honor. Also, it was to show thankfulness for their courage in battle and for the way they protected him and his family.

Paul and other prisoners were being taken to Rome to be tried by Caesar for crimes they had been accused of. They were on a ship that was tossed hither and yon by a wind of hurricane force. The men on the ship were in great danger. The sailors had thrown much of the cargo overboard to lighten the load, but the wind was so strong, they could not go where they needed to go. The men had gone without food for many days. On the fourteenth night of the storm, they believed they were getting close to shore. They were afraid of being dashed against the rocks, so they dropped down the anchors of the ship.

> Just before dawn Paul urged them all to eat. "For the last fourteen days," he said, "you have been in constant suspense and have gone without food—you haven't eaten anything. Now I urge you to take some food. You need it to survive. Not one of you will lose a single hair from his head." After he said this, he took some bread and gave thanks to God in front of them all. Then he broke it and began to eat. They were all encouraged and ate some food themselves.
>
> Acts 27:33–36 (NIV)

Paul was a prisoner aboard this ship, but he was the one to encourage the sailors and guards to eat. Paul certainly set an example of how we are to be thankful for all things as he blessed the food before them. He began to eat and the others were encouraged by what he did and they began to eat. Their strength was restored because Paul encouraged them to eat.

Paul was telling the Christians at Rome to be understanding of those who were weak. There were those who were weak in their faith and thought it was wrong to eat certain foods. Others' faith allowed them to eat everything. Paul encouraged those who were strong in their faith not to look down on those who were weak. Some people believed one day was sacred to the Lord and others another day. They were not to pass judgment on one another. Believers should accept and help those who are weak.

> May the God who gives endurance and encouragement give you a spirit of unity among yourselves as you follow Christ Jesus, so that with one heart and mouth you may glorify the God and Father of our LORD Jesus Christ. Accept one another, then, just as Christ accepted you, in order to bring praise to God.
>
> Romans 15:5–7 (NIV)

We are familiar with the story of the exodus of the children of Israel out of Egypt. Moses was chosen by God to lead them out of slavery in Egypt into the promised land. As they journeyed through the wilderness, there were times they were without food and water. On one particular occasion, they lacked water. God told Moses he should go and stand before him on the rock at Horeb and he was to strike the rock with his rod and water would come out of the rock. Moses did as he was instructed. Later, in the wilderness of Zin, the people had gathered when Miriam, Moses's sister, died. There was no water for the congregation of people. The people came complaining to Moses and Aaron once again. This time, God changed his instructions to Moses.

> "Take the rod; and you and your brother Aaron assemble the congregation and speak to the rock before their eyes, that it may yield its water. You shall thus bring forth water for them out of the rock and let the congregation and their beasts drink." Then Moses lifted up his hand and struck the rock twice with his rod; and water came forth abundantly, and the congregation and their beasts drank. But the LORD said to Moses and Aaron, "Because you have not believed

me, to treat me as holy in the sight of the sons of Israel, therefore you shall not bring this assembly into the land which I have given them."

Numbers 20:8, 11–12 (NASB)

Because of disobeying God's instruction, Moses would not be allowed to lead the people across the Jordan into the promised land. Later on, just before the Israelites were ready to cross over the river and possess the land, Moses sought the Lord's permission to enter the land.

"Let me, I pray, cross over and see the fair land that is beyond the Jordan, that good hill country and Lebanon." But the LORD was angry with me on your account, and would not listen to me; and the LORD said to me, "Enough! Speak to me no more of this matter. Go up to the top of Pisgah and lift up your eyes to the west and north and south and east, and see it with your eyes, for you shall not cross over this Jordan. But charge Joshua and encourage him and strengthen him; for he shall go across at the head of this people, and he shall give them as an inheritance the land which you will see."

Deuteronomy 3:25–28 (NASB)

Instead of being able to enter the good land beyond the Jordan, Moses was to encourage and strengthen Joshua to lead the people. Joshua would need this encouragement as he faced what was ahead of him.

Encourage means to inspire with courage and hope. I challenge you to be an encourager.

Where is Your Dependency?

These past two years, God has led me to reflect back on my life and the many things he has done. I can see the very fingerprints of God as he has taken me as a lump of clay and molded me into the person I am today. Do I think it has been an easy job for the Lord? No, I think not. I have always been a confident person and felt like I could accomplish anything I set my mind to do. As I look back, I question whether I was trusting God to do it through me or if I felt I was capable of doing it on my own. At times, I attempted things on my own and I failed. God came along and picked up the pieces and shaped me once again into a vessel to be used for his honor and glory. This would come about only if I was willing to relinquish control to the Lord. When I was left a widow with two small boys, I came to realize I could not do it alone. If I was going to be the mother or the teacher I needed to be, I must depend on the Lord. "And he has said to me, 'My grace is sufficient for you, for power is perfected in weakness.' Most gladly, therefore, I will rather boast about my weaknesses, that the power of Christ may dwell in me" (2 Corinthians 12:9, NASB).

God took me at my very weakest point in life and got my undivided attention. God rained down his loving kindness, goodness, and mercy on me, completely changing my life. Embedded in my heart and mind is "With men it is impossible, but not with God; for all things are possible with God" (Mark 10:27b, NASB).

In the Book of Nehemiah, Ezra led the people in a time of open confession to the Lord. They did not simply confess their sins in private, but they confessed them before the whole congregation. The Scripture tells us that the people came together and they sat listening to the law of God being read for two to three hours. The

Word of God lays the groundwork for confession because as we read and study the Bible, it convicts our heart of sin in our life. Ezra read from the law of God for several hours and then the people stood confessing their own sins and the sins of their ancestors for several hours. Ezra prayed a lengthy prayer, reminding the people of the events God had brought about in their lives. He reminded them of God hearing their cries of suffering in Egypt. He heard their cries as they neared the Red Sea and Pharaoh was approaching. God parted the Red Sea and they walked across on dry ground. God led them by a pillar of fire by night and by a pillar of cloud during the day. God came down on Mount Sinai and spoke to them from heaven. Through Moses, God commanded them to follow his instructions. When they were hungry in the wilderness, God provided manna and quail for them to eat. God provided water from the rock when they were thirsty. They forgot about God's miracles, they refused to listen to him and worshiped other gods. God still loved them and when they repented, God forgave them. God enabled them to conquer many enemies. Prosperity caused them to stray from God.

> Our kings, princes, priests, and ancestors did not obey your law or listen to your commands and solemn warnings. Even while they had their own kingdom, they did not serve you even though you showered your goodness on them. You gave them a large, fertile land, but they refused to turn from their wickedness.
>
> Nehemiah 9:34–35 (NLT)

God showed his goodness and mercy towards the Israelites, but they continued to forsake him. They entered the promised land, a land flowing with milk and honey, yet they refused to turn from their wickedness. They were now being oppressed by the kings and princes of these nations. Ezra led the people in a time of confession of their sin and then led their princes, Levites, and priests to place

NEVER THE SAME AGAIN

their seal on this covenant stating they would serve the Lord. They vowed to accept the punishment of the Lord if they failed to keep the law of God. They promised to follow the commands of God. The law of the Lord convicted the people's hearts of their sin.

Jehoshaphat, king of Judah, led the people of Judah to follow the Lord and not foreign gods. He led them to make decisions in the fear of the Lord and to have no part of wrongdoing. If they did, God would be with them and help them. The sons of Moab, the sons of Ammon, and some of the Menunites came to make war against Jehoshaphat.

> Then some came and reported to Jehoshaphat, saying, "A great multitude is coming against you from beyond the sea, out of Aram and behold, they are in Hazazon-tamar (that is Engedi)." And Jehoshaphat was afraid and turned his attention to seek the LORD; and proclaimed a fast throughout all Judah. So Judah gathered together to seek help from the LORD; they even came from all the cities of Judah to seek the LORD.
>
> 2 Chronicles 20:2–4 (NASB)

Jehoshaphat realized he could not stand against this army in his own strength. He realized he was powerless without God. He prayed to the Lord. He spoke about God being the ruler over all kingdoms and nations and no one could stand against him. They had faced many things and God was always there to help and rescue them.

> And now see what the armies of Ammon, Moab, and Mount Seir are doing. You would not let our ancestors invade those nations when Israel left Egypt, so they went around them and did not destroy them. Now see how they reward us! For they have come to throw us out of your land, which you gave us as an inheritance.
>
> 2 Chronicles 20:10–11 (NLT)

Jehoshaphat knew God would hear his prayer. The last part of Jehoshaphat's prayer shows his dependence on the Lord. "O our God, won't you stop them? We are powerless against this mighty army that is about to attack us. We do not know what to do, but we are looking to you for help" (2 Chronicles 20:12, NLT).

The Spirit of the Lord came upon Jahaziel, who was a Levite. He told them to not be afraid of this mighty army because the battle was not theirs, but God's. They were to march out against them to the end of the valley in front of the wilderness of Jeruel. The instructions he gave next demonstrate their dependence on God for victory. "But you will not even need to fight. Take your positions; then stand still and watch the Lord's victory. He is with you, O people of Judah and Jerusalem. Do not be afraid or discouraged. Go out there tomorrow, for the Lord is with you!" (2 Chronicles 20:17, NLT).

What did Jehoshaphat lead the people of Judah to do next? They fell with their faces to the ground and worshiped the Lord. The Levites then stood and praised the Lord with a loud shout. As they journeyed to battle the next morning "Jehoshaphat stopped and said, 'Listen to me, all you people of Judah and Jerusalem! Believe in the Lord your God, and you will be able to stand firm. Believe in his prophets, and you will succeed'" (2 Chronicles 20:20b, NLT).

Singers were appointed to walk in front of the army and the moment they started singing and praising the Lord, the Lord caused great confusion amongst the armies of Moab, Ammon, and Mount Seir. They began fighting among themselves, killing one another. By the time the people of Judah arrived all they found were dead bodies lying all around and not one of their enemies were left alive. Because of their dependence on and obedience to the Lord, the battle was won by God.

Recall some times in your life you failed to succeed because you were doing it in your own strength.

How has it made a difference in your life since you have learned to lean on Jesus for strength?

What have you learned concerning the Lord through these times?

What's on the Inside?

The keyboard and screen I use for my computer collect an unbelievable amount of dust. You wonder where all the dust comes from. This morning I wiped the screen with a soft cloth and I used Gust Easy Duster to blow the particles of dust from the keyboard. It reminded me of what I discovered when I took the cover off of my computer to install some new memory modules. Hidden there in my computer was an amazing collection of dust and lint on all the different parts, particularly the filter at the back of the fan that runs when the computer is on. It is frightening enough for someone such as me to take the cover off of a computer because I have no idea what I am looking at or looking for. With the help of the man from Dell Computers, after many tries at installing the parts, putting the cover on, starting up the computer, and it failing to perform, we finally completed the task. I asked him how I could clean the inside and he said with the hose of a vacuum cleaner. I could just see it sucking parts off and swallowing them. The following day I took it apart and removed the collection of dust. To the naked eye, looking at the outside of the computer, one would not see the dirt on the inside. It is hidden from sight. By this time, I am sure you are wondering where I am going with this illustration and some of you probably already have an inkling of what I am going to write about.

Think about your life. People look at you and they may see one who is well dressed, with her hair held neatly in place with hair spray and makeup put on very nicely, complimenting your appearance. On the outside, you look great, but what about on the inside? "For as he thinks in his heart, so is he" (Proverbs 23:7a, AMP).

The very inner core, the heart, of a man shows exactly what kind of man he is. He may look handsome or she may look beautiful, but the inner heart of a person reveals his or her true identity. Think about being in the high mountains of California and you come to a cool, clear stream flowing down the mountain. The sun is shining and as you look in the clear water, you see the reflection of your face. Is what you see in the water truly what you are? "As water reflects a face, so a man's heart reflects the man" (Proverbs 27:19, NIV).

We see a wealthy person who is dressed in the finest quality of clothes and everything matches perfectly, but if we look at his heart, it might be a cold heart and possibly a heart of stone. We might see a street person who is dressed in old, dirty clothes. At night, the person sleeps in a shelter made of cardboard boxes and plastic bags to shield him from the cold. If we could look into his heart, we might see a loving, gracious person who has met with hard times, but he has a soft and moldable heart. Some may be at their very lowest point in life, but yet, they still see some good in everyone and everything. Others may have cobwebs, dust particles, or streaks of dirt running through their heart, feeding their mind with filthy thoughts. They may be harboring hatred for someone or they may have an unforgiving heart for some hurt they have suffered. What you see on the outside is not always what is on the inside.

You remember what happened when Saul became king. Samuel was a judge and a prophet, and when the people asked for a king, his heart was grieved. He felt like the people were rejecting him. The people chose Saul to be their king, and he reigned thirty-two years over Israel. Saul was getting ready to go into battle against the Philistines. Samuel was to come within seven days and offer the burnt offering and the peace offering to the Lord, but he had not come. Saul decided to assume the duty of priest, even though it was against God's teaching. He took it upon himself to offer the burnt offering, but as soon as he did this, Samuel came. Immediately, he asked Saul what he had done. He said he was afraid the Philistines would come against him at Gilgal and he had not asked the favor of the Lord. He said he forced himself to offer the offering.

"You acted foolishly," Samuel said. "You have not kept

the command the LORD your God gave you; if you had, he would have established your kingdom over Israel for all time. But now your kingdom will not endure; the LORD has sought out a man after his own heart and appointed him leader of his people, because you have not kept the LORD's command."

1 Samuel 13:13–14 (NIV)

Because Saul had been disobedient, the Lord sought for one who would obey him with all his heart. Saul had become impatient and took matters into his own hands. By doing this, he acted in disobedience to the Lord. When under pressure, the true character of a man or woman comes out. Sometimes we do things claiming the name of Jesus, but really our hearts are far from him.

Judah's sin was so evident to the Lord: "Judah's sin is engraved with an iron tool, inscribed with a flint point, on the tablets of their hearts and on the horns of their altars" (Jeremiah 17:1, NIV). The disobedient ways of the people of Judah had become such a part of their lives they appeared to be written on their hearts. "The human heart is most deceitful and desperately wicked. Who really knows how bad it is? But I know! I, the Lord, search all hearts and examine secret motives. I give all people their due rewards, according to what their actions deserve" (Jeremiah 17:9–10, NLT). God is aware everything in our life, even those things we think we are hiding from him.

The Pharisees and teachers of the law came from Jerusalem to where Jesus was and saw the disciples eating without washing their hands. They questioned Jesus concerning why the disciples did not hold to the tradition of their elders. Jesus accused them of honoring him with their lips, but their hearts were far from him. Jesus explained to the people what makes a man unclean. "Again Jesus called the crowd to him and said, 'Listen to me, everyone, and understand this. Nothing outside a man can make him 'unclean' by going into him. Rather it is what comes out of a man that makes him unclean'" (Mark 7:14–15, NIV).

The disciples questioned Jesus concerning what he had said. He explained to them how nothing entering into the man from outside would make him unclean. These things do not go into the heart, but into the stomach and out of the body. Jesus explained more clearly what he meant.

> He went on: "What comes out of a man is what makes him 'unclean.' For from within, out of men's hearts, come evil thoughts, sexual immorality, theft, murder, adultery, greed, malice, deceit, lewdness, envy, slander, arrogance, and folly. All these evils come from inside and make a man 'unclean.'"
>
> Mark 7:20–23 (NIV)

What comes out of the heart of man will make him unclean. We must be very careful what we allow to clutter our heart because things sitting idle will gather dust and lint. When these things come out of our heart, they are unclean. My computer sits close to the floor on a shelf and gathers all kind of lint and dust. My computer must be cleaned out every so often so the dust and lint does not cause things to malfunction. We must do the same thing with our heart. If we harbor sin in our heart, it will grow and infect our whole body. We must daily come to the Lord for cleansing. David wrote about this in the Book of Psalms. "I acknowledged my sin to thee, and my iniquity I did not hide; I said, 'I will confess my transgressions to the Lord;' and thou didst forgive the guilt of my sin" (Psalm 32:5, NASB).

Our sin cannot be hidden from the Lord because he sees into the very depths of our heart. He promises if we will confess our sin to him, he will forgive us of our sin.

When God looks into your heart, what does he see? Does he see a love for him or for worldly pleasures?

Do you have sins in your heart collecting dust and lint, or do you daily confess your sins to the Lord?

The Sun Rises and Sets

I attended the funeral of an older cousin who had seen many sunrises and sunsets. We all know the sun rises in the east and goes down in the west. My vision is not good in the early morning just before the sun rises, and it makes it difficult to drive. It is comforting when the sun begins to rise over the mountains in the east. The farther up in the sky the sun gets, the brighter the day becomes. The rising of the sun enables us to see everything. We can be certain the sun will rise in the morning and it will set at night. As I was driving home yesterday evening, dusk (twilight) was coming. When I looked to the west, the sun was down behind the mountains, but the sky reflected brilliant colors of pink, orange, and blue. It was as if God had painted a beautiful masterpiece across the western sky. The sunset appeared as a colorful blanket in the sky and looked as though you could lie down on it, pull it around you and lie there all warm and cozy.

I want to compare a person being born physically to the rising of the sun.

And God said, "Let bright lights appear in the sky to separate the day from the night. They will be signs to mark off the seasons, the days, and the years. Let their light shine down upon the earth." And so it was. For God made two great lights, the sun and the moon, to shine down upon the earth. The greater one, the sun, presides during the day; the lesser one, the moon, presides through the night. He also made the stars.

Genesis 1:14–16 (NLT)

The sun gives a radiant glow of light over the earth and warmth to mankind. Think about the radiant glow on the faces of the new parents as they look into the face of their newborn baby. It is difficult to find words to describe this radiance. It might be compared to the time of the morning when you know the sun is rising because the darkness begins to lift and the sky begins to lighten up in color. If you are driving toward the west, you can look in your rearview mirror and see what looks like a huge ball of fire rising in the sky behind you. It is the beginning of a new day. When the baby is born, it is the beginning of new life here on earth. When the baby was conceived approximately nine months earlier, God began a new creation within the womb of the mother.

My cousin who died would have been eighty-nine in April. His life began many years ago in the little town of Kinta, Oklahoma. "Oh yes, you shaped me first inside, then out; you formed me in my mother's womb. I thank you, High God—you're breathtaking! Body and soul, I am marvelously made! I worship in adoration—what a creation" (Psalm 139:13–14, MSG). God did an amazing work as he formed his small body within the womb of my aunt. I am sure if his mother were living today she could tell us how the birth of Mitchell brightened her day. She knew full well the work of the Lord in her life. I believe she saw a greater brilliance in the rising of the sun the following morning than ever before. A new day dawned and she began the day as the mother of a bouncing baby boy. Nothing is greater in the life of a family than giving birth to a new baby conceived in love.

Let's compare those who live to be eighty to one hundred years old with the setting of the sun. When you look at the life of a saint of God who has lived a productive life for the Lord, one can observe a beautiful masterpiece painted by the hand of God the Father. I have seen this personally in the life of my mother. She loved the Lord passionately and desired more than anything in the world to serve him with all her heart, soul, and strength. My mom had a passion for Women's Missionary Union. She loved missions and wanted others to learn about what God was doing in other places. She spent many hours leading women in this capacity. She loved to sing and was always active in the church choir. She loved to play the piano, although she was not what people would consider an accomplished musician, but she took lessons until she was eighty-eight years old. My dad served as a director of missions several times, and Mom would accompany him to the small country churches and play the piano or lead the congregational singing. My mom was always there to meet the needs of her family. She spent time in the Word of God and prayed continually for her husband, children, grandchildren, and people around her.

> Serve the LORD with gladness; come before him with joyful singing. Know that the LORD himself is God; it is he who has made us, and not we ourselves; we are his people and the sheep of his pasture. Enter his gates with thanksgiving, and his courts with praise. Give thanks to him; bless his name.
>
> Psalm 100:2–4 (NASB)

I believe these verses paint a picture of my mom's life. The beautiful sunset I saw yesterday driving home could represent the masterpiece painted by our Lord in the life of my mom. She was ninety-one years old when she died. She had lived a good life and as the sun went down on the horizon of her life, I could just hear our Lord say, "Well done, my good and faithful servant."

When the sun comes up in the morning, it is the beginning of a new day of opportunity. For one who is lost without Jesus, the Lord has extended his life one more day so he might come to know Jesus. "The Lord is not slow about his promise, as some count slowness, but is patient toward you, not wishing for any to perish but for all to come to repentance" (2 Peter 3:9, NASB).

Jesus has promised to come again, but he delays his coming allowing time for more people to be saved. He does not desire for any to be lost and spend eternity in hell. "Jesus said to the people, 'I am the light of the world. If you follow me, you won't be stumbling through the darkness, because you will have the light that leads to life'" (John 8:12, NLT).

The life spoken about in this verse is everlasting life. "For God so loved the world that he gave his only Son, so that everyone who believes in him will not perish but have eternal life" (John 3:16, NLT). The person who accepts Jesus receives eternal life. At the time of his death, when the sun goes down on the horizon of life, he will be taken immediately to heaven to live eternally with the Lord. It will not be so for those who refuse to accept Jesus as Savior and Lord. They are destined for the everlasting fires of hell.

On my way home one night, I observed a magnificent sunset; the sky was streaked with pink, blue, and orange, but it can't compare to the beauty we will see when we enter heaven and see the streets of gold and the gates made of pearls. "And the city has no need of sun or moon, for the glory of God illuminates the city, and the Lamb is its light" (Revelation 21:23, NLT).

What is the condition of your life today? Where will you spend eternity? When you close your eyes for the last time will you be ushered into heaven where a sun or moon is not necessary for light, or will you be ushered into hell "where their worm does not die, and the fire is not quenched" (Mark 9:44, NASB).

If you do not know Jesus as Savior and Lord, admit you are a sinner in need of God. Believe that Jesus died for your sins and rose again that you might have everlasting life. Confess Jesus as Lord of your life. Pray, asking Jesus to be your Savior, and allow him to be Lord of your life. Write below any decision you make.

If you are already a Christian, thank God daily for his great love.

What is Your Story?

My husband is a real storyteller. He remembers things when he was three and four years old. He not only remembers them, but he knows every detail, as well as the names of the people involved in the situation. His memory is amazing. Doyal's life was very different from mine. His family traveled from place to place, working the crops and living in a government camp. Many times they would come to Oklahoma to live during the time the crops were not in season. He talks about coming here to Wilburton because they had a small house on the property we own. They cleared the land by hauling the rocks to the creek and cutting all the sprouts. The family was a working family. Doyal's grandparents lived in this area, so they helped. He would attend school here, but he might come home from school and the pickup would be loaded. The family would take off for western Oklahoma or California once again to work the crops. His father was a mechanic and often he would work that job while the rest of the family worked in the fields. Doyal learned a lot about mechanics from his father. Even as a young boy, he learned to take an engine apart and put it back together. If you want to hear some sort of a tale, all you have to do is sit a few minutes with Doyal. He truly has a story to tell from all the family adventures. We all have a few stories of our own. The most important one is to tell others about Jesus. If someone asked you to tell what Jesus has done for you, what would you say?

Inside the city of Jerusalem, near the Sheep Gate, was the pool of Bethesda with five porches. People who were sick, blind, lame, and withered were lying there. They were waiting for the water to be stirred. During certain seasons, the angel of the Lord would come and stir the waters. The first to step in the waters was healed. Many had to have assistance in order to get in the pool.

> One of the men lying there had been sick for thirty-eight years. When Jesus saw him and knew how long he had been ill, he asked, "Would you like to get well?" "I can't, sir," the sick man said, "For I have no one to help me into the pool when the water is stirred up. While I am trying to get there, someone else always gets in ahead of me." Jesus told him, "Stand up, pick up your sleeping mat, and walk!" Instantly the man was healed.

> John 5:5–9a (NLT)

The man picked up his pallet and walked and the Jews reprimanded him because it was the Sabbath. He told them the one who had healed him told him to pick up his mat and walk. The Jews wanted to know who this was. The man did not know because Jesus had immediately slipped away after he healed him. Jesus saw and spoke with the man after this and the man knew it was Jesus who had healed him. The man had a story to tell about what Jesus had done in his life. He told the Jews it was Jesus who had healed him. Imagine the excitement in his voice when, after being crippled for thirty-eight years, he could walk. Can't you just feel the excitement in the story he had to tell about his healing?

Jesus was teaching in the synagogue on the Sabbath. There was a woman in the crowd who was very sick.

> One Sabbath day as Jesus was teaching in a synagogue, he saw a woman who had been crippled by an evil spirit. She had been bent double for eighteen years and was unable to stand up straight. When Jesus saw her, he called her over and said, "Woman, you are healed of your sickness!" Then he touched her, and instantly she could stand straight. How she praised and thanked God!

> Luke 13:10–13 (NLT)

The people rejoiced with the woman for what Jesus had done. She had a story to share with all the people she met about the wonderful work of Jesus in her life.

When Jesus received news of John the Baptist being beheaded, he withdrew in a boat to a place where he could be alone. The crowds in the city heard he was there and they followed him. When Jesus saw them, he had great compassion on them and healed the sick among them. After this had taken place, it was late in the evening and the people had nothing to eat. The disciples told Jesus to send the people away, but Jesus had a different idea. "But Jesus said to them, 'They do not need to go away; you give them something to eat!' And they said to him, 'We have here only five loaves and two fish.' And he said, 'Bring them here to me'" (Matthew 14:16–18 NASB).

I can imagine the bewilderment on the faces of the disciples as Jesus told them to give him the five loaves of bread and two fish. I am sure there were many questions running through their minds. Notice carefully what happened next.

> And ordering the multitudes to recline on the grass, he took the five loaves and the two fish, and looking up toward heaven, he blessed the food, and breaking the loaves he gave them to the disciples, and the disciples gave to the multitudes, and they all ate, and were satisfied. And they picked up what was left over of the broken pieces, twelve full baskets.
>
> Matthew 14:19–20 (NASB)

If you really allow the Holy Spirit to lead you as you read this incident, you can see the amazement on the faces of the disciples and the 5,000 people as Jesus looked up toward heaven and blessed the food he had been given. He was given power to perform miracles when he came to earth. He was fully God and fully man. After blessing the bread and fish, he gave it to the disciples to pass out. Every time they gave bread or fish to the people, the amount in the basket was replenished. All the people had been fed and there were still twelve baskets of food remaining. Imagine the headlines in the newspaper the day after Jesus fed the people: "An Unbelievable Feat: 5,000 Fed with Five Loaves and Two Fish." I can hear the buzz at the neighborhood market as they talked about Jesus feeding all these people with five loaves and two fish. What a story all those who were present had to tell their children, grandchildren, and neighbors.

What is the most exciting story you could tell about your life?

You may not know Jesus as Savior, so you do not have a story to tell about what Jesus did for you. Admit you are a sinner. Believe Jesus is God's Son and he has the power to save you from your sin. Confess your sin to God and confess to people around you that Jesus saved you from sin and he is your Savior and Lord. You now have a story to tell to everyone you meet. This is your testimony. Write out your testimony on a separate sheet of paper.

Lament or Grieve Because of...

The word lament in Webster's Dictionary means "crying out in grief; to feel or express sorrow for." Many of us can think of times when we have cried out to God because of some event or happening that has literally grieved our soul and spirit. I remember when I was a freshman in college, and as we were walking back from chapel one day, we heard the news about President Kennedy being shot and killed. The nation lamented over the loss of our president. I remember when my father died. It was the first time I had one so close to me die. I lamented over the loss of my very dear friend, my dad. His girls were always the apples of his eye and he always made us feel very special. I mourned because I would not have him with me anymore even though I knew he was in a much better place. I think of times our children strayed from the Lord and how my heart was grieved over what they had done and their rebellious spirits. I prayed God would do whatever was necessary to bring them back to him. We received news yesterday about the possible murder of a single lady, Cyd Mizell, a missionary serving in Afghanistan. She had been kidnapped in January along with Muhammed Hadi, another relief worker. It is believed both of them have been murdered. We grieve over the loss of one of our faithful missionaries and the one working with her.

Jesus grieved over the condition of Israel. Jesus had been addressing the teachers of the law and the hypocrites. They were so bound by being obedient to the law, they forgot to display justice, mercy, and faith. He accused them of being; "Blind guides! You strain your water so you won't accidentally swallow a gnat; then you swallow a camel!" (Matthew 23:24, NLT). He accused them of being beautiful on the outside, but on the inside being filled with dead people's bones and impurities. He told them in the future they would kill some of the prophets; others they would crucify and others would be whipped in their synagogues. Jesus lamented over the condition of the city and the people within the city. "O Jerusalem, Jerusalem, who kills the prophets and stones those who are sent to her! How often I wanted to gather your children together, the way a hen gathers her chicks under her wings, and you were unwilling" (Matthew 23:37, NASB). Jesus was grieved when he saw how his people had rebelled against him. Many times, he had given them opportunity to return to him, but yet, they refused.

God lamented over the condition of the children of Israel as he spoke to Solomon when he finished building of the house of the Lord. "But if you or your descendants abandon me and disobey my commands and laws, and if you go and worship other gods, then I will uproot the people of Israel from this land I have given them" (1 Kings 9:6–7a, NLT). The children of Israel continually refused to walk in the ways of the Lord. They chose to worship the gods of other nations. They forgot what God had done for their ancestors in the past. Isaiah, the prophet, had also written about what would happen because of Israel's refusal to follow him. "I revealed myself to those who did not ask for me; I was found by those who did not seek me. To a nation that did not call on my name, I said, 'Here am I, here am I.' All day long I have held out my hands to an obstinate people, who walk in ways not good" (Isaiah 65:1–2a, NIV).

Because of the Jews' refusal to accept the gospel of Jesus Christ, the message was delivered to the Gentiles and many believed. The Israelites had been given every opportunity to return to the Lord and follow his teachings, but they were an obstinate, rebellious people. I see in these scriptures the call of our Lord to our nation to return to him. If we do not, what do you think will happen? Consider carefully the scriptures you have just read. Do you think there will come a day when the Lord will reject the United States of America if we do not return to him and serve him wholeheartedly?

Do you ever shed a tear over America and the lostness that pervades our land? Jesus was grieved over the condition of Jerusalem and the behavior of the people.

The king lamented over Vashti's refusal to come to the banquet at his request. Esther was crowned as the new queen after Vashti refused to appear at the banquet. The king did not know Esther was a Jew, but Esther was beautiful and she found favor in his eyes. The king promoted Haman, giving him authority over all the princes in the area. Haman was upset with Mordecai because he refused to bow down to him and show him respect. The king's servants asked him why he would not obey the king's command, but Mordecai would not listen to them. Haman went to King Ahasuerus and offered to put money in the treasury if he would put out a decree to destroy all who would not obey the laws of the king. The day was set when all the Jews would be killed because they refused to bow down to Haman and live in obedience to the king's laws. "When Mordecai learned all that had been done, he tore his clothes, put on sackcloth and ashes, and went out into the midst of the city and wailed loudly and bitterly" (Esther 4:1, NASB). Mordecai knew his life and the lives of his people were in danger. He grieved because of the decree sent out to destroy all the Jews on a day set.

God laments over the condition of his children when they turn from him to worship idols and live an immoral life. The church at Corinth was surrounded by idolatry and all types of immorality. Paul wrote a letter to them instructing them concerning many personal aspects of life. He did not hold back any words, but spoke very boldly to them.

> Even if I caused you sorrow by my letter, I do not regret it. Though I did regret it—I see that my letter hurt you, but only for a little while—yet now I am happy, not because you were made sorry, but because your sorrow led you to repentance. For you became sorrowful as God intended and

so were not harmed in any way by us. Godly sorrow brings
repentance that leads to salvation and leaves no regret, but
worldly sorrow brings death.

2 Corinthians 7:8–10 (NIV)

Paul was not sorry for having written his letter, even though it did
grieve their hearts, because it brought repentance in the hearts of
many. They were in pain for a time, but often this type of pain is
good because it causes us to stop and look at the condition of our
heart and life. When God is the director of the grief and pain, it
will bring about repentance, ending in salvation.

Think of some times when you were grieved. Where did you
find comfort?

What is the difference when God directs your grief than when
the world directs your grief?

My Will or Yours

Daisy is our blue heeler, and the older she gets, the higher she is able to jump. She seems to have a destructive nature as she tries to entertain herself. When she was younger, she could not jump up into my flower bed. My flower bed is made of railroad ties, two ties high. As she grew, she got more spring in her jump and finally was able to jump into the midst of my flowers. I took a decorative fence and put it around the outer edge of the bed, thinking she would not be able to jump over the fence. I was in the house working, and all of a sudden, I heard loud whining and recognized it was Daisy. I went outside and there she was in the midst of my beautiful flowers. Well, let's say they were once beautiful. Where she was at the time, the flowers were broken and laying flat on the ground. She had managed to jump up on the railroad tie and then spring over the fence into the flowers, but she could not jump out because the dirt was lower than the ties. Needless to say, I was a bit upset with her. I had spanked her several times for getting in the flowers before I put the fence up. She had forgotten her punishment because she was determined to do what she wanted, not what I desired. I retrieved her from the flower bed and administered very strong discipline.

I realize this is a simple illustration about an animal rather than a person. However, I think we can make a comparison to help us understand what happens when we seek our will instead of God's. The Book of Nehemiah has a good example of what we are talking about. Nehemiah led the people to rebuild the wall around Jerusalem. The wall was finished and the people had returned to live in Jerusalem because now they had protection. Ezra stood to read the law and lead the people in a time of confession of their sins.

On the twenty-fourth day of the same month, the Israelites gathered together, fasting and wearing sackcloth and having dust on their heads. Those of Israelite descent had separated themselves from all foreigners. They stood in their places and confessed their sins and the wickedness of their fathers.

Nehemiah 9:1–2 (NIV)

The Levites led the people in a time of praise to the Lord God and in a time of reflection of all the things God had done for them as he led them through the wilderness. God had provided for all their needs and protected them from their enemies. They then reviewed the reaction of their ancestors. "But they, our forefathers became arrogant and stiff-necked, and did not obey your commands. They refused to listen and failed to remember the miracles you performed among them. They became stiff-necked and in their rebellion appointed a leader in order to return to their slavery" (Nehemiah 9:16–17a, NIV).

How many times did the children of Israel rebel against the will of God? They are too numerous to count, but then so are the number of times we have rebelled against God's will for our life.

Think about a time in your life when God spoke to your heart, leading you to serve him in some capacity but you said, "Not me Lord. This is not what I desire to do." You refused to do what God said. How did you feel? Did you rejoice over your decision or did you try to hide from the Lord because you knew you had been disobedient? Reading in 1 Kings 13, we find a man of God, a prophet, who came out of Judah to Bethel. King Jeroboam was there beside the altar and he heard what the prophet said.

Then at the LORD's command, he shouted, "O altar, altar! This is what the LORD says: A child named Josiah will be born into the dynasty of David. On you he will sacrifice the priests from the pagan shrines who come here to burn incense, and human bones will be burned on you." That same day the man of God gave a sign to prove his message, and he said, "The LORD has promised to give this sign: This altar will split apart, and its ashes will be poured out on the ground."

1 Kings 13:2–3 (NLT)

King Jeroboam was standing nearby and became very angry with the prophet. He pointed towards the prophet and told his servants to seize him. Immediately, his hand was paralyzed in that position and he could not pull it back to him. In an instant, the altar began to split apart and the ashes were poured out on the ground, just as the prophet had predicted. The king asked the prophet to call out to his God and ask him to restore his hand. The man of God prayed to the Lord and the king's hand was normal once again. When the king asked him to come to the palace and eat and drink with him, the prophet said he could not because God told him not to eat or drink in this place. He left Bethel and began his journey home. The sons of the old prophet who lived in Bethel came and told their father what had happened. The prophet of Bethel inquired as to which way the man of God went. He told them to quickly saddle his donkey and he went after him. The old prophet found him sitting under an oak tree. He questioned him as to whether he was the prophet from Judah. The prophet from Bethel invited him to come to his house and eat and drink, but the man of God refused, telling him he was not to eat or drink in this place. Then the old prophet of Bethel told him a lie.

The old prophet answered, "I too am a prophet, as you are. And an angel said to me by the word of the LORD: 'Bring him back with you to your house so that he may eat bread and drink water.'" (But he was lying to him.) So the man of God returned with him and ate and drank in his house.

1 Kings 13:18–19 (NIV)

While they were sitting there eating and drinking, the old prophet received a message from the Lord.

He cried out to the man of God who had come from Judah, "This is what the LORD says: 'You have defiled the word of the LORD and have not kept the command the LORD your God gave you. You came back and ate bread and drank water in the place where he told you not to eat or drink. Therefore your body will not be buried in the tomb of your fathers.'" When the man of God had finished eating and drinking, the prophet who had brought him back saddled his donkey for him. As he went on his way, a lion met him on the road and killed him, and his body was thrown down on the road, with both the donkey and the lion standing beside it.

1 Kings 13:21–24 (NIV)

Because of disobeying God's command, he lost his life. The Lord fulfilled his word in sending the lion to attack and kill him. We must be careful to obey the Lord's command because we do not know how God will discipline us for our disobedience.

The Lord gives us thorough instructions as to how we are to live. "How can a young man keep his way pure? By keeping it according to thy word. With all my heart I have sought thee; do not let me wander from thy commandments. Thy word I have treasured in my heart, that I may not sin against thee" (Psalm 119:9–11, NASB). We are to live our life in obedience to the commands of our Lord whether we are at home or on a mission field far away. We must surrender to the will of God.

My dog did not want to be obedient to my command. She

found herself in a predicament she did not know how to get out of. I came to her rescue, but at the same time, I disciplined her. She needed to learn from her mistakes. When we run from God and his will for our life, we will suffer the consequences of our actions. God will forgive us and lead us in the right way if we will return to him. Think of all the blessings we may have missed during our time of rebellion when we could have been living and serving in the will of God.

Have you refused to surrender to God's will for your life? What did God call you to do? Did you finally surrender to God's will? What happened after you decided to do the will of God?

How do we discern the voice of God so we know when God is calling us to a specific task?

An Attitude of Gratitude

As a child, I was always taught to say please and thank you. My parents instilled those words deep in my heart and mind. When my boys were little, I taught them to be polite and always use these special words. Hopefully, they still use them with sincerity. It bothers me today when you are sitting at the table with someone and they do not preface what they ask for with "please" or when you pass it to them, they do not say "thank you." I firmly believe we are to be polite and use manners in every situation. I want us to think about showing gratitude or thankfulness to others. Gratitude is acknowledging something good we have received from another. We express appreciation for something someone has done. "No matter what happens, always be thankful, for this is God's will for you who belong to Christ Jesus" (1 Thessalonians 5:18, NLT).

What is your attitude today? Are you grateful for what God is doing in your life or do you take it for granted? Are you thankful for the good husband or wife you have and for the comfortable home you live in? This thought came to me today as I was doing a Bible study by Jennifer Rothschild entitled *Fingerprints of God.* Jennifer has been blind since she was fifteen years old. At that time, she was diagnosed with a rare degenerative eye disease that gradually destroyed her sight. Jennifer still had the ability to tell whether it was daylight outside at the time she wrote this book. One day when she went to church, she was grumpy and feeling sorry for herself. She met Bobby Smith, who she had always wanted to meet. While serving as a Louisiana law enforcement officer, he lost his sight from a gunshot wound. He was totally blind, in utter darkness. He asked Jennifer about her sight, and she said she had a little light perception because she could tell when it was daylight. She heard a heavy sigh and could tell he would have great pleasure in being able to perceive when it was daylight. Jennifer said she realized how blessed she was because at least she had some light perception. "Enter his gates with thanksgiving; go into his courts with praise. Give thanks to him and bless his name" (Psalm 100:4, NLT).

Jesus healed many different people throughout the Gospels. "And behold, a leper came to him, and bowed down to him, saying, 'Lord, if you are willing, you can make me clean.' And he stretched out his hand and touched him, saying, 'I am willing; be cleansed.'" (Matthew 8:2–3a, NASB). How do you think this man felt as he went away cleansed of his leprosy? I think he had an attitude of gratitude for what Jesus had done for him.

In the Bible study I was doing today, I was asked to write down ten reasons for gratitude. One reason is God's holy Word, the Bible. I love the Word of God and I am so thankful God inspired men to write the Bible. The more I study God's Word, the deeper my faith becomes. "Let your roots grow down into him and draw up nourishment from him, so you will grow in faith, strong and vigorous in the truth you were taught. Let your lives overflow with thanksgiving for all he has done" (Colossians 2:7, NLT).

As I am writing this morning, I can hear the rain hitting the metal roof of our home. I am thankful God is sending the rain to give water to the animals, fill the lakes to keep fresh water for the fish, to water the flowers, grass and trees, and to refresh the whole earth. When the rains come, the earth is saturated with refreshing moisture. The roots of a tree soak up the rainwater, so when drought comes again, it will be able to stand strong. However, the roots continue going deeper in the ground searching for moisture. As I have dug deeper into the Word of God, I have learned more about him and what he desires me to be. I receive encouragement from his Word and my faith is strengthened as I allow the Holy Spirit to control my life. The only way I can learn the characteristics God desires for my life is to spend time allowing my roots to sink deeper into God's Word. I will be more prepared for the trials of life and those times of spiritual drought. I am thankful for every opportunity I have to study the Bible.

I am grateful for the peace I have because of my relationship with Jesus Christ and the leadership of the Holy Spirit in my life. "And let the peace that comes from Christ rule in your hearts. For as members of one body you are all called to live in peace. And always be thankful" (Colossians 3:15, NLT). When we allow Jesus Christ to control our life, he brings about a peace far beyond our understanding. It is a feeling of contentment to know whatever we may face, he is in control. "And the peace of God, which surpasses all comprehension, shall guard your hearts and your minds in Christ Jesus" (Philippians 4:7, NASB).

I have peace from knowing Jesus Christ as Savior. It reminds me of sitting by a cool stream of water in the mountains of California and listening to the water flow down the mountainside. All is quiet. Every so often, you might hear the chirping of birds or the rustling of the leaves as the wind gently blows. It has a very calming, peaceful effect as one comes away from the busyness of life. "You lead me to streams of peaceful water, and you refresh my life" (Psalm 23:2b–3a, CEV).

I am grateful for prayer. I am able to commune with the Lord at all times, whether I am in Oklahoma or Malawi, Africa. God is always with me and he hears my prayers. He is never too busy to hear what I have to say. "Devote yourselves to prayer with an alert mind and a thankful heart" (Colossians 4:2, NLT).

Too many times we come to the Lord and fail to voice our thanksgiving for all he has done in our life. We are not to take lightly these special times of prayer we have throughout the day, but we are to devote our mind and heart to him as we pray. We are to come with a tender heart, seeking his guidance in our life. I have an attitude of gratitude because I do not need an appointment to speak with my Father.

What is your attitude today? Is it an attitude of gratitude or do you come to the Lord demanding him to act on your behalf? What are you most thankful for today?

414

Oh, Lord! I Wish I Had Not . . .

Have you ever done something you wish you had not done? Have you spoken a word to someone you wish you had not said? Have you treated someone with contempt or disrespect and immediately you felt terrible for what you had done? The past couple of weeks have been extremely frustrating for me. The first week of January I decided I needed a new printer because I was using so many ink cartridges printing ministry projects. Doyal and I went to McAlester to Staples where they have everything you need for an office. They had a printer that used larger ink cartridges, and according to them would give me more copies. Instead of using two ink cartridges at a time, I would use four. I did not install the printer until the last week of February. Everything was going just fine with the installation until I got to the last step where I was to click on a button and then restart the computer. All of a sudden a box for my virus protection appeared saying it did not recognize the file and did I want to accept it. I clicked yes because it was a file on my printer. Oh my! How I wish I had not done that! Now, when first booting up the computer, you cannot click on an icon and start work immediately. You have to hit control, alternate and delete to end the task and then you can begin work. The computer technicians have helped me completely restore my computer and it is still the same. I have literally been consumed with computer problems, particularly the past three days. Several times I have said to myself, "I sure wish I had not purchased this printer." I have spent hours daily and into the night talking to Dell and Hewlett Packard technical support concerning the problems. Why did I think I had to have the new printer? Why was I not content with what I had? I have not convinced myself, as yet, that I am getting more copies out of these cartridges. I suppose time will tell. How many times in life have we said to ourselves, "Oh, Lord! I wish I had not…"?

I think of Judas Iscariot betraying Jesus. He was paid thirty pieces of silver to identify Jesus to the host of people sent by the chief priests and elders.

> And while he was still speaking, behold, Judas, one of the twelve, came up, accompanied by a great multitude with swords and clubs, from the chief priests and elders of the people. Now he who was betraying him gave them a sign, saying, "Whomever I shall kiss, he is the one; seize him." And immediately he went to Jesus and said, "Hail, Rabbi!" and kissed him.
>
> Matthew 26:47–49 (NASB)

We know from the scripture Jesus was arrested and was put on trial before different people in authority. Jesus was condemned to die on the cross.

> Then when Judas, who had betrayed him, saw that he had been condemned, he felt remorse and returned the thirty pieces of silver to the chief priests and elders, saying, "I have sinned by betraying innocent blood." But they said, "What is that to us? See to that yourself!" And he threw the pieces of silver into the sanctuary and departed; and he went away and hanged himself.
>
> Matthew 27:3–5 (NASB)

Judas realized he had done a horrible thing. Possibly before Judas Iscariot hung himself, the thought may have crossed his mind, "Oh, Lord! I wish I had not…"

Peter was a man who was headstrong and sometimes spoke before he thought. He loved Jesus greatly and followed him faithfully. Peter, James, and John were considered to be Jesus's inner circle of disciples. They were the ones Jesus took farther into the garden of Gethsemane to pray for him as he prayed to the Father concerning the events ahead. At the Last Supper with the disciples, Jesus made this statement: "Then Jesus said to them, 'You will all fall away because of me this night, for it is written, 'I will strike down the shepherd, and the sheep of the flock shall be scattered'" (Matthew 26:31, NASB).

Peter was disturbed by what Jesus said and told him that even though others would fall away, he would not. The statement Jesus then made would come back to haunt Peter very shortly. "Jesus said to him, 'Truly I say to you that this very night, before a cock crows, you shall deny me three times.' Peter said to him, 'Even if I have to die with you, I will not deny you.' All the disciples said the same thing too" (Matthew 26:34–35, NASB).

After Jesus was betrayed and arrested, he was tried before Caiaphas. Peter followed at a distance, and he was in the courtyard with the soldiers and others, warming himself by the fire. Three times Peter was asked if he was one of the followers of Jesus the Galilean and he emphatically said no. When he said this the third time, he heard the cock crow. Peter ran from the courtyard and wept bitterly. I believe the thought certainly went through Peter's mind, "Oh, Lord! I wish I had not…"

Several times, I have wished I had not purchased the printer that threw my computer into a tailspin. Except for having to go to control, alternate, and delete every time the computer is booted up, both the computer and printer are functioning well at this time. But, still yet, I wonder if I should have purchased the printer. All of these Bible characters I mentioned probably felt they would have been much better off if they had not done what they did. I have always heard the old adage, "Hindsight is better than foresight." I believe there is a lot of truth in this statement.

What about you? Are there things in your life you have done

that when you have looked back, you have said, "Oh, Lord! I wish I had not ... "?

When we come to know Jesus, we are forgiven of our sin. Even now, when we do something wrong how does the Lord treat us?

Covering from Above

Our area of Oklahoma has been blanketed with a covering of snow. Everything looks so quiet and peaceful. In my younger days, I loved the snow. I remember when we lived in northwestern Oklahoma in the wheat-farming community of Driftwood; we loved to see the snow come. An older friend would hook a trunk lid of a car with a chain to a tractor and pull us across the wheat fields. We had the thrill of our lives. Even in my young adult years, we would go to the mountains in California and rent big truck inner tubes and literally fly down the mountain. To us, it was so exciting. Our children always loved the snow, and as good parents do, we would take them sledding. They would build snowmen and have the time of their lives. As I have grown older, my enjoyment of the snow comes by looking at it through the picture window of our home. We live out in the country so it appears like a winter wonderland. Only God could put a covering such as this across our land. "He spreads snow like a white fleece, he scatters frost like ashes" (Psalm 147:16, MSG).

The covering of snow over the ground makes everything around us appear so clean and pure. Jeremiah used the word snow in reference to the princes of Israel. "Our princes were once glowing with health; they were as clean as snow and as elegant as jewels" (Lamentations 4:7, NLT). He continued to say they were no longer this way because of the sin they allowed to control their thinking and the way they lived. He then compared their faces to being as black as soot, so much so that no one could recognize them.

David was engulfed by his sin with Bathsheba. Nathan the prophet came to deliver a rebuke from the Lord to David. In Psalm 51 David cried out to God as the heaviness of his sin became so great. "Purify me with hyssop, and I shall be clean [ceremonially]; wash me, and I shall [in reality] be whiter than snow" (Psalm 51:7, AMP). David wanted his sins to be erased and his heart and life to be whiter than snow.

The Scriptures have much to say about God's protective covering.

He will shield you with his wings. He will shelter you with his feathers. His faithful promises are your armor and protection. If you make the Lord your refuge, if you make the Most High your shelter, no evil will conquer you; no plague will come near your dwelling. For he orders his angels to protect you wherever you go.

Psalm 91:4, 9–11 (NLT)

Think about this. If you search the Bible, you will find the many promises of God. When danger comes, you can recall those promises and they will be as armor to shield and protect you.

The Bible speaks about love being a covering. "Hatred starts fights, but love pulls a quilt over the bickering" (Proverbs 10:12, MSG). When there is discord, it is amazing how things can change if we respond with love rather than hatred or anger. "Above all, keep fervent in your love for one another, because love covers a multitude of sins" (1 Peter 4:8, NASB). One paraphrase expresses it as love covering many of our faults. Even though we do wrong, others will love us because they can overlook the wrongs we have done and love us for who we are. What did Jesus say about love? "Jesus replied, 'You must love the Lord your God with all your heart, all your soul, and all your mind.' This is the first and greatest commandment. A second is equally important: 'Love your neighbor as yourself'" (Matthew 22:37–39, NLT).

Jesus was very specific when he spoke about love. We are to love him with all our heart, soul, and mind. Can you honestly say you love the Lord with all your heart, soul, and mind? We are to allow Jesus to be our first priority in life. When we put the Lord first, everything else will come right in line with our obedience to him. If we love him, we will love our husband, our children, our employer, our fellow workers, our friends, and our neighbors. We will even love the people who live on the streets, under bridges, and those who come from foreign lands. "A new commandment I give to you, that you love one another, even as I have loved you, that you also love one another. By this all men will know that you are my disciples, if you have love for one another" (John 13:34–35, NASB). As a disciple of our Lord, we are to spread a covering of love over all people as he would love them.

The Bible dictionary defines glory as the visible sign of God's greatness. Webster's Dictionary defines glory as "honor and praise rendered in worship." The glory of God is referred to as a covering. "But [the time is coming when] the earth shall be filled with the knowledge of the glory of the Lord as the waters cover the sea" (Habakkuk 2:14, AMP).

God had allowed the Babylonians to capture the people of Judah because of their continual sinfulness and rebellion against the Lord. Habakkuk questioned the Lord as to why he would allow this to happen and God assured him that in time the Babylonians would be punished also. God's mission here on earth is for every person to be aware of the visible sign of God's greatness. Every person must hear about the saving power of Jesus Christ. The knowledge of God's greatness will be as vast as the waters of the seas or the oceans. It reminds me of when we were out on Lake Malawi. Because it was fifty miles wide, we came to a point where we could not see land in any direction. Had we been dropped from a helicopter at that point in the water, we would have thought the whole earth was covered with water. This is how great the knowledge of the Lord will be at the specific time God chooses. "For the earth will be full of the

knowledge of the Lord as the waters cover the sea" (Isaiah 11:9b,
NASB).

The covering of the snow on the ground is pure white and beautiful.
Regarding your relationship with Jesus, what does the word covering
mean to you? As a believer, what do you desire God to cover you
with in your life?

How Do You Respond?

Doyal always took the two younger boys to work with him from the time they were four up through their teenage years. When they were in their early teens, the younger one had a music tape belonging to the older one. The older one said, "You had better give that back or you are going to be dead meat." Knowing the younger one, I am sure he probably said something back daring the older one to try to make him dead meat. As they have grown older and have recalled this time, it has brought a big laugh. Neither of them was real tough and prone to fight, but the older sibling usually tried to keep the younger one under his thumb. They enjoyed the feeling of being in control of someone. If their dad had not been there in this situation, I am sure they might have scuffled a bit trying to make the other one do what they wanted. How we respond in situations determines what others think about us. If we reflected on our past and even on the present, we could all think of times when we felt we were treated unfairly. How did we respond to what they said or did? Were we a good witness for the Lord or did we treat them in the same way they treated us? "My dear brothers, take note of this: Everyone should be quick to listen, slow to speak and slow to become angry, for man's anger does not bring about the righteous life that God desires" (James 1:19–20, NIV).

How do we respond when trials continually come into our life? Do we retreat into our shell or do we lash out at others? Do we give up and feel life is useless? "Consider it all joy, my brethren, when you encounter various trials, knowing that the testing of your faith produces endurance. And let endurance have its perfect result, that you may be perfect and complete, lacking in nothing" (James 1:2–4 NASB).

James' statement here is just the opposite of how most people feel. How can we be joyful in the midst of trials? When we are being wronged or put in difficult situations, it is hard to be joyful.

We must try to look beyond the particular situation we are in and look to what God has in store for us because of our faithfulness to him. We know trials will come in life and if we respond in the way God would respond, we bring glory to him. Through these times, our faith is strengthened and we come to know him better. "As we know Jesus better, his divine power gives us everything we need for living a godly life. He has called us to receive his own glory and goodness!" (2 Peter 1:3, NLT).

Even when people lash out against us and our relationship with Jesus is challenged, we must stand in the assurance that our Lord is there with us. "I will never desert you, nor will I ever forsake you" (Hebrews 13:5b, NASB). If we know the promises of God, we can claim these promises and they will help us to stand strong.

Moses recounted for the children of Israel the different events in their wilderness wanderings. "Remember how the Lord your God led you through the wilderness for forty years, humbling you and testing you to prove your character, and to find out whether or not you would really obey his commands" (Deuteronomy 8:2, NLT). They grumbled about having nothing to eat and God provided manna. God was trying to teach them they needed more than just food for their physical life. He wanted them to understand real life came by feeding on every word the Lord spoke. He told them the Lord was bringing them into a rich land where the streams flowed in abundance and many different crops produced a great harvest. Everything was plentiful in the land God had promised to them. He then made a very important statement. "But that is the time to be careful! Beware that in your plenty you do not forget the Lord your God and disobey his commands, regulations, and laws" (Deuteronomy 8:11, NLT). He warned them about becoming proud and forgetting the Lord when they became prosperous. Their response to God's abundance was not always what God desired.

One of the greatest illustrations of one found faithful to God during a time of testing was Abraham.

Now it came about after these things, that God tested
Abraham, and said to him, "Abraham!" And he said, "Here
I am" And he said, "Take now your son, your only son,
whom you love, Isaac, and go to the land of Moriah; and
offer him there as a burnt offering on one of the mountains
of which I will tell you." So Abraham rose early in the
morning and saddled his donkey, and took two of his young
men with him and Isaac his son; and he split wood for the
burnt offering, and arose and went to the place of which
God had told him.

Genesis 22:1–3 (NASB)

Abraham immediately obeyed the Lord, doing exactly what God
told him to do. They took the wood and the fire and proceeded
to the place God told them. They built the altar and Abraham
arranged the wood on the altar. He then bound his son and laid
him on the altar on top of the wood. God allowed him to even go
so far as to raise the knife in the air to kill his son. An angel of the
Lord spoke to Abraham.

But the angel of the LORD called to him from heaven, and
said, "Abraham, Abraham!" And he said, "Here I am." And
he said, "Do not stretch out your hand against the lad, and
do nothing to him; for now I know that you fear God, since
you have not withheld your son, your only son, from me."

Genesis 22:11–12 (NASB)

Abraham looked around and there was a ram caught in the thicket
to serve as the sacrifice. Abraham's faith was greatly tested, but his
response of obedience was exactly what God desired from him.

When times of testing come into your life, what is your response?

When someone says or does something that hurts us, do you
think as a child of God we sometimes have to "bite our tongue and
hold back harsh words we are inclined to say?" Why do you think
this is so?

Decisions, Decisions, Decisions

Throughout our life, we are faced with many different decisions. Little children begin making decisions when they are about one year old. They choose to obey or not to obey. They get to the time when they are old enough to dress themselves, and they have a favorite shirt, pair of jeans, or dress they want to wear. They begin choosing the foods they want to eat. As they become teenagers, the fun really begins for parents as their children begin making decisions about their life. Some of these decisions are good and some bad. Before they reached this stage of life, we tried to teach them the right way to live according to the teachings of God. We pray continually for them to abide by our instruction. They graduate from high school, and they choose the college they want to attend. Our prayers become even more intense as we untie the apron strings and allow them to make their own decisions. Even as adults, we have many decisions to make. God calls us out to do things far beyond our expectations, and we are continually faced with decisions. My greatest comfort comes as I pray and strive to make my decisions according to God's Word. "If the Lord delights in a man's way, he makes his steps firm" (Psalm 37:23, NIV).

When we walk with the Lord, abiding in his teachings and seeking to live our life accordingly, God is able to direct our steps and keep our footing sure on the strong foundation of his Word. This only comes when we totally surrender all we are to the Lord. Decisions still are not easy to make because we must be sure we are listening to the Lord and not to the thoughts in our mind or the desires of our heart. "I waited patiently for the Lord; and he inclined to me, and heard my cry" (Psalm 40:1, NASB).

All of us would like to know what the future holds. If we knew, it would be much easier to make decisions. The children of Judah had a strong desire to know their future, so they tried to discern it through horoscopes. Jeremiah the prophet spoke to the people of Judah delivering God's message to them. He encouraged them not to seek their future in the stars, but to seek their future from God who created the stars. They had turned to worshiping idols rather than the one true God.

> But the LORD is the only true God, the living God. He is the everlasting king! The whole earth trembles at his anger. The nations hide before his wrath. Say this to those who worship other gods: "Your so-called gods, who did not make the heavens and earth, will vanish from the earth."
>
> Jeremiah 10:10–11 (NLT)

Because of their sinfulness, God told them to pick up their bundle and get ready to leave because the siege was about to begin. They would be thrown into a distant land where their lives would be full of great trouble. Jeremiah loved the Lord and desired to serve him with all his heart, soul, and strength. "I know, Lord, that a person's life is not his own. No one is able to plan his own course" (Jeremiah 10:23, NLT).

We must come to realize our life is not our own. It belongs to the Lord. Very truthfully, we cannot plan our own course. God our Father created us with a purpose and he will seek to carry out his plan for our life. We are as clay in the potter's hands.

> But the vessel that he was making of clay was spoiled in the hand of the potter; so he remade it into another vessel, as it pleased the potter to make. Then the word of the LORD came to me saying, "Can I not, O house of Israel, deal with you as this potter does?" declares the LORD. "Behold, like the clay in the potter's hand, so are you in my hand, O house of Israel."
>
> Jeremiah 18:4–6 (NASB)

This message is for you and me today. It is reassuring to know that if we make a wrong decision in life, we can come to the Lord and ask him for help. Our Father will take us as a marred vessel, shape us into a lump of clay once again and proceed to remold us into a beautiful vessel. What a loving and forgiving God we serve!

When Jesus was brought to Pilate, a very important decision was to be made. Pilate did not want anything to do with this case, but the people forced him to proceed. He came to them with a very important question. "When therefore they were gathered together, Pilate said to them, 'Whom do you want me to release for you? Barabbas, or Jesus who is called Christ?'" (Matthew 27:17, NASB).

The scripture tells us the chief priests and elders persuaded the people to ask for Barabbas' release and to have Jesus put to death. "Pilate said to them, 'Then what shall I do with Jesus who is called Christ?' They all said, 'Let him be crucified!'" (Matthew 27:22, NASB). I imagine their answer cut to the inner core of Jesus's heart. I know he must have felt great pain when they asked for his crucifixion. This was a major decision made by the people that day.

The rich young ruler came to question Jesus. "And as he was setting out on a journey, a man ran up to him and knelt before him, and began asking him, 'Good teacher, what shall I do to inherit eternal life?'" (Mark 10:17, NASB).

Jesus questioned him as to why he called him good because there was no one good except God. He reviewed the commandments for him and the rich young ruler said he had kept all the commandments from his youth up. Jesus then asked him a question that required a major decision.

And looking at him, Jesus felt a love for him, and said to him, "One thing you lack; go and sell all you possess, and give to the poor, and you shall have treasure in heaven; and come, follow me." But at these words his face fell, and he went away grieved, for he was one who owned much property.

Mark 10:21–22 (NASB)

The decision the ruler made at this time determined whether he would be destined for heaven or hell. He loved his material possessions here on earth more than he wanted the promise of living eternally with the Lord. His decision was not what Jesus desired from him.

Jesus was speaking to his twelve disciples and others who were following him, explaining different things they needed to know. "I am the true bread from heaven. Anyone who eats this bread will live forever and not die as your ancestors did, even though they ate the manna" (John 6:58, NLT).

Jesus spoke these things while teaching in the synagogue in Capernaum. Jesus was explaining to them how he was the bread of life, the bread sent from heaven. If they would partake of this bread, they would live forever. "Many therefore of his disciples, when they heard this said, 'This is a difficult statement; who can listen to it?'" (John 6:60, NASB).

Jesus knew many were grumbling and complaining about what he was saying. Jesus then asked a very direct question. "At this point many of his disciples turned away and deserted him. Then Jesus turned to the Twelve and asked, 'Are you going to leave too?'" (John 6:66–67, NLT). The twelve disciples who had been companions of Jesus as they moved from place to place had a decision to make at this time. Were they going to continue following Jesus or were they going to do as others of Jesus's followers and turn back? What would you have decided to do if you had been in the position the twelve disciples? Decisions, decisions, decisions; it always seems we must make decisions in our lives daily.

How do you approach decision making in your life? What is the process you go through?

I have some major decisions to make concerning the ministry

God has called me to do and I am sure you are faced with decisions concerning what God desires for your life. "Let your light shine before men in such a way that they may see your good works, and glorify your Father who is in heaven" (Matthew 5:16, NASB). What does this verse tell us we are to be? Who is to receive the glory for what we do?

Unending Journey

We are at the end of another incredible journey with the Lord through the Holy Bible. Once again, this has been a learning experience for me as God has led me deeper and deeper into his Word. I love the scripture "Thy word is a lamp to my feet, and a light to my path" (Psalm 119:105, NASB). I know in my life this is so true. He sheds light upon my path and goes ahead of me preparing the way for my journey through life! "I will go before you and make the rough places smooth" (Isaiah 45:2a (NASB).

In the Bible, our Father promises to take care of all we need in life if we will simply trust him. In the New Testament, Jesus sent the twelve disciples out with definite instructions as to what they were to take with them.

> And he instructed them that they should take nothing for their journey, except a mere staff; no bread, no bag, no money in their belt; but to wear sandals; and he added, "Do not put on two tunics." And he said to them, "Wherever you enter a house, stay there until you leave town."
>
> Mark 6:8–10 (NASB)

Jesus wanted the disciples to be totally dependent on him to give them the provisions they needed. It reminds me of how much stuff we take with us when we embark on our mission trip to Malawi. We take things for every situation we might face. We pack our bag full of snacks to have out on the field if we must go without a meal. We try to take every item of clothing we might need whether it is cold or hot. We take plenty of money with us just in case something should happen. I can just see the Lord looking down to earth and shaking his head as we go to ship our bags to our destination.

"Trust God from the bottom of your heart; don't try to figure out everything on your own. Listen for God's voice in everything you do, everywhere you go; he's the one who will keep you on track" (Proverbs 3:5–6, MSG). God probably wants to ask us, "Did you hear what I just said?"

My Bible is the most precious possession I have. I have often said if my house caught fire, and I could choose one thing to take, it would be my Bible. God's Word is written specifically for you and me. Every part of the Scripture is applicable to our lives today as it was during the time it was written. "For the word of God is full of living power. It is sharper than the sharpest knife, cutting deep into our innermost thoughts and desires. It exposes us for what we really are" (Hebrews 4:12, NLT).

God's Word is powerful and it is sharper than any two-edged sword, able to cut deep and reveal the innermost thoughts and desires of our heart and mind. *The Message* talks about God's Word being as sharp as a surgeon's scalpel that is able to lay us open where we can listen to what God has to say to us. It reveals who we are and exactly what we are made of.

The Word of God is food for my soul. "Thy words were found and I ate them, and thy words became for me a joy and the delight of my heart; for I have been called by thy name, O Lord God of hosts" (Jeremiah 15:16, NASB).

Through these writings, I have enjoyed learning so much more about God the Father, God the Son, and God the Holy Spirit. Learning to sit and partake of the inspired Word of God is like sitting down to an exquisite, seven-course dinner. It has not been easy for me to do because it takes much discipline and time. I have not accomplished all I desire and definitely not all the Father expects me to know. Isaiah wrote about a great banquet to be given to celebrate the defeat of evil and the reality of living eternally with the Lord. It will be for all Jews and Gentiles. "In Jerusalem, the Lord Almighty will spread a wonderful feast for everyone around the world. It will be a delicious feast of good food, with clear, well-aged wine and choice beef. In that day he will remove the cloud of gloom, the shadow of death that hangs over the earth" (Isaiah 25:6–7 NLT).

They will be served the very best foods, aged wine, and choice beef. People of all nations will be included. When we partake of the luscious meal our Father spreads before us in his Word, we will go away filled to the brim. We will be more knowledgeable of God and what he wants us to do. We will be more likely to walk in his ways and not go astray if we feast on God's Word and digest it as we would delicious food. " … Like newborn babes, long for the pure milk of the word, that by it you may grow in respect to salvation, if you have tasted the kindness of the Lord" (1 Peter 2:2–3, NASB).

The Bible is the inspired Word of God. The words written were given to men by God. Nothing is to be added to it and nothing is to be taken away from it. "Every word of God is tested; he is a shield to those who take refuge in him. Do not add to his words lest he reprove you, and you be proved a liar" (Proverbs 30:5–6, NASB).

God spoke his Word and we must not be guilty of teaching or speaking his Word falsely. "The words of the Lord are pure words; as silver tried in a furnace on the earth, refined seven times" (Psalm 12:6, NASB). Silver is tried in a furnace and purified by the fire, so God's Word has been tried and found to be pure. "As for God, his way is blameless; the word of the Lord is tried; he is a shield to all who take refuge in him" (Psalm 18:30, NASB). Seeking the Lord through his Word will bring joy and contentment in our life. He will reveal things to us we never knew. He will open our eyes to see the truth.

I believe the reason God led me to write these devotional books was to encourage people to spend time in the Word of God, to pray, and to seek him continually in all they do. The desire of my heart has been to speak the truth of the Bible. "Be diligent to present yourself approved to God as a workman who does not need to be ashamed, handling accurately the word of truth" (2 Timothy 2:15, NASB).

The prayer of my heart is that I have not in any way added to or taken away from the Word of God in these writings.

Appendix

Translations and paraphrases of Bible used in manuscript:

AMP–Amplified, Copyright 1987 by The Zondervan Corporation and the Lockman Foundation. All rights reserved.

CEV - Contemporary English Version, Copyright 1995 by American Bible Society.

GNT - Good News Translation, Copyright 1992 by American Bible Society.

HCSB - Holman Christian Standard Bible, Copyright 2004 by Holman Bible Publishers. All rights reserved.

The Living Bible, Copyright 1971 owned by KNT Charitable Trust. All rights reserved.

J. B. Phillips, The New Testament In Modern English, Copyright 1972 by Macmillan Publishing Company. All rights reserved.

NASB - New American Standard Bible, Copyright 1985 by Holman Bible Publishers. All rights reserved.

NIV - New International Version, Copyright 1986 by Holman Bible Publishers. All rights reserved.

NKJV - New King James Version, Copyright 1997 by Thomas Nelson, Inc. All rights reserved.

NLT - New Living Translation, Copyright 1996 by Tyndale Charitable Trust. All rights reserved.

MSG - The Message, Copyright 2005 The Message Numbered Edition by Eugene Peterson. All rights reserved.

Endnotes

1   http://www.nyise.org/fanny/bios.html

2   http://www.billysunday.org/timeline.php3

3   http://www.kamglobal.org/BiographicalSketches/amy carmichael.html

If you wish to contact me:

Nancy Rowland
3212 NW Ash Creek Rd.
Wilburton, Oklahoma 74578

nancyrowland44@gmail.com